A CLINICIANS GUIDE TO MYOFASCIAL PAIN IN THE CANINE PATIENT

IV

A CLINICIANS GUIDE TO MYOFASCIAL PAIN IN THE CANINE PATIENT

Dr. Michele Broadhurst D.C.
I.C.C.S.P; FIAMA acu; I.V.C.A;
Mtech Chiro (RSA); C.C.R.P.

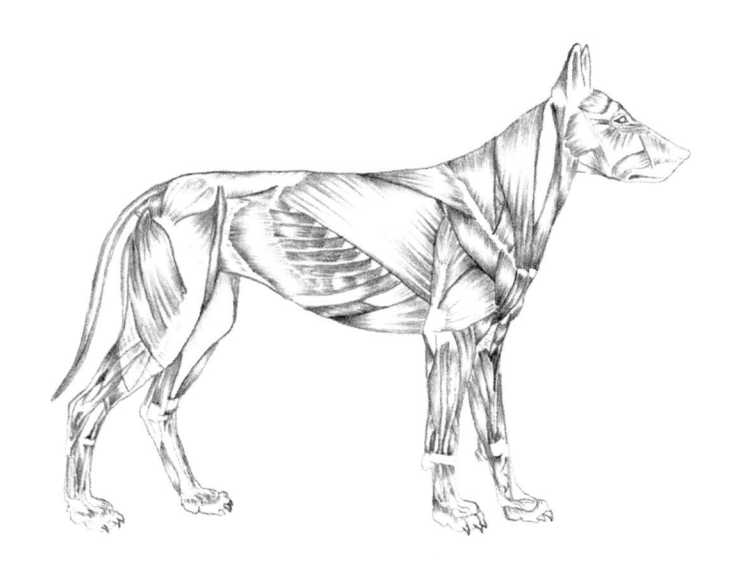

Illustrations by
Dr. Antony Angus D.C.; FIAMA
Mtech Chiro (RSA)

1st edition

COPYRIGHT

Copyright © 1st edition 2019 by Michele Broadhurst
All rights reserved.

All rights reserved. No part of this publication may be reproduced or utilized in any form, or by any mechanical or electronic means, including photocopying, recording or by any information storage or retrieval system, without the permission from the authors, copyright owner and publishers.

ACKNOWLEDGMENTS

Many thanks are owed when a book that has been in my head for the last ten years finally makes its way to print. I would like to thank my husband Antony for his continual support and belief in this project and for his incredible work on the illustrations. My mom and dad who have always been my biggest cheerleaders and taught me that the only thing standing in your way is you. To all my professors and mentors that have walked a path with me, teaching me and enhancing my knowledge as a professional and as a person.

To all the animals that have entered my clinic and my life. You have been my greatest teachers and I have learned something from each of you. To all the owners who entrusted their animals to me, I thank you for the belief and trust you had in me and the process. Without that ,this book would not have been created to help others who are in the same position that you once were.

To you the practitioner, who has decided to embark on this journey and fill your toolbox with a phenomenal skill that even after 16 years still surprises me every day as to how miraculous the results are. I hope that this makes you a better practitioner and encourages you to think outside the box and be an integral part of the body healing itself with the right tools.

PREFACE
ABOUT THE AUTHORS

Dr Michele Broadhurst DC; ICCSP, IVCA, FIAMA; CCRP; Mtech Chiro (RSA): Dr Broadhurst graduated from Chiropractic College (DIT) at the end of 2003. She learned about myofascial dry needling in her third year at university and used it extensively in her two-year residency. After graduating from Chiropractic College Dr Broadhurst then went on to study further and was awarded her diploma as an Internationally Certified Chiropractic Sports Physician from the International Federation of Chiropractic Sports. Dr Broadhurst joined Dr Angus and his West Coast Chiropractic team in 2005. The practice continued to flourish and grow, many families, ranging from babies to those nearing a century, athletes and chronic pain sufferers visited the practice expectant of pain relief. We were very blessed to offer this to our patients.

Dr Broadhurst branched out in 2006 and went over to the USA to Options for Animals and certified with them and the International Veterinary Chiropractic Association as an Animal Chiropractor. Dr Broadhurst built an exceptionally busy and prominent small and large animal practice, specializing in stud, racehorses and canines.

Dr Broadhurst worked for prominent stud farms such as Drakenstein Stud, Klawervlei, Maine Chance, Highlands, Lammerskraal, Sandown, Nutfield, Varsfontein stud and many others. Her resume includes working for the best South African thoroughbred racehorse trainers including the J&B Met and Queens Plate winners. She was one of the first animal chiropractors to practice in South Africa and has mentored some of the animal chiropractors that have subsequently started practicing in SA. She has helped thousands of humans and animals with myofascial work and chiropractic.

In 2018 Drs Angus and Broadhurst moved to the USA where they currently reside. She qualified under Dr John Amaro (IAMA) as a

Chiropractic acupuncturist and certified as a Canine Rehabilitative Practitioner through the University of Tennessee.

Dr Antony Angus DC; FIAMA, Mtech Chiro (RSA): Dr Angus graduated from Chiropractic College (Durban Institute of Technology) in 1996. He then went on to study acupuncture, and under the tutorage of Dr Ishmael Patel, he qualified as an acupuncturist in 2000. Dr Angus's love for myofascial dry needling started in his third year of Chiropractic College when he received extensive instruction in dry needling as a modality in treating pain and dysfunction. He studied dry needling extensively over the remaining three years of college and it inspired him to study acupuncture.

Dr Angus opened West Coast Chiropractic Centre in 1998 in Bloubergstrand South Africa. The practice quickly got a reputation as a holistic, multifaceted practice where people got better very quickly. The combination of acupuncture, dry needling and chiropractic is incredibly fast and effective in treating myofascial pain syndromes.

Dr Angus has treated Nobel prize laureates and their families, South African rugby captains and players and many others. The practice has over 15000 current patients on file. In 2017 Dr Angus moved to the USA to further his acupuncture studies and studied under Dr John Amaro at the International Academy of Medical Acupuncture. Dr Angus has over 25 years of dry needling and acupuncture experience.

With over 40 years of combined experience in the field of chiropractic, acupuncture and dry needling, Dr Angus and Broadhurst bring an extensive and fresh understanding to myofascial dry needling, pain patterns and how to use it on a daily basis in practice.

They continue to work and practice their art and every day they are grateful to be taught something new by their wonderful patients who have been and continue to be their greatest teachers.

They decided to write this book to teach practitioners the "missing link" in pain management and relief. This book will add a very needed and greatly lacking aspect to your toolbox of treatment options for myofascial pain syndromes. It is quick, effective and easy to use and understand. We hope you enjoy it and find it helpful.

For further information on course dates and further books please consult the website www.drmicheleb.com.

Other publications by these authors:
A clinician's guide to dry needling for myofascial pain (for people)
A clinician's guide to myofascial pain in the equine patient.

HOW TO USE THIS MANUAL:

Reader please note: This book is intended to be an educational and informative guide. It is a quick reference for therapists, providers and instructors. It assumes that the reader is receiving or has received thorough training in anatomy and diagnostic procedures. The techniques in this book are meant to supplement, and not substitute, professional veterinary care and treatment. They should not be used to treat serious and undiagnosed ailments, nor without consultation with a qualified veterinarian or health care provider. The information in this book is compiled from sources deemed to be reliable and all efforts have been made to ensure that the book is as accurate as possible. The contents serve as a guide only, and professionals should use sound judgment and individualized therapy for each specific patient. This text is sold without warranties of any kind, expressed or implied, and the publishers, authors and editors disclaim any liability, loss or damage caused by the contents.

It is highly recommended that prior to embarking on dry needling your patients, that you attend a seminar where you are taught both theoretical and practical techniques on dry needling. Please ensure that you are treating within the scope of your profession and that the laws of the country or state are being followed.

For books and courses please go to www.drmicheleb.com.

All rights reserved. No part of this publication may be reproduced or utilized in any form, or by any mechanical or electronic means, including photocopying, recording or by any information storage or retrieval system, without the permission from the authors, copyright owner and publishers.

TABLE OF CONTENTS

ACKNOWLEDGMENTS	VII
PREFACE	IX
ABOUT THE AUTHORS	IX
HOW TO USE THIS MANUAL:	XII
INTRODUCTION:	1
DEFINING THE RELATIONSHIP OF MUSCLES & TRIGGER POINTS	5
FASCIA	16
MYOFASCIAL PAIN SYNDROMES IN THE CANINE	25
HOW TO TREAT MYOFASCIAL PAIN SYNDROME (MPS)	33
PALPATION	38
DIAGNOSIS	44
TREATMENT:	49
NEEDLING USE AND TECHNIQUE	53
ACUPUNCTURE VS DRY NEEDLING	65
EXTRACORPOREAL SHOCK WAVE THERAPY (ESWT)	73
LASER THERAPY	85
PRACTITIONER INTEGRATION AND LEGISLATION	96
NEEDLE SAFETY AND CONSIDERATIONS	98
MUSCLES OF THE NECK AND FORELIMB:	110
STERNOCLEIDOMASTOID MUSCLE (SCM)	113
OMOTRANSVERSARIUS (OMOTRANSVERSE)	118
TRAPEZIUS	121
RHOMBOIDEUS (RHOMBOIDS)	124
SUPRASPINATUS (SUPRASPINOUS)	126

INFRASPINATUS (INFRASPINOUS) *129*
DELTOID *133*
BICEPS BRACHII *136*
TRICEPS *140*
TERES MINOR and MAJOR *143*
LATISSIMUS DORSI *146*
PECTORAL *149*
MUSCLES OF THE HINDLIMB: *153*
SUPERFICIAL GLUTEAL MUSCLE *157*
MIDDLE GLUTEAL MUSCLE *160*
TENSOR FASCIAE LATAE (TFL) *163*
PIRIFORMIS *166*
HAMSTRING *169*
HIP ADDUCTORS *175*
THE FEMORAL TRIANGLE *179*
QUADRICEPS *180*
SARTORIUS *187*
GRACILIS *190*
QUADRATUS LUMBORUM (QL) *193*
ERECTOR SPINAE or PARASPINALS *197*
CRANIAL TIBIAL *203*
GASTROCNEMIUS *206*
CONCLUSION *210*
BIBLIOGRAPHY *211*

INTRODUCTION:

Myofascial pain is a term that has been bantered around for many years. It is often unclear to people exactly what this means or how to fix it. Veterinarians, physical therapists, chiropractors and other practitioners are starting to acknowledge the importance of myofascial pain syndromes and collaborate to figure out how to treat it.

Acupuncture, which is older than 2000 years old, is resurfacing in the western world as an incredibly effective way to treat organic and musculoskeletal pain. The only trouble with acupuncture is that most insurances do not cover it, it takes time to perform and many patients require ongoing treatment that they cannot afford.

Complementary medicine is often defined as a group of diagnostic and therapeutic disciplines that are used together with conventional medicine. An example of this would be using dry needling to lessen a patients' discomfort following spinal surgery.

Complementary medicine is different from alternative medicine. Whereas complementary medicine is used together with conventional medicine, alternative medicine is used in place of conventional medicine. An example of an alternative therapy is using a special diet to treat cancer instead of undergoing surgery, radiation, or chemotherapy that has been recommended by a veterinarian.

Veterinary care is becoming more and more competitive, with many fads cropping up on a monthly basis. Many of these have no scientific basis, and yet in the technological age that we are living in, a good marketing strategy can convince you to try anything. I have heard hundreds of patients say that they have tried this and that, with little or no result other than emptying their wallet.

This manual is an essential resource for anyone who is interested in treating pain in their respective practices. For the veterinarian who spent

Introduction

only a few weeks in college learning about the musculoskeletal system and wants to understand it better and treat their patients more effectively, for the veterinary dentist, who is struggling to help patients with temporomandibular joint dysfunction, or the physical therapist who feels like massage isn't quite cutting it, or for the chiropractor who can't understand why their adjustment isn't holding and the patient is still suffering. No one has time in their busy offices to lug out an enormous textbook and start paging through it for 15 minutes while their patient and client sit waiting.

This has been designed as a quick reference text for those practitioners that have a patient presenting with a myofascial pain syndrome and need to quickly recap what muscles can be causing it, where those trigger points are, how to treat it and what to do post treatment.

The author has more than 16 years of practical hands on experience and has worked on thousands of patients (human and animal) to bring you the most valuable and concise information that you will need to be successful in dry needling in your practice.

The authors have assumed that you have a strong and solid grasp of anatomy and physiology, so they have not done a full recap on the basics of these subjects. Travell and Simons and P. Baldry, have all done incredible works on myofascial pain and are easily referenced in their respective texts. (311,1). In the small animal world ,Millis and Levine have covered some of the more commonly seen pathologies and how to treat them in their text (378).

We begin with an overview on the relationship of muscle and trigger points as well as fascia and its role and function in the body. This is a useful review about the functionality, integrity and uses of muscles, fascia and the trigger points that form and reside in them.

Next, we cover myofascial pain syndromes in canines and go over several ways to treat it.

Introduction

The palpation chapter is one of the most important chapters in this book, as most practitioners are deficient in this skill. There are fundamental tools in this chapter that will help you quickly and effectively, master palpation.

The diagnosis and treatment chapter outlines the fundamentals in evaluating and treating patients with myofascial pain syndromes. This helps to marry all the different health professionals together by realizing that there is commonality in the basics of how we evaluate and treat our patients. Therefore, the acupuncturist, osteopath and orthopedic surgeon, while differing in their treatment approaches and perspectives, will all share a similar pattern in evaluating and possible treating a patient.

Needling use and technique will give you the foundations on what and where to needle as well as the how. This chapter incorporates different needling techniques as well as post treatment protocols. It teaches you how to be safe, and what contraindications are important to keep in mind when evaluating a patient for dry needling.

Next, we cover the differences and similarities between acupuncture and dry needling. A brief discussion that will help you answer the question you will encounter many times a day as to what the differences between these two treatment protocols are.

Other modalities for eliminating MFTPs are discussed briefly. Treating patients is not a "one size fits all" scenario, therefore one must be aware of alternative treatments that are beneficial when dealing with myofascial pain and trigger points. We have touched on the efficacy of some of these treatments but have not gone into great detail.

Needle safety and consideration covers everything you need to know regarding clean needle technique and how to be safe when working with needles.

Each muscle that is discussed covers the attachments, action, how to palpate the muscle, the relevant pain pattern for that specific muscle,

Introduction

needling technique, causative and perpetuating factors and accessory/associated trigger points relating to that muscle. (311-320, 375-378) were used as references for the muscle attachments and anatomical importance.

In conclusion, this manual is for the practitioner who wishes to deepen their understanding of myofascial pain syndromes and wants to help their patients in a quick and incredibly effective manner. This book focuses on the how, not the why. It is a quick way of referencing pain patterns and finding out how to treat it immediately.

DEFINING THE RELATIONSHIP OF MUSCLES & TRIGGER POINTS

Motion and functional movement are an exceptionally important part of life. Movement results, in part, due to a complexity of contractions and relaxations of muscles. Musculature, if regarded, as a single entity is the largest internal organ of the body and on average makes up almost 50 percent of the total body weight.

Muscles have 3 primary functions:

1: They create a support structure for the body and protect the internal organs.

2: They allow movement of the skeletal system as a whole as well as movement of organs and associated structures.
The maintenance of a correct posture and being able to perform everyday movements, sitting, breathing, chewing, walking etc. takes place due to correct muscular functioning.
Organic functioning, heartbeats, peristalsis, bladder control and elimination and breathing is all due to muscular interaction.

3. Muscles regulate body temperature by producing heat as a result of movement.

There are three classifications for muscle: visceral, skeletal and cardiac.

Muscles all have the same characteristics:

1: Irritability: the ability to receive and respond to stimuli resulting from a nerve impulse.

2: Contractility: the ability to shorten in response to an internal or external stimulus.

Defining the relationship of Muscles and Trigger points

3: Extensibility: the ability to stretch.

4: Elasticity: the ability to return to a normal shape or length after contraction or elongation.

The only muscles we will be dealing with in this book are voluntary skeletal muscle. Skeletal muscle is defined as either phasic or tonic muscles.

Phasic muscles create a phasic contraction, which allows the muscle to move at its attachments. Phasic muscles are predominantly made up of fast twitch fibers that create rapid contractions and resulting in fast movements. These muscles fatigue quickly due to a low blood supply and the degree of contraction required by them.

Due to rapid fatigue these muscles are very prone to weakening and dysfunction.

Phasic muscles include:

Rhomboids
Middle and lower trapezius
Inferior portion of Pectoralis
Triceps Brachii and fore limb extensors
Vastus medialis, intermedius and lateralis
Gluteus muscles
Rectus abdominus
Short cervical flexors

Tonic muscles are responsible for posture. These muscles produce a partial contraction of the muscle known as a tonic contraction. A tonic contraction results in contraction of a certain portion of the muscle and a relaxation of other portions of the muscle. This is not as powerful a contraction as phasic muscles and does not produce movement of the skeletal attachments.

Defining the relationship of Muscles and Trigger points

During a tonic contraction, individual muscles do NOT function continuously like phasic muscles, instead individual motor units fire independent of the whole muscle which results in a non-uniform contraction and relaxation that prevents early onset fatigue. These tonic muscle fibers that are primarily responsible for posture and working against gravity to maintain a certain position, are comprised of slow twitch fibers.

There is an abundance of blood supply to these muscles and as a result they take much longer to fatigue as compared to fast twitch fibers. When there is a disturbance in these muscle groups, the result is often shortening and bunching of these postural muscles.

Tonic Muscles include:

Sternocephalic
Brachiocephalic
Cleidocephalic
Omotransverse
Upper trapezius
Scalenes
Suboccipitals
Pectoralis
Biceps brachii and fore limb flexors
Quadratus lumborum
Cervical and lumbar Erector Spinae/paraspinals
Iliopsoas
Hamstrings (semimembranosus, semitendinosus, biceps femoris)
Rectus femoris
Tensor fasciae latae
Adductor magnus, brevis, longus
Piriformis

Both phasic and tonic muscles are very prone to injury due to overuse and postural dysfunction such as moving incorrectly, compensations due to joint and bone dysfunction, limping, strains and sprains etc.

Defining the relationship of Muscles and Trigger points

Musculature is still one of the most under rated and overlooked causes of pain and dysfunction.

NORMAL MUSCLE:

In order to understand abnormal muscle, one needs to familiarize oneself with normal muscle.

Normal muscle is soft, pliable and supple. It has an elastic quality and underlying structures should easily be palpable through the muscles. There is no pain or tenderness on palpation and a healthy muscle will contract as a response to a nerve stimulus, thereafter, returning to a normal shape.

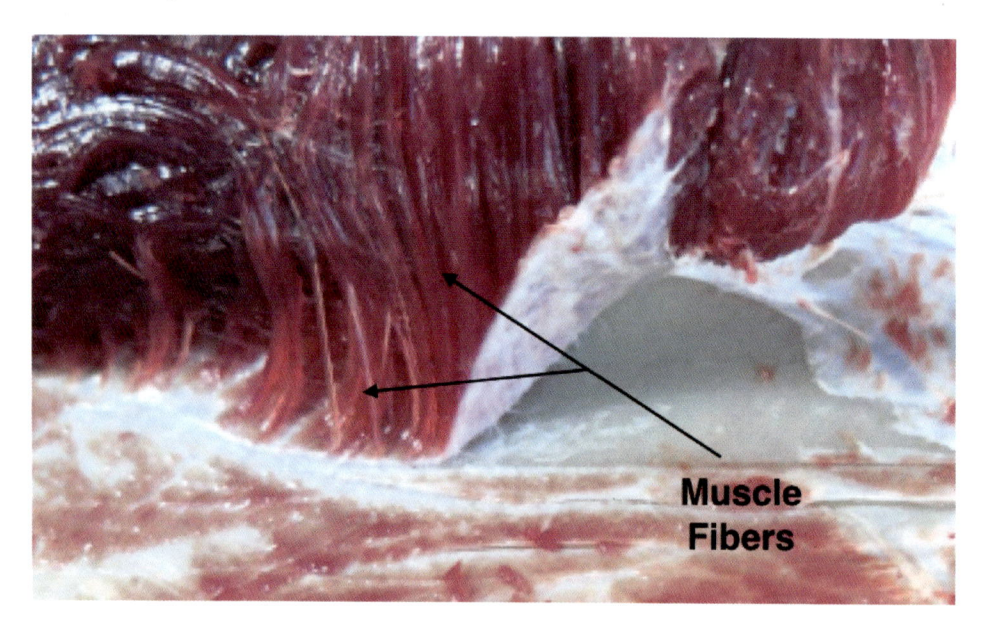

Muscle Fibers

A dysfunctional muscle on the other hand will contract but is not capable of returning to its normal shape after contracting. It remains fixed in a shortened position and due to this shortened position, there is a reduction in blood and lymph flow to the area and a resultant decrease range of motion.

Defining the relationship of Muscles and Trigger points

Within a short period of time, these muscles change in integrity and present with:
Increased muscle tone.
Resistance to palpation.
Stiffer and harder as compared to a soft, supple muscle.
As a muscle shortens the range of movement of the affected area is impaired which results in a weaker and impaired function.

Taut muscle bands may feel ropey or cord like, they can vary from thick bands to thin strings. These tight contracted muscles often feel painful or tender on palpation, the muscle itself is less elastic and supple and in severe cases one may be unable to palpate the underlying structures.

Muscle integrity directly determines the posture that one is capable of holding and maintaining. These postures can result from physical or psychological causes. When there has been constriction of the muscle for a long period of time and is now deemed as chronic. Compensations result as the bodies coping mechanism kicks in, resulting in changes in blood flow, lymph drainage and neural functioning.

This in turn affects the many systems of the body including the immune system, the neuromusculoskeletal system and others, therefore drastically affecting the animal's overall health.

Dr Janet Travell – the leading authority on myofascial pain in humans, defines a trigger point as a "hyperirritable locus within a taut band of skeletal muscle, located in the muscular tissue and /or its associated fascia"(1).
Myofascial trigger points (MFTP's) are located both in muscle and in fascia and are palpable and symptomatic in their character.
There is a resistance felt on palpation of the muscle and the area is tender and painful.

Often the pain felt and associated with myofascial trigger points can result in a referred pain pattern and autonomic symptoms such as visual disturbances, nausea, dizziness, tearing of the eyes, skin temperature changes and many more. Referred pain has often been disregarded when evaluating a patient's condition, however the implications of such extensive symptomatology are critical in examining, diagnosing and treating many complaints that were previously not considered to be musculoskeletal.

Muscle size is irrelevant when determining the extent of pain caused by MFTP'S. The level of hyperirritability is the key determinant in defining the degree of pain. The more irritable it is, the more pain the animal experiences, both locally and throughout the referral pain pattern.

Trigger points can form in any muscle of the body, however there are certain muscles that are more prone to myofascial trigger points due to the mechanical strain and overuse that they are subjected to. This results in an increase in the sensitization of nerves, an accumulation of cellular metabolism, a decrease in circulation and impaired lymphatic drainage.

Trigger points can be active or latent. They present almost the same: stiffness and tightness through the muscle, pain and tenderness on palpation and a resultant weakness in the muscle. MFTPs are divided into active and latent trigger points dependent upon the degree of irritability. Active MFTPs are spontaneously painful, while latent MFTPs are only painful when stimulated, for example, with digital pressure.

MFTPs can be visualized by magnetic resonance imaging and sonography elastography (2-6), which has shown that active MFTPs are larger than latent MFTPs and feature a reduction in circulation (3). MFTPs are physiological contractures, characterized by local ischemia and hypoxia (3,8) a significantly lowered pH (active MFTPs only) (9-11) a chemically altered milieu (active MFTPs only) (9-11) local and referred pain(12-14) and altered muscle activation patterns (15,16). Although latent MFTPs are not spontaneously painful, recent research has shown that they do contribute to nociception, therefore they need to be included in the treatment plan.

MFTPs are associated with dysfunctional motor endplates (17,18) endplate noise (19) and an increased release of acetylcholine (20-24). MFTPs activate muscle nociceptors and are peripheral sources of persistent nociceptive input, thus contributing to the development of peripheral and central sensitization (25-28). Stimulation of MFTPs activates the periaqueductal grey matter and anterior singular cortex in the brain (29-31) and enkephalinergic, serotonergic, and noradrenergic inhibitory systems associated with A-δ (A delta) fibers through segmental inhibition (32,33).

Active trigger points are differentiated from latent trigger points by their pain pattern. Active trigger points are considered more clinically relevant due to the pain and the referral patterns that are associated with them.

Referral from these active trigger points tends to be away from the affected muscle in a specific pain pattern. Travell and Simons were pioneers in establishing relationships between active myofascial trigger points and its characteristic referred pain pattern.

Myofascial dysfunction may be due to an acute or gradual onset, such as a specific incident is noted to be the cause of pain or from long standing overuse and overload of a muscle.

The characteristic of the pain is also important. It is very difficult to determine in animals, as they are unable to verbally communicate, however, the presentation of the pain is often clear in its character. For example: Pain from MFTP's are generally described as achy, deep, dull and steady. Very seldom is it described as burning, throbbing or tingling. A horse or dog may present with a lameness, that doesn't induce screaming or crying, instead it presents as non or altered weight bearing, resting more, lying on the affected side, and several other factors. Pain varies in intensity and may occur with motion or at rest.

As previously discussed, the pain and tenderness elicited from a trigger point are not always found at the specific trigger point but is distributed to other areas, i.e.: referred pain. A good example of this is lick

Defining the relationship of Muscles and Trigger points

granulomas that are often a result of a spinal subluxation (chiropractic term) in the cervical spine that produces a biomechanical compensation in the cervical muscles, MFTP form in those muscles resulting in a neurological and myofascial referral into the paw. By addressing both the abnormal biomechanics of the cervical spine and needling the MFTP's, the referral to the paw diminishes and the lick granuloma heals.

The pain experienced at the trigger point itself is considered to be a local pain pattern. This tenderness will dissipate after the trigger point is treated and starts to diminish. Shortening or lengthening the muscle that contains the trigger point, cold weather, infections, and stress will increase the intensity of the pain from the trigger point.

Passive stretching, moist heat and rest help to reduce the degree of pain experienced from the trigger point.

Latent trigger points are thought to be more common than active trigger points. They are more predominant in constricted muscle and arise from maintaining a particular posture for long periods.

Latent trigger points become active due to acute overload and fatigue, chronic overload due to sustained contraction of the muscle, trauma, compression or sustained cold affecting the muscle.

Indirect activation occurs more than ever from lifestyle circumstances such as animals maintaining a shortened position of the muscle for long periods of time, such as sleeping, eating or sitting in one fixed position, jumping or working from one side only, walking on cambered or uneven surfaces, limping, abnormal growth, etc.
This indirect activation may also be attributed to viral and visceral disease, stress and anxiety and muscular strain from managing dysfunctional joints such as arthritic joints.

A trigger point can go between active and latency, improving with rest and stretching. However, trigger points will not be fully eradicated without specific treatment.

Defining the relationship of Muscles and Trigger points

Efficient palpation techniques are essential to identify the active trigger point that you will be needling. Focused, specific palpation is the most important tool when identifying trigger points in a muscle.
One examines the muscle for tightness and feel for the specific taut band within the muscle. Intense tenderness within the taut muscle band is the most important feature when identifying an active trigger point.

When applying manual pressure to the trigger point, a local twitch response (LTR) should be elicited (34), where the muscle literally twitches, and a patient jumps or shows some reaction to pain.
When extended pressure is applied to the trigger point, a referred pain pattern may be felt by the animal.

The LTR has been shown to be associated with alleviation and mitigation of spontaneous electrical activity or motor endplate noise (18,19,42,43); a reduction of the concentration of numerous nociceptive, inflammatory, and immune system related chemicals;(10,11,45) and relaxation of the taut band(46). Deep dry needling of myofascial trigger points is associated with reduced local and referred pain, improved range of motion(15,16) and decreased MFTP irritability both locally (19,49)and more remotely (44,50). Dry needling normalizes the chemical milieu and pH of skeletal muscle (9-11) and restores the local circulation(51).

Superficial dry needling is thought to activate mechanoreceptors coupled to slow conducting unmyelinated C fiber afferents, and indirectly, stimulate the anterior cortex (52). Superficial dry needling may also be mediated through stimulation of A-delta fibers (53) or via stretching of fibroblasts in connective tissue(33). Superficial dry needling is associated with reduced local and referred pain and improved range of motion (55-56) but it is not known at this time whether superficial dry needling has any impact on normalizing the chemical environment of active MFTPs or reducing motor endplate noise associated with MFTPs in general.

Defining the relationship of Muscles and Trigger points

There is a definitive difference between a trigger point and a generally tight muscle. Focused palpation along a taut muscle band will lead to an area of exquisite tenderness, i.e.: a myofascial trigger point. This varies in the character of the pain when a trigger point is compared to a tight muscle. A MFTP has a specific, isolated area of tenderness with or without a referral pattern, relative to its activity level, whereas a tight muscle has generalized tenderness when palpated throughout the extent of the muscle. Muscle tension is determined by a combination of the basic viscoelastic properties of a muscle and its surrounding fascia, and the degree of activation of the contractile apparatus of the muscle(56).

There is some evidence that excessive muscle tension, as seen for example in spasticity, can be alleviated with dry needling (57,58). Scar tissue has been linked to myofascial pain (59) and fibroblasts (60,61). Fibroblasts are specialized contractile cells within the fascia that are of particular interest, as they synthesize, organize, and remodel collagen, dependent upon the tension between the extracellular matrix and the cell (62,63). Dry needling, especially when used in combination with stimulation of the needle, can place fibroblasts in a high-tension matrix, at which point the fibroblast changes shape and assumes a lamellar shape, and increases its collagen synthesis and cell proliferation(64,65).

Dry needling has been shown to directly activate fibroblasts through mechanical manipulation of the needle, (32,66,67), which in turn activates the release of cytokines and other pro-inflammatory mediators (68-72). Dry needling can play a substantial role in the process of mechano-transduction, which is described as the process by which the body converts mechanical loading into cellular responses.(21,73-78) Fibroblast activation with a solid filament has been shown to result in pain neuromodulation(33,68).

The reduction of a trigger point may be done by various methods, the preferred method (by these authors) is by inserting a needle and releasing the trigger point. There is also ischemic compression, injecting the trigger point, spray and stretch techniques, cold laser, extracorporeal shockwave therapy and many more.

Defining the relationship of Muscles and Trigger points

Once the trigger point is reduced, a practitioner will introduce stretching or gentle functional movement to the patient that needs to be done multiple times a day in order to prevent the muscle from reverting back to a shortened state, and depending on the degree of weakness, strengthening exercises may be prescribed.

The sustainability of the muscle is entirely dependent on daily activities done by the animal. If overload or overuse is ignored, these trigger points may return.

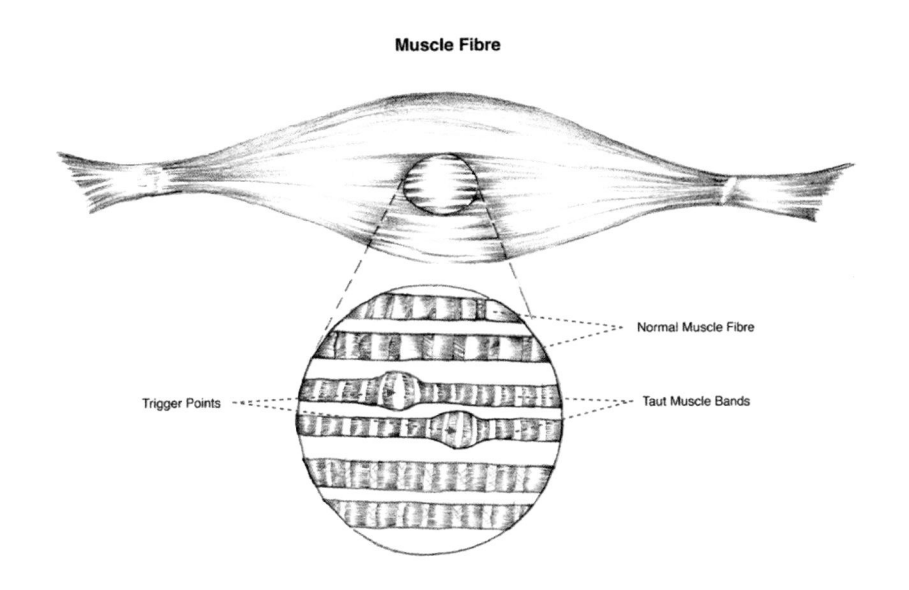

Muscle Fibre

FASCIA

Fascia has been defined as the connective tissue system that permeates the body, forming a whole-body continuous three-dimensional matrix of structural support. It penetrates and surrounds all organs, muscles, bones, and nerve fibers. Every muscle fiber and every muscle belly are surrounded by fascia. This is extremely important because it transmits almost 40% of the force of a muscle contraction and possibly more importantly, the fascia is a sensory organ that communicates with the CNS. Muscle spindle cells that help regulate muscle function are found in the fascia. If the fascia is too dense and unable to slide over and within muscle, then the spindle cell cannot provide normal feedback to the CNS. There will be abnormalities in muscle function, leading to eventual pain and dysfunction.

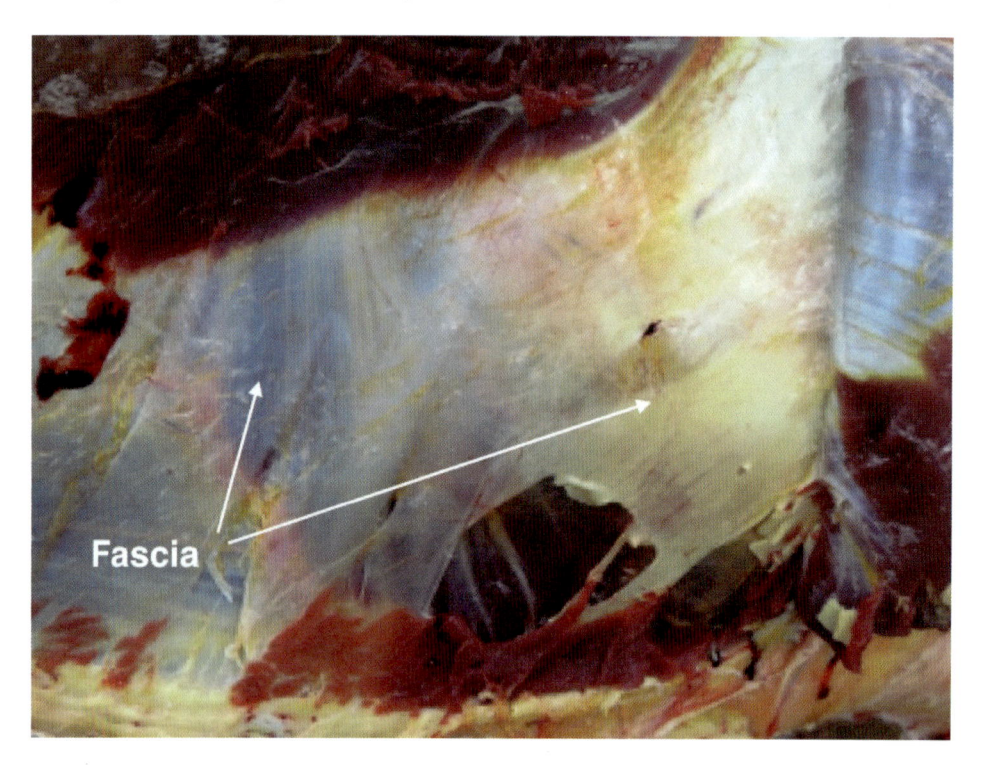

Fascia

Dr Warren Hammer and Thomas Myers are the some of the leading human fascial specialists in the USA .The knowledge that normal muscle function depends on the fascial system and between 30 and 40 percent of the force generated by muscle is due to its surrounding fascia. Science has dismissed the value of a connective tissue structure that encompasses our whole body both internally and externally.

Current research shows that more than 30 percent of the force generated from the muscle is transmitted not along a tendon as previously thought, but rather by the connective tissue within the muscle and fascia, and both of these contain mechanoreceptors and proprioceptors. When a muscle is in use, the fascia that is connected to spindle cells stretches. The normal stretching of fascia communicates the force of the muscle contraction and the status of the muscle regarding its tone, movement, rate of change in muscle length and position of the associated body part to the central nervous system (CNS).

Every person and every animal is born with a connective tissue covering which encompasses them from head to toe and encases all organs, muscles, nerves etc. Fascia is the connective tissue network that extends throughout the body, not only lying beneath the skin but also surrounding and connecting every organ, muscle, bone, nerve and blood vessel.

Fascia is comparative to a spider's web that surrounds, separates, supports and protects the body down to the cellular level, while allowing the body to move freely. If you touch one portion of the web, the whole web moves, providing the spider with information that it then reacts to. Fascia is a whole-body communication system where, if stimulated, transmits a signal to every part of the body.

Fascia evolves into tough, flexible supporting structures like ligaments and tendons, and forms the bursae that reduces friction and allows free movement over joints. The most essential job that fascia has is to

Fascia

produce scar tissue after an injury and help stabilize the area while it's being repaired.

Another vital job is to keep the muscles separate so that they can slide past each other as they work in different directions. In animal dissection you can remove different layers of muscle due to the covering of the fascia over each group. Muscles are covered by specific types of deep fascia, called epimysial or aponeurotic fascia.

In the extremities, a thin layer of epimysial fascia called the epimysium covers the surface of each muscle. It surrounds the entire surface of the muscle belly and separates it from adjoining muscles. It gives form to all of the extremity muscles.

Fascia

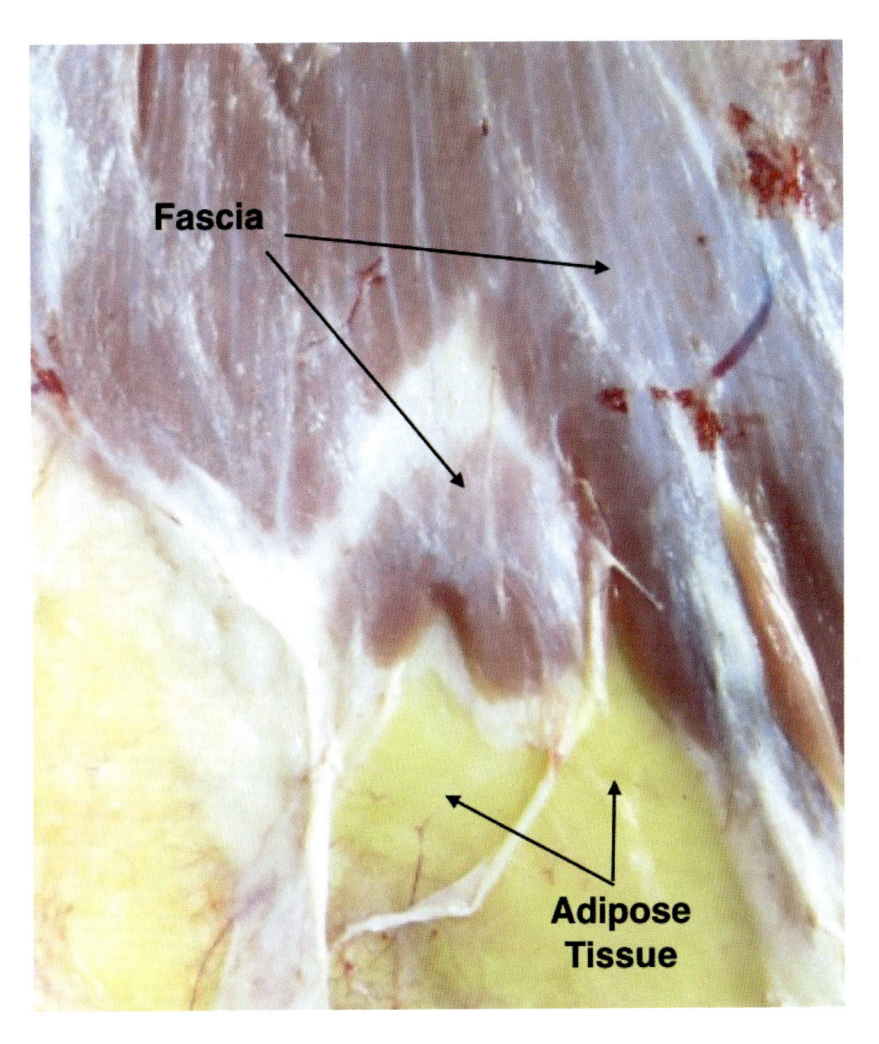

Fascia (labeled in image)

Adipose Tissue (labeled in image)

Aponeurotic fascia aids in transmitting the force of the muscles it covers and is innervated predominantly in the superficial layer. Fascia helps with delivery of fluids, nutrients and oxygen as well as removal of toxins and waste. Electrical impulses flow through it and it is thought that the energy or life force known as "chi" in Chinese medicine flows through it as well.

When fascia is injured or challenged, an inflammatory response changes it from a squishy soft, pliable gel to a stiff solid material that has an effect on electrical conductivity, all of this congestion impacts the animal's ability to move and results in compensations and biomechanical changes. Stiffened fascia leads to poor posture and abnormal or dysfunctional biomechanics as well as lowered strength and endurance. With an inefficient or painful nervous system, it can lead to reactive or unusual behavior.

Maintenance and repair of fascia is adversely affected by poor or unbalanced nutrition. Chronic pain or stress impacts the fascia by causing constant tension in the muscles, resulting in a reduction in circulation, causing the fascia to become stiff and dry. Fascia is often damaged by trauma such as strains, tears or lacerations.

As a natural part of healing, scar tissue forms at the site of damage, then disappears during the repair process. Poor circulation, lack of movement, inadequate nutrition and other factors don't allow the healing process to be completed, leaving behind adhesions i.e. tissue that is stuck together and stiffness. Those adhesions are fascial trigger points and have referral pain patterns.

Chronic overwork or reinjuring an area also affects the fascia. If an animal is trained into an aberrant way of standing or moving, worked beyond his ability to recover completely, or kept in a constant state of tension, the fascia is stressed along with overused muscles, tendons and ligaments.

When identifying fascial tightness, it is important to note that the skin doesn't slip over the body, and movement is stiff and shortened. The body has a memory of its proper constitution and healthy movement patterns and strives to move freely and pain free. It has the ability to change dysfunctional fascia into normal fascia, from a solid, unmoving tissue back to a gel.

"Myofascial release" has been a catch phrase for a while and there is little understanding of what that truly is. As fascia is worked on, there is a decrease in tension in the fascia and surrounding muscles. This lowers the resistance to flow and reduces pressure that is placed on pain sensitive tissues such as nerves and blood vessels. This allows the body to restore the proper length and alignment to the affected muscles. As a result, the joints have freedom of movement and the animal's flexibility, coordination and strength improve dramatically.

While there has been a great deal of basic scientific work done on the microscopic structure and chemistry of fascia, the work still needs to be done to verify what other alternative therapist such as Rolfers have always proposed: 1) that restriction in a small area of fascia can be propagated across long distances and across firm attachment points to cause global movement dysfunction and 2) that deep manual intervention is actually able to stretch or "free" fascial restrictions deep in the tissues. As time has gone on, I have seen some prominent human myofascial authors back away from these theories after participating in anatomical dissections. I was taught twenty years ago, that I could stretch the human quadratus lumborum fascia with my hands, yet even a cursory look into dissection at that depth and overlying muscle would lead one to question the possibility of achieving that outcome.

I was also taught that I could have an effect on the TFL and the very tough fibrous fascial attachments around the hip joint with manual intervention. Having actually palpated and felt tissues in dissection many times, I have to doubt the possibility. Given the strength and organization of those tissues and the forces they are designed to withstand, any gross change in them whether manual or surgical would amount to tissue damage and joint capsule injury and would require substantial healing. This is why myofascial dry needling is so effective for releasing fascia. It produces very minimal damage or adverse effects within the fascia while releasing the adhesive trigger point, increasing blood supply and aiding to remove noxious by products.

There are several conflicting theories that call into question our hypothesis about fascia and the effects that it has on the body. One such theory is that deep fascial intervention, as a secondary byproduct, causes mast cell degranulation in superficial tissues and that the released histamine granules cause extravasation of intravascular fluid into the tissues which "hydrates" those tissues, bringing about better sliding between fascial planes. The redness you see on the skin after fascial treatment and dry needling is partially due to this phenomenon of mast cell degranulation.

Moshe Feldenkrais, repeatedly showed that supposed "physical restrictions" in the human body were actually habitual muscle tensions that could be eliminated simply through a few minutes of low amplitude client-directed movements to bring awareness to those actions.

Joanne Elphinston in her text Stability, Sports and Performance Movement guides the reader through many of the typical abnormal movement patterns that therapists have always credited to fascial "restriction." She shows how these are often related to and corrected by addressing weakness in stabilization strength. She also shows how weakness in stabilization in one area of the body can demand compensatory and inefficient movement patterns elsewhere in the body.

Movement strategies are global whole-body phenomenon, and weakness in one area can result in compensations across joints distant from the weakness. Not only are these compensations clearly visible, but being inefficient, often lead to pathology and injury, once again distant from the underlying problem. Without fascial work there is still a possibility that these problems can be reversed through skill and strength acquisition.

Where physical restriction and tension are actually palpable and measurable, current scientific research seems to implicate vascular, neural and local chemical mediators all playing an interrelated role in initiating, sustaining and propagating such restrictions. Fascial adhesion may be an end point, but to what extent from the initial insult its effects can travel are still unknown. Further research is required in this field.

How to identify and treat problem areas.

Fascia

- Fascia allows the entire body space to move. As injuries as well as ageing occurs, this superficial fascia may shrink, pucker or tear, becoming tight or twisted.

- Scan for areas where the skin does not move over the body. You might find these on the upper shoulders or neck, the back, and over the upper rib cage or the hindquarter.

- The middle layer of fascia holds the organs, vessels, nerves, bones, and muscles in place.
  It forms compartments within the body and surrounds every layer of muscle fiber. When it is tight, it prevents full muscle contraction and relaxation, lowers circulation and nerve conductance, leading to compromised tissues and organs all over the body. To clear fascial restrictions a focused acupuncture needle inserted into a trigger point is used to eradicate the MFTP and release it from surrounding tissue. Scar tissue can disappear over time as you bring back circulation and help the body heal the area.

  Gentle movement and stretching are important to restore a healthy gait pattern and good posture. You can release fascia by moving a part of the body or helping the animal move into a release position.

- Normal muscle function requires that it's surrounding fascia is sufficiently hydrated so as to allow normal tissue gliding.

- Improper tissue gliding is directly related to mechanoreceptive and proprioceptive failure and muscle incoordination.

- Dysfunction occurs over myofascial kinetic chains, which is related to both the myofascial and acupuncture meridian fascial planes.

Fascia

- A full case history should be considered in areas of previous trauma or surgery which could reveal fascial thicknesses responsible for present complaints.

- Practical testing and palpation of fascial planes are a major diagnostic method.

- Treatment of affected points should be continued until normal thickness is palpated and negative testing improves.

Fascia is still a very misunderstood and ignored organ. I use the word organ intentionally because it is as important as a liver, kidney, heart or the skin. Considering the direct effect that it has on muscles and joints we cannot ignore the fact that dysfunction in the fascia opens a door to many abnormalities and changes that we see on a muscular and joint level. This results in biomechanical changes, gait abnormalities and compensations that create issues elsewhere.

By treating the MFTPs in the fascia and surrounding muscle with dry needling, one eradicates the dysfunction that is occurring in that area, reducing the risk of perpetuation and recurrence and helps the body heal itself and return to normal functioning. This information is just the tip of the iceberg with regards to fascia but to get to the nitty gritty of it, will require another book.

MYOFASCIAL PAIN SYNDROMES IN THE CANINE

David Simons, MD, a well-known expert in muscle pain and dysfunction in people, and coauthor of Travell and Simons' – *Myofascial Pain and Dysfunction -The Trigger Point Manual,* referred to muscle as an "orphan organ". He said, "No medical specialty claims it. As a consequence, no medical specialty is concerned with promoting funded research into the muscular causes of pain, and medical students and physical therapists rarely receive adequate primary training in how to recognize and treat myofascial trigger points."

The previous absence of research evidence validating a set of reliable diagnostic radiologic markers, continues to relegate the existence of myofascial trigger points, and perhaps myofascial syndromes in general, to being recognized by some, but rejected by others.

In dogs skeletal muscle makes up approximately 44% of live body weight in mixed breed and purebred dogs. In greyhounds' muscle to live weight is approximately 57%.(70) Yet, there continues to be a deficiency in both veterinary education and veterinary literature, about skeletal muscle and its role in pain and dysfunction.

Muscle pain or myalgia is described as an aching, cramping pain that is difficult to localize and can refer to deep somatic tissues. Myalgia activates cortical structures and is inhibited by descending pain-modulating pathways. Activation of muscle nociceptors is very effective at inducing neuroplasticity in the dorsal horn neurons that occur in chronic pain.(71)

Myalgia strongly activates the anterior cingulate cortex and periaqueductal gray matter(PAG). These areas are known to be associated with emotions in humans, and depression often accompanies chronic myalgic conditions such as fibromyalgia. These areas of the brain are not affected by cutaneous pain.(72,73)

Muscle pain often occurs as a result of joint injury or dysfunction. If the joint is not functioning properly, mechanical stress can be placed on the functional muscle unit of that joint (flexors, extensors, adductors, abductors, etc.). However, muscle pain and dysfunction can also lead to joint dysfunction. Muscle pain can also follow nerve injury or dysfunction. Muscles innervated by an irritated or injured nerve can become painful.

Myalgia is defined as pain in a muscle and may result from:

Overuse resulting in muscle injury.
Inflammatory myopathies
Trauma
Metabolic/Endocrine disorders
Nutritional insufficiencies
Myofascial pain

Skeletal muscle is one of the most adaptable tissues in the body. It is well recognized that the main reason change is created in skeletal muscle is the level of muscle activity in relation to normal muscle activity. (82) Every structural aspect of muscle can change given the proper stimulus.

Muscle plasticity is an important consideration as changes in the muscle occur due to injury and disease. Plasticity is also important in training and conditioning of the canine athlete.

Characteristics of Myofascial Trigger Points

MFTPs have three major characteristics, sensory, motor and autonomic. The muscle pain or myalgia associated with MFTPs is described in humans as diffuse, deep and difficult to localize with defined referred pain patterns. When the MFTP is stimulated manually a localized pain is appreciated. Very often palpation of a MFTP in dogs can result in a "jump sign", a pain response resulting in vocalization and/or withdrawal as pressure is applied. Other sensory aspects include peripheral and central sensitization. Peripheral sensitization can be described as a reduction in threshold and an increase in responsiveness of the peripheral ends of nociceptors. Central sensitization is best explained as a physiochemical change resulting in increased excitability of neurons within the central nervous system.(79)

Motor abnormalities of MFTPs include the development of a taut band within the muscle, a local twitch response (LTR) with stimulation, muscle weakness without atrophy and loss of reciprocal inhibition.(84)The taut band is a localized, band of hardened muscle within the softer homogeneous muscle. Taut bands are identified running parallel to muscle fibers and can be described as a localized contracture within the muscle without nerve-initiated activation of the motor endplate or neuromuscular junction.(85)

What is the difference between MFTPs and muscle spasm?

Muscle spasm is the result of increased neuromuscular tone of the entire muscle due to a nerve-initiated contraction. A muscle spasm that is painful is referred to as a muscle cramp. The contracture associated with the taut band also results in reduction in range of motion. The MFTP is located within the taut band and is what distinguishes it from other painful areas within muscle(86).

The local twitch response (LTR) is another motor component of MFTPs that we have already spoken about. The local twitch response is a unique involuntary spinal cord reflex resulting in a rapid contraction of the taut band following manual stimulation of the MFTP. Manual stimulation can be accomplished by direct palpation or introduction of a needle. The LTR in dogs can also serve as verification of the presence of a MFTP.

In people, weakness is recognized in muscles that have MFTPs. This weakness occurs without atrophy and is not related to neuropathy or myopathy.(83) Weakness is usually rapidly reversible immediately upon inactivation of the MFTP. This rapid reversal suggests that weakness is a result of inhibited muscle activation. Remember that MFTPs in one muscle can inhibit function or contractile force in another muscle proving a central inhibition process.(85) Additional motor or muscle dysfunction from MFTPs is brought about by disordered recruitment or altered muscle activation patterns in muscles that work together to produce a specific action.(86,87)

Reciprocal inhibition is defined as inhibition of antagonist muscle contraction during contraction of the agonist muscle. This central inhibition of muscle activity results in coordinated quality movement. Reciprocal inhibition becomes reduced when the agonist or the activated muscle contains a MFTP resulting in co-contraction and subsequently altered gait and decreased quality of movement.

In dogs, several helpful tests that can illuminate weakness are: Sit to stand and one leg weight bearing. With a dog in standing position, slowly slide limb backward until non-weight bearing. A slight to profound drop of the contralateral side can be indicative of muscle weakness and/or altered muscle firing patterns associated with MFTPs within the anti-gravity muscles of that limb. In humans, this is known as Trendelenburg sign or test. Sit to stand exercise can serve as a subjective assessment of weakness by observation of dog's ability to both sit and stand.

Etiology of Myofascial Trigger Points

Trigger points can be described as segments of muscle fiber with intensely contracted sarcomeres and increased diameter. It is unknown as to why these MFTPs occur. It is postulated in *Integrated Trigger Point Hypothesis* that there is a problem at the motor endplate resulting in excessive release of acetylcholine. This excess of acetylcholine results in sarcomere shortening that has been observed histopathologically.(88) Contraction knots or areas of concentrated focal sarcomere contraction have been described in animals and humans.(89)

Muscle overuse or overload and direct trauma are the most common causes of MFTPs. Low-level muscle contractions, uneven intramuscular pressure distribution, direct trauma, unaccustomed eccentric contractions, eccentric contraction in unconditioned muscle, and maximal or submaximal concentric contractions can lead to muscle injury and subsequent development of MFTPs.(79,90)

The *Integrated Trigger Point Hypothesis*(1981), was the first scientific hypothesis to attempt to explain MFTPs based on both electrophysiological and histopathological data.(91) The hypothesis postulates that muscle injury leads to increased calcium concentrations outside the sarcoplasmic reticulum, possibly due to mechanical rupture of the sarcoplasmic reticulum or the sarcolemma. Increased calcium concentrations result in sustained muscle fiber contraction. This hypothesis was later refined, in 2004, to include a dysfunctional motor endplate occurring secondary to muscle injury and resulting in excessive release of acetylcholine.(92)

Sustained maximal contraction of the muscle fibers in the vicinity of the dysfunctional endplate causes increased metabolic demand and decreased concentrations of adenosine triphosphate (ATP). The calcium pump that returns calcium to the sarcoplasmic reticulum is ATP dependent, as is the un-crosslinking of actin and myosin, therefore calcium concentrations and contractile activity remain increased.

Muscle injury alters the normal equilibrium between the release and breakdown of acetylcholine, and its removal by acetylcholinesterase from acetylcholine receptors in the postsynaptic membrane. Substances such as calcitonin gene related peptide (CGRP) and Substance P (SP), released during muscle injury, facilitate increased release of acetylcholine, inhibition of breakdown, and up regulation of acetylcholine receptors. (92) A persistent muscle fiber contraction develops leading to the development of the taut band and subsequent MFTP.

Perpetuation of MFTP formation in dogs

Mechanical stresses cause chronic muscle overload. Postural changes in the dog due to orthopedic injury, postoperative surgical trauma and pain, neuropathy, joint dysfunction, and pain related to osteoarthritis create muscle overload. Many of the same muscle-related mechanisms that lead to development of MFTPs also perpetuate them.

Chronic osteoarthritis creates compensatory changes that activate and perpetuate MFTPs in numerous muscles. Moderate to severe osteoarthritis of the coxofemoral joints activates and perpetuates MFTPs in the functional unit muscles of the coxofemoral joint, flexors (including iliopsoas), adductors, and extensors. The cranial shift in weight overloads the infraspinatus, deltoideus, and the long head of the triceps brachii. Repeated lateral flexion of the spine, which assists in ambulation by advancing the pelvis and pelvic limb while limiting coxofemoral flexion and extension, results in overloading of the iliocostalis lumborum.

A dog that presents with a non-weight bearing pelvic limb lameness, adopts hopping actions in the contralateral pelvic limb, resulting in unusual eccentric contractions of the coxofemoral and stifle extensors in an attempt to limit flexion. Lumbar paraspinal muscles become overloaded, as they must now assist with ambulation and not solely spinal stabilization. The iliopsoas develops MFTPs and this results in a kyphotic posture.

In the case of osteoarthritis, MPS occurs and MFTPs form because of sustained low-level contractions in a muscle or a group of muscles. When a muscle needs to perform a low-level contraction, only a few muscle fibers are enlisted for that action.
When these low-level contractions occur, the same few muscle fibers are always used, and even if they become exhausted, no other muscle fibers attempt to help out and work. This has been referred to as the "Cinderella hypothesis." The rest of the muscle, just like Cinderella's sisters, never help out: the same fibers are the first to activate, do all the work on their own and are the last ones to retire.

If you want to understand this better, pick up a dinner plate and hold it in your hand, extending your arm horizontally in front of you. It probably weighs only a few grams or ounces. Within several minutes your muscles will begin to ache and eventually it will become impossible to hold your arm out in front of you.

Now think about doing arm curls in the gym, where you might be curling 20 pounds or more and not feeling the same degree of exhaustion as you just felt with the plate. That's because the entire muscle is working together to help you do that curl not just individual muscle fibers.

The first example with the plate is similar to what a dog with a painful limb will experience, but the pain of putting full weight on the limb is often less than the pain of the "muscle cramp" that comes about from protecting the injured leg by keeping it non-weight bearing. Eventually these constantly cramped and exhausted muscle fibers develop myofascial trigger points and the dog is constantly in pain.

Ultimately these few muscle fibers become permanently contracted. There is a lack of adenosine triphosphate (ATP), which is necessary for the sarcomere within this taut band of muscle to relax. We always think of muscles needing energy to contract, but the opposite is also true, they need it to relax. This is why we see muscles go into rigor mortis upon death when all the existing ATP is used up.

When these taut muscle bands occur, the entire muscle becomes shortened, the joint is compressed from the constant contraction, causing dysfunction in the joint dynamics. So not only is there muscle pain, but the reduced width of the joint space causes increased wear and tear on the joint.

The insertion of a needle results in the relaxation of the taut band of muscle by utilizing a spinal reflex pathway that bypasses the ATP cascade.

Other methods include cold laser therapy and massage, which both increase blood flow to the affected area, thereby allowing for the mitochondrial production of ATP and the relaxation of the sarcomere. Dry needling is instant, with immediate relief. The other methods take time to get results.

In people additional perpetuating factors are identified, nutritional, metabolic, nerve impingement and visceral-somatic pain, nutritional insufficiency of vitamin B12 (cobalamin) and folic acid have been described as perpetuating factors for myofascial pain syndrome.(79,83,86)

There are no references in the veterinary literature with regards to insufficiency of these substances causing pain of any type. This is due to lack of research in this area.

Hypothyroidism, a metabolic and endocrine disorder, is recognized in people as a perpetuating factor for MFTP. Clinical signs for people include myalgia, stiffness, weakness, cramps, and pain upon exertion.(83) Hypothyroidism is the most common endocrine disorder in dogs and is associated with a variety of clinical signs; however, the veterinary literature does not mention pain as a consequence of hypothyroidism.

In people visceral pain can activate and perpetuate MFTPs in the area of referred pain. Neurons in the dorsal horn of the spinal cord receive input from the viscera, from receptors in the skin and deeper soft tissues.(93) As a result of this overlap, visceral nociceptive activation of the dorsal horn neurons may result in muscle pain and may also be a cause of MFTPs in animals.

HOW TO TREAT MYOFASCIAL PAIN SYNDROME (MPS)

One always needs to look at the originating cause of the MPS, whether it's osteoarthritis (OA), a torn or strained bicep tendon or a cruciate tear. In this case, if you address only the underlying cause, with a NSAID or surgical repair for example, and ignore the associated compensations the patient may not have a good response to treatment. If the MPS is mild, aggressive treatment of the causative factor, such as OA, may allow the MFTPs in the muscles to relax on their own as the muscles are used in a normal manner over time.

I have seen many cases where OA treatment has been unsatisfactory until the MPS was addressed. In addition to this, "successful surgeries" can result in compensations in the myofascia that prevents the animal from weight bearing and healing successfully. I have had several cases where the surgery, according to all diagnostics, was successful and the dog is still refusing to use the leg. The surgeons are baffled, the owners get angry and emotional and think of suing everyone involved, and the dog is in constant pain. One or two dry needling sessions later, where the myofascial pain was addressed correctly and efficiently resulted in the dog walking out normally. The owners are happy, the surgeons are happy and more importantly the dog goes on to live a full, pain free life.

The Canine Athlete

Muscular injury can occur from trauma or biomechanical overloading. Injured muscles are shortened with increased tone and tension due to varied states of over contraction and contracture.(108). In people, myofascial pain, characterized by the presence of myofascial trigger points (MFTPs), is estimated to account for 85% of muscle pain (myalgia) due to injury.(83) Myofascial pain and MFTPs are now being recognized as clinical entities in veterinary patients, however, minimal literature exists.(129-133)

With the exception of spontaneous pain there is no difference between active and latent MFTPs. The later only produces pain when stimulated; however other MFTP characteristics remain the same. MFTPs produce muscle weakness, thought to be due to central inhibition. The muscle contracture brought about by the development of taut bands shortens muscle length and reduces joint range of motion. Altered muscle activation patterns and loss of reciprocal inhibition of antagonist muscles can directly affect coordinated limb and body movement.(86,134)

More recent findings in people suggest accelerated muscle fatigue and overloading of active muscle motor units close to the MFTPs. Combined or alone these MFTP characteristics potentiate decreased performance in the athlete.

The etiology of muscle injury in the canine athlete can be caused by eccentric muscle contractions, maximal concentric muscle contractions, and unaccustomed muscle contraction; poorly conditioned canine athletes maybe at greater risk, especially those with insufficient core strength. Core body strength can be defined as the balanced development of muscles that stabilize, align and move the trunk of the body. In dogs this is primarily the dorsal and ventral paraspinal muscles and to a lesser degree the abdominal muscles.

A classification system for muscle injury by European sports medicine physicians may more clearly define muscle injury.(76)

Functional muscle disorders – acute indirect muscle disorder without macroscopic evidence of muscle tear.
Fatigue-induced muscle disorder and delayed onset muscle soreness.
Spine-related and muscle related neuromuscular muscle disorders.

Structural muscle injury – any acute indirect muscle injury with macroscopic evidence of muscle tear.
Partial muscle tears.
(Sub)total muscle tears and tendinous avulsions.

How to Treat Myofascial Pain Syndrome

In the canine athlete functional muscle disorders appear more common. Canine athletes are often treated empirically, without benefits of advanced diagnostic imagining or ultrasound that would define a structural problem. Muscle injury resulting in the development of taut bands and MFTPs would be defined as a functional muscle disorder.

Two of the more commonly reported muscles injured in the canine athlete are the iliopsoas (formed by the joining of the psoas major and the iliacus near its insertion on the lesser trochanter of the femur) and the teres muscle. The iliopsoas is very important for core muscle strength.

The teres aids in flexion of the shoulder, draws the humerus caudally and medially rotates the shoulder preventing lateral rotation. It is most likely injured during rapid lateral movements while attempting to stabilize the shoulder. Just below the scapula the teres major joins the latissimus dorsi. Some injuries classified as teres major may actually be latissimus dorsi or a combination of both.

The Orthopedic and Neurologic Patient

The development of myalgia and muscle dysfunction in the orthopedic patient can be the result of mechanical stress resulting in muscle overload. Changes in posture, compensatory movements and altered limb loading are likely the etiologies related to the development of MFTPs. The neurologic patient is similar with the addition of MFTP development in muscles innervated by irritated nerves and/or spinal cord segments.

In the non-weight bearing pelvic limb patient, MFTPs can develop in the muscles of contralateral limb (rectus femoris, vastus group, gluteals, biceps femoris, semitendinosus) due to eccentric contractions brought about during hopping movement. Continuous hip flexion maintains non-weight bearing resulting in low-level muscle contractions in the flexors of the hip, including the iliopsoas. MFTPs develop in these muscles creating contracture and limiting coxofemoral joint range of motion often accompanied by a kyphotic posture. The later can be due to MFTP development in the iliopsoas. These functional problems in the muscle can exist long after the initial orthopedic structural problem resolve.

When treating MPS it is imperative to treat the causative factor first but not neglect the compensatory mechanisms that have occurred such as myalgia or MFTPs in a muscle. It needs to be a fully inclusive treatment. For example: a dog with hip dysplasia needs a full hip replacement to resolve the joint dysfunction, then within the first few weeks post-surgery all the compensatory muscles need to be addressed to ensure that the dog does not fall back into its old compensatory movement pattern and to eradicate any MFTPs that would result in the muscles not regaining their full length or function. If that were to be neglected, the pain and dysfunction that would result would be due to a functional issue now not a structural one.

PALPATION

The success of treating myofascial disorders lies solely in the hands of the practitioner and their ability to palpate, identify and treat the dysfunction that has been diagnosed.

Palpation is the most overlooked technique by practitioners today and in so doing, it allows for many misdiagnoses and incorrect treatment protocols. Examination of muscles for myofascial pain and MFTPs is not part of the standard physical, orthopedic, or neurologic examination in veterinary medicine. Identification of taut bands and hypersensitive MFTPs within muscle is an acquired skill that requires understanding of these changes, skilled instruction, and repeated practice.

There are three basic palpation techniques employed in a myofascial examination:

Flat Palpation: Examination by finger pressure that proceeds across the muscle fibers at a right angle to their length while compressing them against a firm underlying structure, such as a bone. This technique could be used for the infraspinatus, supraspinatus, and psoas major.

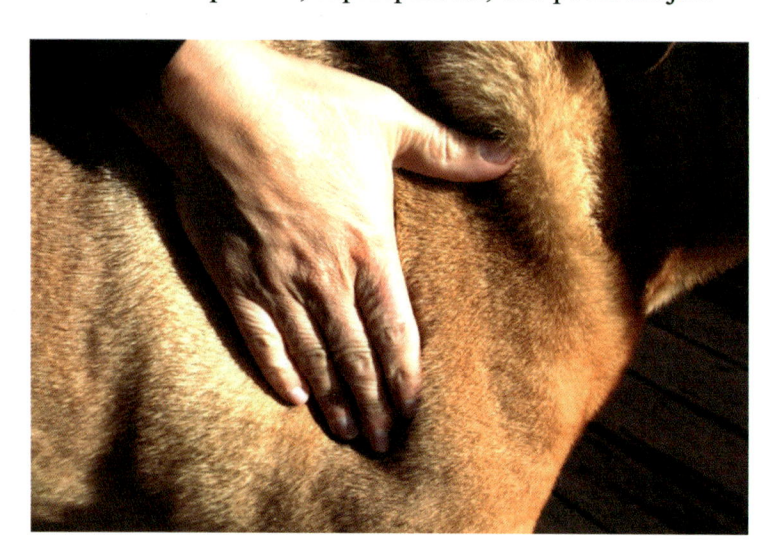

Palpation

Pincer Palpation: Examination of a part of a muscle by holding it in a pincer grasp between the thumb and fingers. Groups of muscles fibers are rolled between the tips of the digits to detect taut bands. This technique could be used for the triceps, sartorius, and tensor fascia latae.

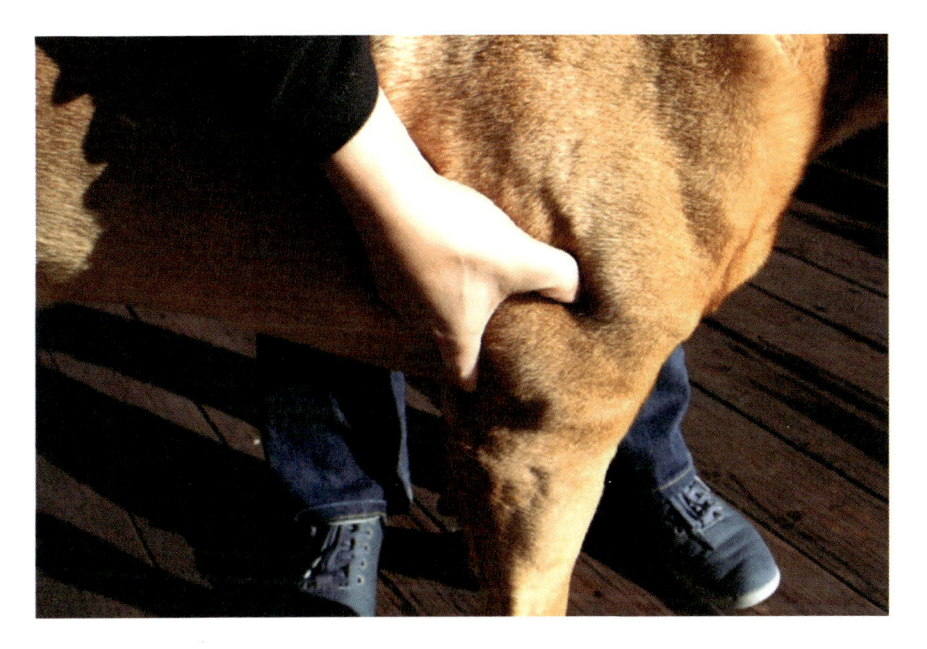

Palpation

Deep palpation: Examination of a part of a muscle by positioning the finger into the fleshiest and most tender area of the muscle and identifying the myofascial trigger points that lie deep in the muscle. This technique can be used for rectus femoris and the gluteal muscle group.

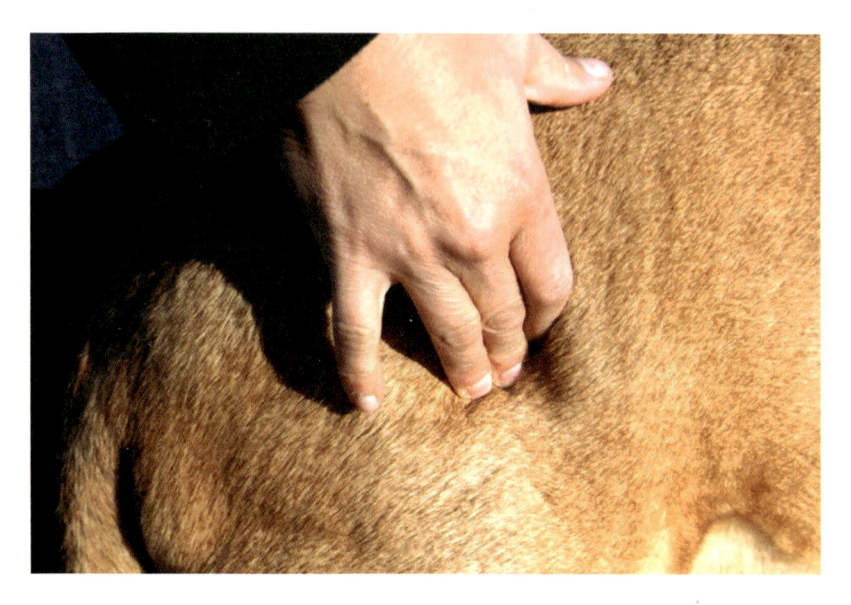

Myalgia can be appreciated in individual muscles with examination of the patient in the standing position. However, taut bands and MFTPs are easier to appreciate in a relaxed muscle by placing patient non-weight bearing position such as lateral recumbency.

In each position, an assistant is needed to provide gentle patient restraint because examination can induce a jump sign. Education of the client prior to the myofascial examination is needed to avoid concern when pain is elicited.

Palpation is viewed as the assessment through touch of the muscles, tendons and fascia, discriminating normal tissue from trigger points, and identifying the source of the myofascial pain. This is achieved by physical touch, that when trained correctly a practitioner can discern structures by feel and identify abnormalities.

Palpation

Anatomical and physiological knowledge is essential in developing a clear mental image of what is being palpated. Knowing the attachment and the action of a muscle is essential in determining whether it is functioning normally or abnormally.

Muscle quality fluctuates significantly. Flaccid or hypotonic muscle, as well as constricted or hypertonic muscle, are both deemed abnormal and sit on opposite sides of the spectrum, with normal muscle in the middle. Healthy muscle is soft, pliable, painless on palpation and allows the underlying structures to be easily palpated.

Tight, harder, ropey muscles are considered constricted. It is very difficult to palpate structures lying beneath this muscle as its "guards" the underlying structures. Discomfort, tenderness or pain may be experienced by the animal when palpating this area. The degree of constriction is dependent on the state of muscle contraction. If there is partial contraction of the muscle, muscle fibers are still discernable and identifiable.

These bands have a ropey feel to them and are tender on palpation and resistant to pressure. Within this partially contracted band of muscle there will be harder, very tender points known (as defined by Travell and Simons) as a myofascial trigger point. When pressure is applied to this trigger point, a radiating pain will occur. This is known as referred pain and is characteristic of a myofascial trigger point.

A deeply contracted muscle is considered to be a muscle that remains in a contracted position without partial relaxation of the muscle. Dysfunctions that cause this could be a neurological condition, trauma, chronic structural abnormalities (structural short leg, post knee surgery (TPLO or TTA), scoliosis- structural or functional, hemivertebra etc. and severe repetitive strain injuries.

When a muscle is contracted for a long period of time, circulation to the area diminishes and can result in a fibrous, and sclerotic muscle that has no elastic properties. The muscle remains in a shortened position. Pain and dysfunction occur due to a loss of normal movement. If this fixed

Palpation

posture persists it will become chronic and the chances of a full recovery and return to normal functioning decreases significantly.

The ability to treat myofascial trigger points effectively is entirely dependent on the practitioner's ability to envision the correct anatomical structures that he or she is feeling. Bony landmarks, insertion points, angles of the muscle fibers, lymph nodes, arteries and veins need to be identified in order to diagnose and treat the dysfunction correctly.

It is imperative that one uses not only touch, but sight too, as a diagnostic tool. Looking and feeling for symmetry of the muscles as well as the anatomical structures are clues as to where the source of the dysfunction is coming from. To use a clinical example: when assessing a dog from behind, one identifies a high riding scapula, contracture of the rhomboid and trapezius muscle on the right side and a flaccid latissimus dorsi muscle. One needs to ask questions regarding posture or trauma. This may present as an overuse or repetitive strain injury from always using the dominant side or it may be a result of trauma from running after balls, doing agility, or turning in one direction.

A full history from the owner will give you clues to the information you need in order to diagnose your patient effectively and lead you quickly to the muscles and fascia that may be involved. Learning and understanding the specific referred pain pattern is essential in identifying the causative active trigger points, treating them and effectively reducing your patients' pain and symptomatology almost immediately.

Ergonomic evaluations, stretching and strengthening protocols will then be introduced to prevent a recurrence of this condition.

The steps to learning palpation are fairly simple, but to be effective in performing palpation takes a lot of practice and an increase in the sensitivity of your hands and fingers is imperative. This takes time and the more you palpate the better you will be at "feeling" the body.

Palpation

Step 1: Anatomically envision the area that you want to palpate.

Step 2: Lightly place your fingers over the muscle that you want to palpate. Always start by palpating the "normal" side first. This is a very important step as one can only diagnose abnormal if one has felt normal first. Identify bony landmarks and the circumference of the muscle.

Step 3: Lightly palpate the muscle fibers that run lengthways and feel for any constrictions within the muscle belly. Repeat this process at ninety degrees to the length of the muscle.

Step 4: As you lightly palpate the muscle you will feel areas within the muscle that are less pliable and more resistant to pressure than others. Deepen your palpation slightly and you may feel the patient instinctively tighten up as a subconscious reaction to pain. The patient may elicit a jump sign or cry out (or try bite you), and if the trigger point is very active you may even see or feel a twitch response. Congratulations you have successfully found the trigger point that you will need to needle.

DIAGNOSIS

As a clinician, you presumably have the anatomical and diagnostic knowledge of the animals' body as well as a working relationship with myofascial pain syndromes. Many diagnostic tools become automatic over time and the more time that one spends in practice, the more subconscious and routine certain protocols become. Below are a few tips outlining some diagnostic criteria that need to be addressed when diagnosing and treating myofascial pain syndromes.

Observe the patient:

Look at a patient's posture- seated, standing, down and ambulatory. This as well as certain body language goes a long way to tell us what the patient is experiencing.

Many owners are not aware of the changes that are going on with their animals, so when asked where the pain is located, duration, onset and presentation, they are unable to answer.

Watching routine movements such as standing from a seated position, lying down, putting the animal through its gaits, climbing stairs or an incline, etc. gives you an indication of where the problem lies.

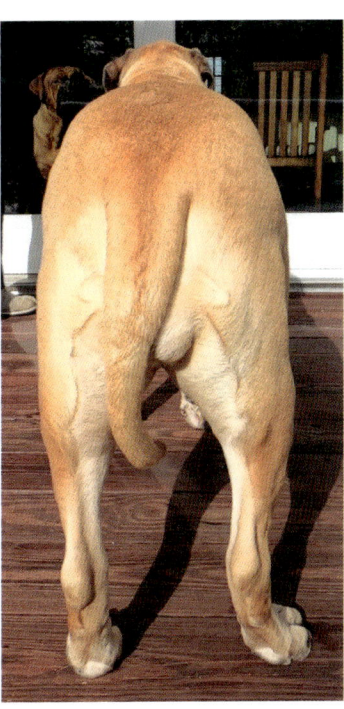

Diagnosis

Diagnosis

It is very rare to find a singular muscle with trigger points; it is normally part of a much bigger, multifaceted system. Multiple muscles, even several joints, nerves, fascial chains and vascularity may be involved in creating the pain syndrome.

Medical history and a detailed history of the current problem will lead you 70 % of the way to determining a diagnosis, treatment plan and prognosis. Therefore, between observation and listening to the owner, you are well on your way to a successful treatment outcome.

There are always some medical outliers, that present with a certain condition that appears simple and ends up being completely different to what you thought.
Keep this in mind when dealing with myofascial trigger points, as they are very often a major cause of pain that may be located locally at the trigger point or within the referred pain pattern or may present completely differently to any pattern that you have learnt.

Listening skills:

The owner (hopefully) knows their animals' body and behavior better than you do, therefore be very attentive to the way the client describes their animals pain, try not to interrupt or put words in their mouth, as it will change the way you and they interpret their animals pain and current condition.

Many clients would have been disregarded by their veterinarian by the time they come to you, so be aware that they may have been told that they are imagining it, it's all in their head or even more disconcerting that their veterinarian doesn't know what is wrong with their animal therefore it cannot be treated. Owners often feel disheartened, hopeless and sometimes angry by the time they get to your office. If an owner feels heard and listened to, you have already started leading them in the right direction to helping their animal on their healing journey.

Educating the owner with regards to myofascial pain, what it is, how do we treat it and their very important role in their animals' treatment with

Diagnosis

regards to ergonomics, stretching and strengthening is crucial in moving forward towards an ultimate success. If someone doesn't understand the WHY they are doing something they will never do it, which will hamper your success in treating their animal. Reassuring the owner that it is real, and they are not "crazy" goes a long way in developing a healing relationship and partnership with your patients and owners.

Myofascial needling is painful. You need to tell the owner this before you even go near their animal with a needle. The animal will react instinctively to pain i.e.: cry out, pull away, try to bite etc. If you don't educate the owner before the treatment, they will ALWAYS think that you have messed up and are trying to "cover it up" after the fact. If you tell them prior to the treatment, what to expect during and after treatment, they will trust you and more importantly be completely on board with the process.

Palpation skills:

Palpation is an art. It is a skill that needs to be honed constantly in order to improve. Many animals have trust issues and do not like to be touched especially by strangers. Be very in tune to the fact that a stranger's touch may make patients guard or develop defensive postures that may hamper your diagnosis. Develop a rapport with your patient and make them as comfortable as possible. In order to be concise and specific with your diagnosis, you need to have felt normal, compared it to abnormal and be able to identify the trigger points, quickly and effectively.

Every patient has a different pain tolerance. Be aware of this and treat them accordingly. For some patients, just soft, light palpation may result in them feeling excruciating pain, whereas others may feel almost nothing. Treat your patients as individuals and do not over treat. When in doubt, doing one or two points instead of every trigger point you find will not aggravate the patients pain level, it will not increase the inflammatory level and result in them not wanting to be treated by you. It is remarkable what a patient will allow you to do if they trust you.

Diagnosis

There are three basic palpation techniques that we have discussed before:

Flat Palpation: Examination by finger pressure that proceeds across the muscle fibers at a right angle to their length while compressing them against a firm underlying structure, such as a bone.

Pincer Palpation: Examination of a part of a muscle by holding it in a pincer grasp between the thumb and fingers. Groups of muscles fibers are rolled between the tips of the digits to detect taut bands.

Deep palpation: Examination of a part of a muscle by positioning the finger into the fleshiest and most tender area of the muscle and identifying the myofascial trigger points that lie deep in the muscle.

MFTPs can be located in individual muscles with examination of the patient in the standing position or in a non-weight bearing position such as lateral recumbency.

In each position, an assistant is needed to provide gentle patient restraint because examination can induce a jump sign. Education of the owner prior to examination is needed to avoid concern when pain is elicited.

Remember that myofascial trigger points are seldom found in isolation in one muscle belly and are generally accompanied by trigger points in antagonistic and agonistic muscles. Examine the affected muscle, the areas surrounding the muscle as well as all known antagonists and agonists and treat what you find.

TREATMENT:

After palpating the various muscles and identifying the active trigger points, treatment needs to be administered. There are many ways of getting rid of trigger points, laser, shock wave, acupressure but we have found a dry needle insertion to be the most effective in treating myofascial trigger points.

When approaching patient care and treatment there are a few things to consider:

Prior to treatment, have the patients' area of pain clearly defined in your mind. Practitioners have trouble identifying where the source of the pain comes from. If a patient presents with pain on a specific movement, ask the owner to have their animal reproduce the movement and pinpoint where in the movement the pain occurs. Often you will need to needle the patient with them holding that specific posture in order to reproduce the referred pain and eradicate the trigger point. For example, if a dog is lame on the left fore on weight bearing, but you are unable to palpate the MFTP with the dog lying lateral recumbent and in a relaxed position , place the dog in a weight bearing position, if the MFTP is palpable then needle the dog weight bearing on the left fore.

There may be more than one muscle involved in the patients' pain presentation. Always ensure that all potential muscles are palpated and evaluated to identify the active trigger point.

Palpate each of the possible muscles extensively. Feel for hard taut bands and specifically for the "exquisite tenderness" that results in a pain reaction, that accompanies active trigger points.
Palpate agonists and antagonists to determine whether there are associated trigger points from compensations; treat these if they are active.

When you find the trigger point, you need to "block" the trigger point. This is done either between two fingers (index and middle) or a thumb

Treatment

and a finger(index). You want to lock that trigger point in place so that it cannot move. This ensures specificity and accuracy when needling the trigger point.

Clean the area to be treated extensively with rubbing alcohol. This is essential to prevent infection and contamination of any kind.

Do not remove all the needles from packages before use. Remove a needle as needed in order to preserve a sterile environment.

Needling techniques will be covered in another section.

Prior to needling the patient, the treatment should be explained to the owner, including what the patient will feel during treatment, possible post needling soreness, side effects, how often the patient needs to be seen and the prognosis and goal of the treatment.

Moist heat is helpful after treatment, not ice. Moist heat should be applied for 10-20 minutes at a time, with a break of at least 1 hr. between applications. You can have them repeat this as often as they like.

Stretching is a great adjunct to treatment. It helps to stretch the muscle, decrease muscle spasms and constrictions and return the muscle to full efficacy. Stretching should be muscle specific and done several times a day.

Provide a strengthening program, once the patients' full range of motion has returned and has been pain free for 1-2 weeks. If you are not a qualified rehabilitation practitioner, I highly recommend developing a good working relationship with a certified canine rehabilitation practitioner. You may not have the time or the skills to rehabilitate a dog correctly and that will affect the final outcome for that patient. It is imperative to have an integrated relationship with the veterinarian or surgeon, the rehab specialist and you as a practitioner. This is the only way to guarantee success and if everyone works together in their area

Treatment

of expertise, the chances of a full recovery of the patient increases exponentially.

Post treatment patient re- education is important. Movement patterns are important to modify, sleeping positions, collar, harness and bed choices, functional movement, impacting activities and stress management are all essential elements to ensure a successful long-term treatment outcome.

Owner feedback will be a very helpful tool in ensuring quick and effective treatment. Often the primary trigger point will resolve, and other secondary trigger points will become more active than the primary. Treat those when they crop up. It is very much like an onion, there are multiple "layers" and compensations to be treated. As you resolve one trigger point, another may present itself and so on and so forth. Keep peeling away the onion until the issue is resolved.

It all comes down to a local twitch response. The difference between success and failure in the treatment of myofascial pain with needles is this: <u>If no LOCAL TWITCH RESPONSE occurs, the treatment is completely ineffective.</u>

Dry needling is as effective as myofascial anesthetic injections for trigger point relief. The only difference in dry needling and anesthetic injection if both are administered correctly, is that the post needling soreness is higher in dry needling as the anesthetic will eliminate that with the injection.

Active trigger points produce pain when they are compressed. Pain is experienced locally and in a referred pain pattern away from the MFTP. Always needle the active trigger points first, once the primary active trigger point has been treated, satellite/associate and latent trigger points can spontaneously resolve due to the eradication of the active trigger points.

There are many ways that trigger points can form. They result from direct stimuli-acute overload, fatigue, trauma, and radiculopathy or

Treatment

from indirect stimuli-other trigger points, organic disease, joint dysfunction, emotional issues. A latent trigger point can become active due to overload and stress.

The most common active trigger points are found in the postural muscles of the neck, shoulder, pelvic girdle, and rotary muscles. The trapezius, triceps, deltoid, rhomboid, SCM, latissimus dorsi, paraspinals/erectors spinae and quadratus lumborum are the most affected.

NEEDLING USE AND TECHNIQUE

Patient positioning, drug or supplement intake (with regards to increasing the tendency to bleed), needle selection, cleansing the area and non-painful needle penetration are all important considerations.

Patient position

In most cases, with a few exclusions such as large animals, it is important for the patient to be recumbent as it makes the animal easier to control and limit movement. Patients are generally more relaxed when recumbent. By asking the owner to identify certain actions that create the onset on pain, you can recreate that action and often identify the muscle that needs to be needled in that very position.

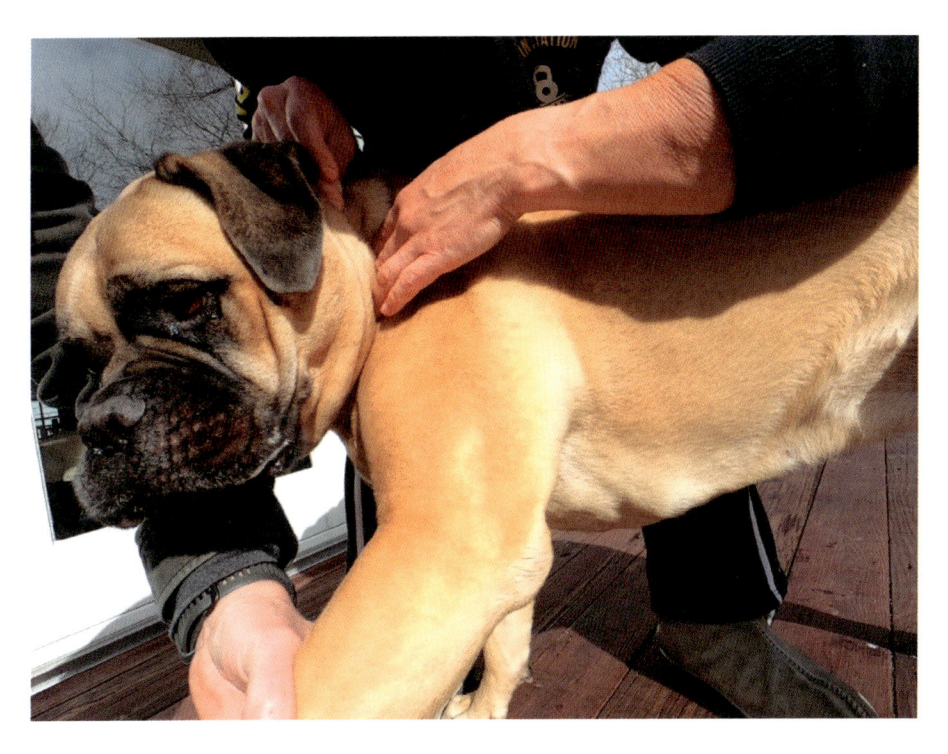

For example, if an agility dog only shows pain and lameness when doing weave poles, watch the dog perform that movement and look for

Needle Use and Technique

symmetry, abnormal weight distribution, head bobbing and compensation on the opposite diagonal or the opposite side. If the lameness or pain is evident on weight bearing when exiting the pole: the shoulder is in external rotation and the elbow is extended with the paw in extension. Put them in that position, locate the trigger points and if the trigger points are not palpable in a neutral position, put the animal in the painful posture and treat them in that position.

Needle Selection

Needle length is very subjective; the most important thing is that it reaches the muscle and the trigger point. The diameter is irrelevant and is purely professional preference. Please be aware that the exception to that is when one is needling in vascular areas or where a pneumothorax is a possibility. If you are not confident in your anatomy or your needle technique rather use alternative ways of ridding those areas of trigger points.

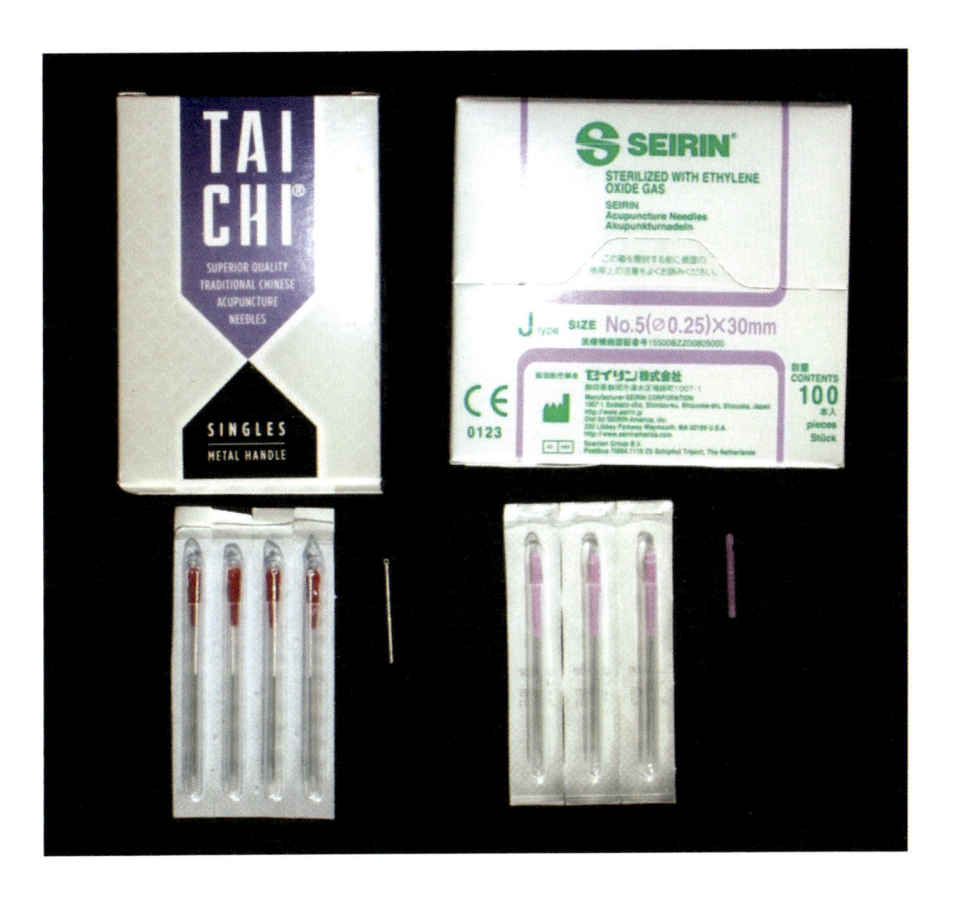

Needle Use and Technique

Cleansing and disinfecting

Unless you have a very hairy animal try not to shave the area. Owners are often put off a procedure that makes their animal look "ugly". Cleanse the skin with an appropriate antiseptic. You may need to cleanse the skin more than once to ensure a clean, sterile area. My recommendation would be to use disposable needles that are discarded into a sharps bin once they are used. These are also known as single use needles. They are sterile and do not require any additional sterilization from you. Always have an ear bud ready when removing the needles in case there is some bleeding. Push the ear bud onto the area for a few seconds or until the bleeding stops.

Needle Use and Technique

Needle penetration

After cleaning the area, make sure that the skin is dry, if wet, as the needle is inserted it will create a stinging or burning sensation that is unpleasant for the patient. Place the applicator on the cleansed skin and sharply tap the needle through the applicator into the trigger point. The trigger point in question has already been trapped by two fingers or by a pinch/pincer grip and as the needle goes in, maintain the tension you have created until you feel the twitch response. Do not use needles over and over again for a number of reasons. 1: The needle is no longer sterile after the first insertion, 2: The needle becomes blunter and blunter with every insertion resulting in a burning sensation that is very unpleasant for the patient and also ineffective from a treatment perspective.

Drug and supplement intake

There are certain drugs that can increase the tendency for the patient to bleed. Blood thinners are anticoagulants, so the patients bleed longer and more profusely. Arnica, turmeric and a depleted vitamin level all increase the patients' tendency to bleed. A supplementation of 500mg/day of vitamin C for a 150lb dog, prior to needling has shown to help reduce the bleeding and bruising that a patient may experience.

Needle Use and Technique

Localizing the myofascial trigger point.

There are typically three types of palpatory techniques, flat, pincer or deep. As you learn more about needling you will develop modifications to these basic techniques.

Flat palpation (Fig 3): push the myofascial trigger points back and forth between 2 fingers, generally the index and middle finger. Pin the myofascial trigger point down midway between the fingertips. Aim the needle halfway between the fingers and insert at the correct angle and to the allocated depth.

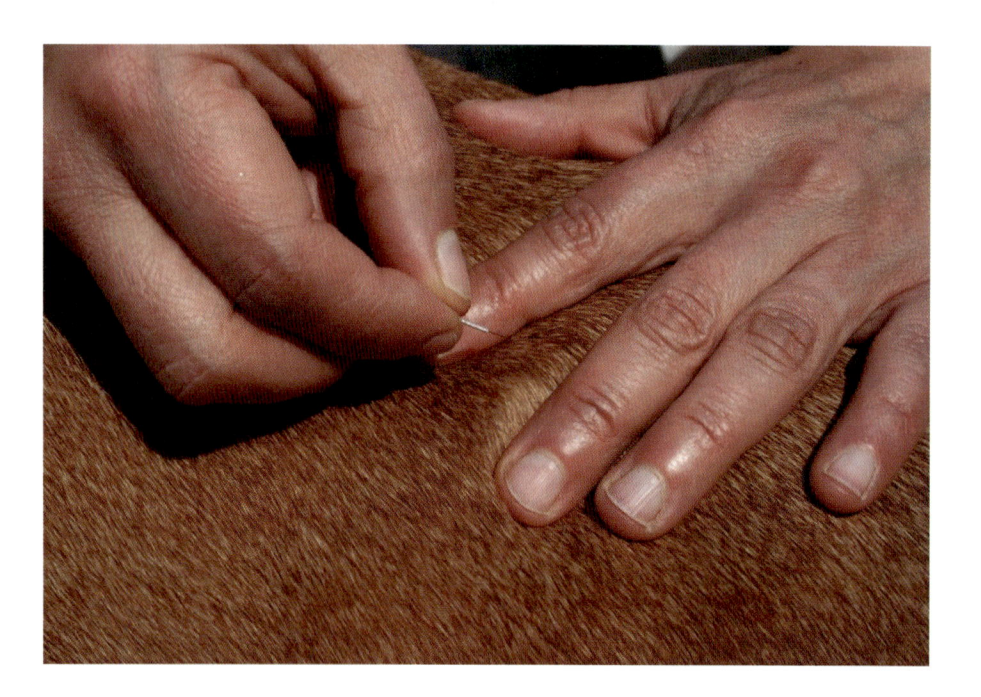

Needle Use and Technique

Pincer palpation (Fig 4): Roll the portions of the muscle between the digits. The nodule is generally found in the center of the muscle fibers. Hold the trigger point between the thumb and the fingertips.

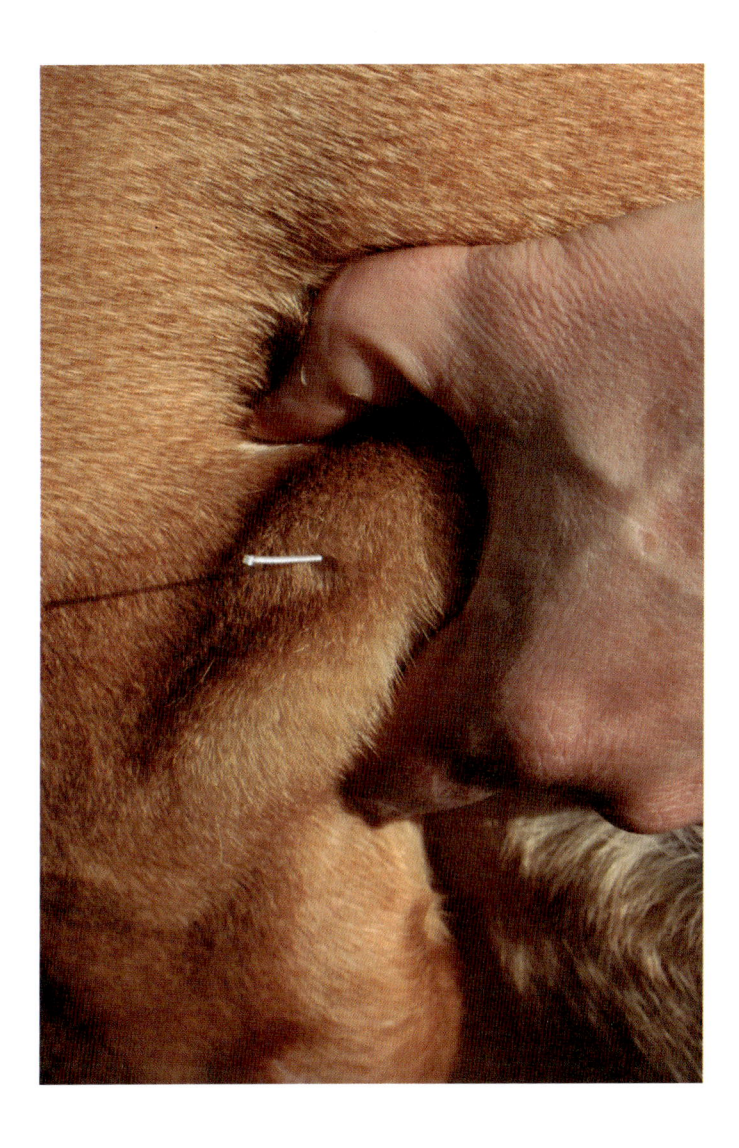

Needle Use and Technique

Deep palpation: position the finger over the most tender area of the muscle and the myofascial trigger points. Needle directly into the tender area.

The filiform needle in its tube is fixed with the non-needling hand against the suspected area by using a pincer grip or flat palpation depending on the muscle orientation, location, and direction of needle penetration. With the needling hand, the needle is gently loosened from the tube. The top of the needle is tapped, allowing the needle to penetrate the skin (Fig 5). With deep needling, the needle is guided toward the MFTP until resistance is felt and a local twitch response (LTR) is elicited. The elicitation of a LTR is essential in obtaining a desirable therapeutic effect (35,36).

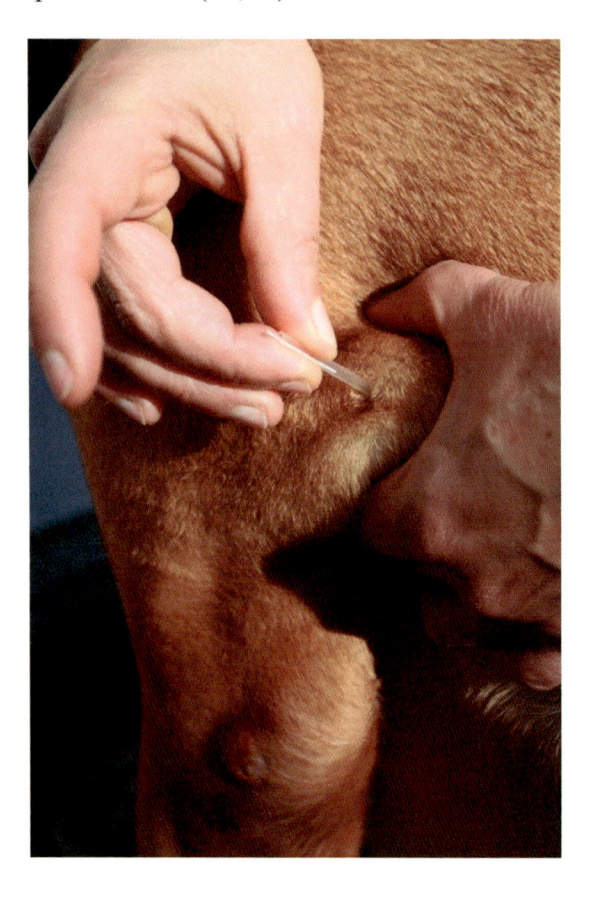

Needle Use and Technique

The needle is then focused in this area or other neighboring areas by drawing the needle back toward the subcutaneous tissue without taking it out of the skin, and then redirecting the needle toward the remaining MFTPs (121)This is known as a fanning needle technique: when there are clusters of myofascial trigger points. Insert the needle into the "primary" trigger point, after each probing movement, withdraw the needle into the subcutaneous tissue and redirect before the next movement (Fig 6). Work in a fanning distribution. Do not withdraw the needle completely as it creates an unsterile environment if it needs to be reinserted and causes the needle to lose its sharpness.

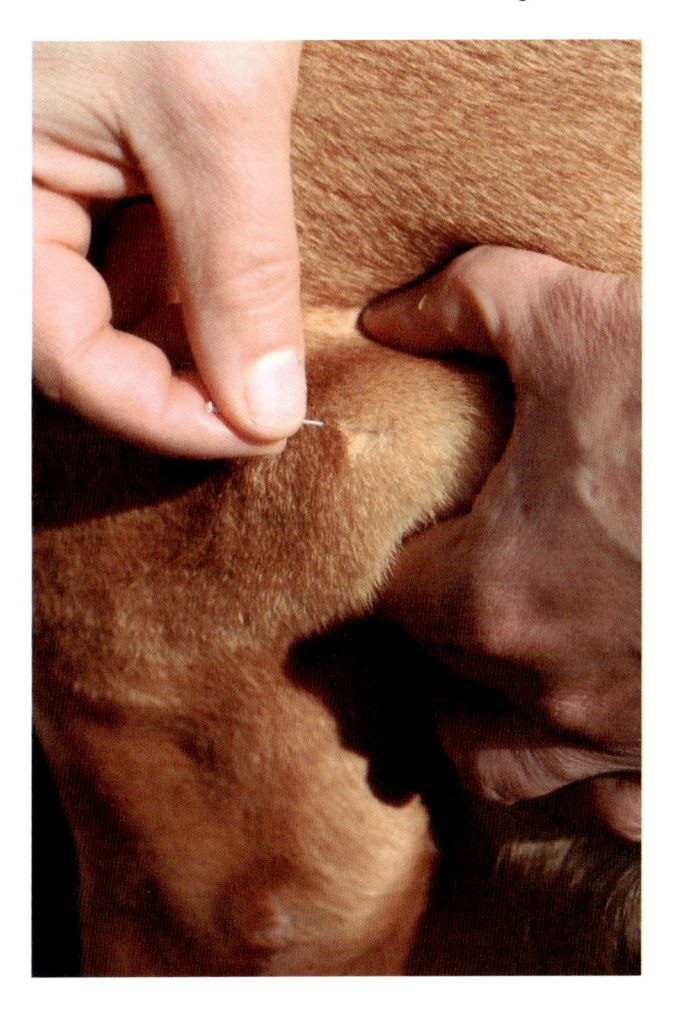

Needle Use and Technique

Generally, numerous LTRs can be elicited. Cessation of a dry needling may occur as a result of notable decreased frequency or eradication of LTRs, decreased resistance to palpation of the underlying tissue, or patient intolerance of continued needling at that particular site.

After needling, the trigger points character should have changed: a reduction in local and referred pain, no local twitch response, reduction of spot tenderness on palpation within 48-72 hrs.

Dry needling can be combined with electrical stimulation in which the needles become the electrodes. To use electrical stimulation combined with dry needling, a minimum of 2 needles is required per channel, but multiple channels can be used simultaneously. The best results are reached when the needles are placed within the dermatomes corresponding to the region of dysfunction(121). Frequencies between 2 and 4 Hz with high intensity are commonly used in nociceptive pain conditions and may result in the release of endorphins and enkephalins. For neuropathic pain, frequencies between 80 and 100 Hz are recommended, which are thought to affect the release of dynorphin, gamma-aminobutyric acid, and galanin (122) The needles can be placed directly in or on either side of a MFTP (123,124).

The dry needling treatment of fascia and connective tissues, including scar tissue, is similar to the approach for MFTPs. The therapist should palpate the tissues for adhesions and movement restrictions. The needle is inserted in the same manner as for MFTPs but after insertion, the needle is directed more superficially toward the adhesion or restriction. Rotating the needle facilitates mechanotransduction and will lead to tissue relaxation.

Post treatment:

Post needling soreness:

It is very important to educate owners about this!! If owners don't understand that their animals are going to be sore post treatment, they are going to be very unhappy for the first 48 hours. Education is very very important. Post needling soreness can last up to 72hrs. Adding a TENS unit or an e- stim to the needle may reduce the post needling soreness, but this is not guaranteed, and many dogs do not enjoy the sensation of an electric current. There is always some palpable pain and discomfort for the initial few days. Tell the owner the best- and worst-case scenarios and then there are no surprises for them.

Avoidance of strenuous activity is important over the initial 72hrs. Patients are encouraged to move as much as possible and do functional movements, sitting, standing, walking etc. Patients need to take care to prevent any shortened or lengthened posture for any period of time. This may exacerbate or reactivate previous trigger points. Ergonomic education is essential- getting in and out of a car, up and down stairs or on and off furniture. Check each muscle group for specific perpetuating factors and ask the owner to ensure that the patient avoid those.

Stretching after treatment is very important. The owner is required to attempt to move the patients affected area through their full range of motion at least three times. Stretching equalizes sarcomere lengths through the muscle, which results in a relief of tension and eliminates tight muscle fibers.

Cold, especially a cold wind from a natural source or artificial such as air conditioning can activate myofascial trigger points. Heat is very helpful, especially a moist heat. Apply it for 20 minutes, then remove for at least an hour and repeat as often as three times a day, continue with this treatment protocol until the symptoms resolve.

Contraindications to myofascial dry needling:

- Patients on anti-coagulation therapy or bleeding disorders.

- Cancer (avoid the area)

- Dangerous animal- a concern for practitioner and/or handler

Needle Use and Technique

- Pregnancy
- Open wounds or skin lesions
- Acute infection sites
- Cellulitis
- Dermatological diseases (rash, dermatitis etc.).
- Lymphedema
- Hyperalgesia or allodynia
- Allergies to metals in the needles- very uncommon
- Vascular disease

- Caution is warranted with dry needling following surgical procedures where the joint capsule has been opened. Although septic arthritis is a concern, dry needling can still be performed as long as the needle is not directed toward the joint or implant.

ACUPUNCTURE VS DRY NEEDLING

When making a comparison between dry needling and acupuncture it is important to note that they are two different treatment modalities. Many owners will arrive at your practice claiming that their animal has had acupuncture whereas they have only had dry needling and vice versa. Please educate your patients and explain that there are significant differences, this chapter will cover the fundamentals that you need to convey to your owners.

Dry needling can be defined as a skilled intervention that uses a thin solid filament needle to penetrate the skin and stimulate underlying myofascial trigger points for the treatment of myofascial pain and muscle dysfunction. The American Physical Therapy Association defines dry needling as an invasive technique used by physical therapists (and other practitioners, where allowed by state law or country) to treat myofascial pain that uses a dry needle, without medication or injection, which is inserted into areas of the muscle known as trigger points.(46)

Similarities exist between dry needling and the Traditional Chinese Medicine (TCM) style of acupuncture, however, there are also very significant differences.

Acupuncture is based on meridians, the movement of qi optimally in the body and the Jing-Luo system. It consists of many complex channels, and focuses on transporting qi, nourishing the body, co ordinating the Zang- Fu organs and connecting the whole body, as well as preventing the invasion of pathogens and resisting illness and disease. The dog in the picture is receiving acupuncture for lumbar and pelvic pain which is treated by needling certain points on the gallbladder and bladder meridian.

Acupuncture vs Dry Needling

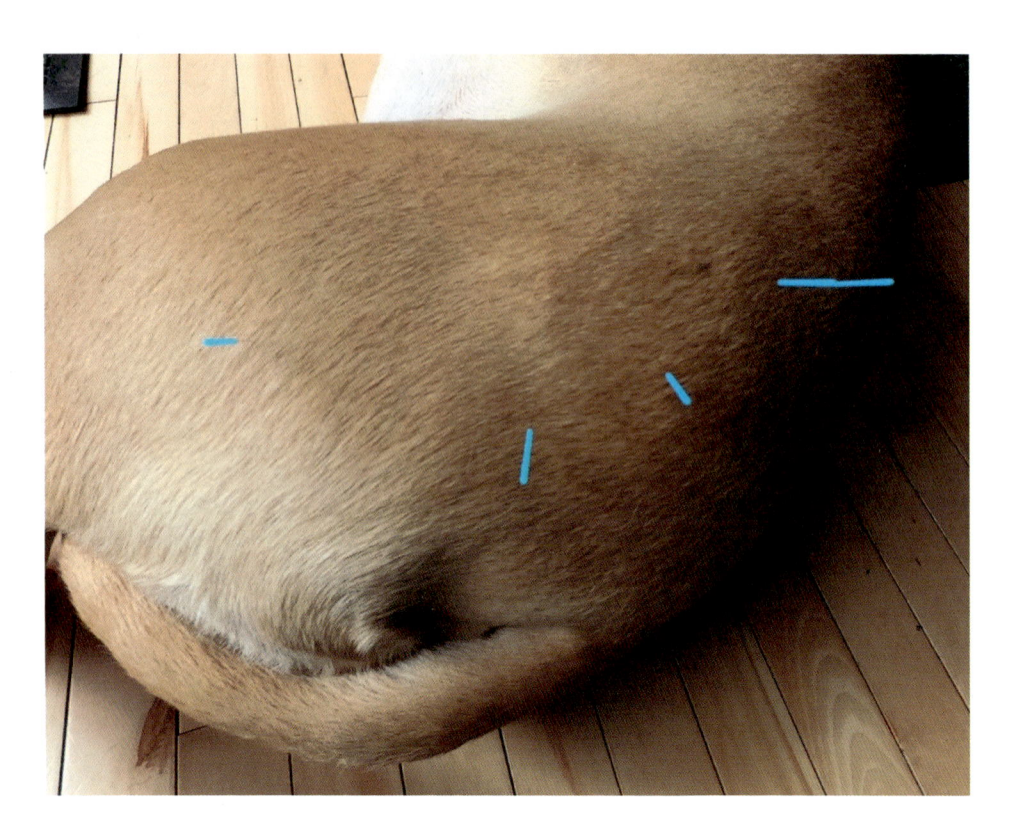

Dry needling is focused on reducing pain pathways caused by myofascial trigger points that create localized and referred pain. This pain leads to dysfunction on an organic and neuromusculoskeletal level. There are certain overlaps with acupuncture, but they are not to be regarded as the same treatment.

Acupuncture follows rules and beliefs developed from ancient times, whereas dry needling does not adhere to this ancient acupuncture philosophy. Dry needling is based more on modern scientific neurophysiology and anatomy.(47)Dry needling has more in common with Western Medical Acupuncture (WMA) since this form of acupuncture is a more modern scientific approach to therapy. WMA still uses mostly predetermined point for needle placement many of which were developed from evaluation of traditional Chinese acupuncture.

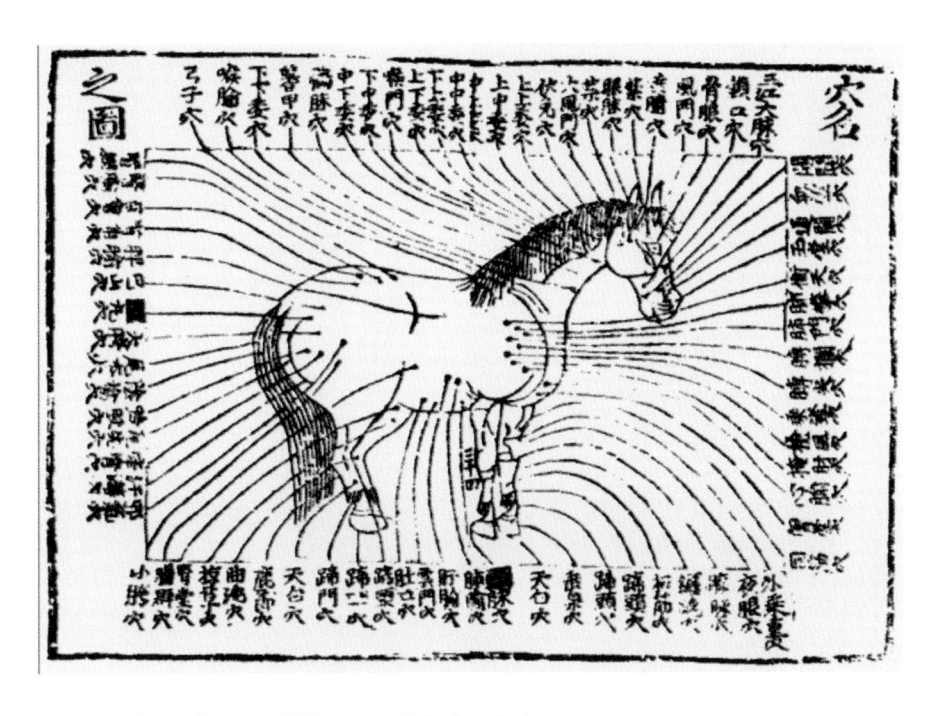

Neurophysiology of Western Medical Acupuncture

The placement of acupuncture needles in the tissue produces therapeutic effects through stimulation of peripheral nervous system and can be divided into four categories local, segmental, hetero-segmental and general.

Local effects: Local effects are brought about by antidromic stimulation of high threshold afferent nerves. This antidromic (conduction of an impulse in an axon opposite of normal directions) leads to release of trophic and vaso-reactive substances within the local area of stimulation. Increased circulation is perhaps one of the most important local factors from needling.

Segmental effects: When the needle is inserted, changes can occur within the dorsal horn of the spinal cord. Within the laminal II, substantia gelatinosa, enkephalinergic interneurons inhibit C fiber pain transmission thus modulating nociception.(48)

Hetero-segmental effects: Placing a needle anywhere in the body can produce actions that result in analgesia. Both the spinal cord and brain process the afferent input from the nociceptive stimulus of the needle. The central nervous system produces a descending pain inhibition and two such pathways have been described. A third analgesic system, induced by noxious stimulation anywhere in the body, is described as Diffuse Noxious Inhibitory Control (DNIC).(49)

Dry needling has been shown to produce short-term anti-nociceptive effects.(55) This effect was limited to muscles innervated by the same spinal cord segment. When a MFTP in the bicep was needled, pain thresholds to pressure were increased in MFTPs in the brachialis (segments C5) while no change in pain threshold to pressure was found in MFTPs in the biceps femoris (tibial branch of sciatic nerve).
Pressure pain thresholds have also been shown to increase in active MFTPs. Improvement in the range of motion of the neck was an additional finding.

The clinician who undertakes dry needling as a treatment option for MFTPs needs not only a thorough knowledge of anatomy, but also must develop the kinesthetic skills to accurately place the needle into the MFTP.

The acupuncture needle is rapidly inserted, with the aid of the insertion tube, into the superficial tissues and then, depending on what muscle is being addressed, directed into the deep tissues and muscle to the taut band. An increase in resistance as the needle enters the taut band is important to note. If needle placement is accurate, a local twitch response (LTR) will be appreciated in the taut band. The needle is moved in and out of the MFTP. In dogs, the LTR confirms the presence of a MFTP.

Two landmark studies in humans have helped to validate invasive MFTP dry needling and the therapeutic importance of the local twitch response (LTR)(57).
In the first study, after induction of the LTR by the needle entering the MFTP, local concentrations of biochemical mediators such as

Substance P and Calcitonin Gene Related Peptide decreased. This may explain the observed decrease in pain in people after release of the MFTP.

In the later study, not only were there similarities in the biochemical makeup of the active MFTPs, but increased concentrations of analytes were found in remote muscle sites that did not contain MFTPs. Study participants with active MFTPs in the trapezius had increased concentrations of inflammatory mediators, neuropeptides, catecholamines, and cytokines in the gastrocnemius, which did not contain MFTPs. The cause of this is not completely understood, however, it could be related to central sensitization.

There is also the possibility that widespread release of these analytes is a precursor to the development of MFTPs. Both studies offer explanations of the therapeutic benefits of invasive therapeutic intervention and the secondary hyperalgesia that is often present in people with myofascial pain syndrome. Due to the similarities shared by humans and dogs with respect to pathways and mechanisms of actions, one can presume that canines would have a similar if not the same response as humans.

"Surround the dragon"

A well-known technique in acupuncture is called "surround the dragon", it has been documented in many acupuncture texts as a form of acupuncture involving inserting needles into palpably painful points.(301,302)

The practitioner would palpate the affected area and if the patient reacts to any localized pain/discomfort then a needle would be inserted at that same point, regardless if it correlated with an acupuncture point or not. This would be repeated in the same area, slowly eliminating whatever painful areas there may be associated with that area.(303,310)

Soft tissue meridians

These form part of the meridian system that is associated with the musculotendinous pathways in acupuncture meridian concepts.

In chapter 13 of Miraculous Pivot,(300) it says, "Where there is pain, there is an acupuncture point". That means that muscle problems can be treated by inserting a needle at the local painful points. When palpating the area of pain and the patient cries out or reacts, that is known as an *a shi* point in acupuncture and the classic Chinese acupuncture treatment for that would be to insert a needle into that spot. Nguyen van Nghi a great French-Vietnamese acupuncturist says that instead of treating the point next to the *a shi* point it is more important to treat the *a shi* point itself to eradicate the patient's symptoms.(304,305)

Trigger point and acupuncture point correlation

As discussed above an *A SHI* point is found in traditional Chinese acupuncture and is defined as any point that, when palpated causes the patient to cry out or cause discomfort. These points are generally treated by needle technique, moxibustion, cupping, acupressure or gua sha.(306)

In Japanese acupuncture, KORI is used to describe an area of the bodily stiffness and constriction with discomfort. Kori is defined as a tight myofascial constriction that may or may not elicit pain when palpated but can be felt as a constriction by the practitioner when palpating. In Japanese acupuncture these points are released by needling into the dense muscular resistance that signals the presence of Kori. Kikko Matsumoto describes this dense myofascial resistance as a gummy feel. A needle is inserted until the gummy feeling is felt and then left there for 10-20 minutes.(307,308)

Modern Japanese acupuncture believes that when kori is present in the muscles or the fascia, they block the area, therefore affecting the lymphatic drainage, circulatory-venous and arterial system and nervous conduction of the body. When these systems get blocked, not only will there be pain and discomfort, but immune function and internal regulation of the body will be interfered with. (309)

Travell and Simons define a trigger point as a focus of hyperirritability in a tissue that, when compressed, is locally tender. If it is sufficiently sensitive, such a trigger point may give rise to referral pain, tenderness and sometimes, autonomic manifestations as well as proprioceptive changes.

Travell and Simons have this to say regarding the relationship between classical acupuncture points and myofascial trigger points:

"Unlike the classical acupuncture points, we do not think of the published trigger point sites as immutable locations, but as a guide for where to start looking. Every muscle can develop trigger points, many muscles have multiple trigger point locations. Only the most common trigger point locations are shown in the published illustrations, individual muscles may have trigger points in other locations. The trigger point sites in a given muscle may vary from patient to patient, no two patients are exactly alike.(1)

The myofascial phenomena described by the ancient acupuncturists correlates directly with the referral patterns seen by Travell and Simons. (34)

Xies Veterinary acupuncture(139) is the leading text for veterinarians and people treating animals through traditional Chinese medicine. Xie talks about conventional acupoints and specifically states that these are used in dry needling, such as ST 36 for weakness. She also talks about A-shi points as originally talked about in Miraculous pivot.

The acupuncture points in animals are thought to be almost identical to those of humans, particularly in the canine. The horse has some differences due to anatomy.

In summation, traditional Chinese and Japanese acupuncture draws a parallel correlation to trigger point therapy. Not only when looking at the original meridian charts, but also based on the description of the pain that those specific points elicited. These painful points (a shi, kori, etc.) are essentially trigger points and are eliminated most effectively by needle insertion.

Acupuncture vs Dry Needling

EXTRACORPOREAL SHOCK WAVE THERAPY (ESWT)

The most common treatment methods for myofascial pain syndromes include medical therapies, superficial and deep heating modalities, electrotherapy, stretch and spray techniques, acupuncture, dry needling, local injections, cold laser, massage, and exercise. However, further research is required to establish more effective and safe treatments.

Shockwave therapy was originally developed to disintegrate urinary stones 4 decades ago. Since then, there has been remarkable progress regarding the knowledge of its biological and therapeutic effects. Its mechanism of action is based on acoustic mechanical waves that act at the molecular, cellular, and tissue levels to generate a biological response.

The shock waves in ESWT are refracted by the tissues with different acoustic impedances. That means that the kinetic energy is dissipated in different tissue passages that can cause changes within the tissues. Apart from the mechanical effects, shock waves can also cause cellular changes, the most important being the reversible damage or the increased permeability in the neuronal membrane(140).

This mechanism explains the analgesic effects of ESWT. Increased blood circulation and hydroxyproline levels have been observed at the application sites. In addition, cellular regeneration is accelerated by the neovascularization of the tissue, and the chemical effects of the shock waves are suggested to be mediated by free radicals.

If used *incorrectly*, shock waves can rapidly destroy cells by means of free radicals. Structural changes occur within the cytoplasm and the mitochondria, with an energy flux density of 0.5 mJ/mm^2, and the mean density level of 0.12 mJ/mm^2, which is significant enough to change the permeability of the cell membrane. The analgesic effects of ESWT have been demonstrated in many clinical studies; however, the mechanism of this effect is not clearly understood(141).

Extracorporeal Shock Wave Therapy

Apart from neuronal membrane damage, some other theories such as the nociceptive blockade or central control of sensory input have been put forward, although no evidence supports these theories. Another mechanism associated with the analgesic effects of ESWT is the depletion of neuropeptides. Apart from these, the effects on growth factors and inflammatory process can be regarded among the biological effects of ESWT.

ESWT may break the vicious cycle of pain-spasm-ischemia-pain by restoring normal vascularization. It is possible that the favorable effects of ESWT on the inflammatory process, the stimulation of tissue regeneration from stem cells, and the depletion of neuropeptides in the painful area may contribute to the clinical improvement in patients.(142)

Physical Principles and Wave Generation:
Two types of technical principles are included in ESWT—focused ESWT (F-ESWT) and radial pressure waves (RPW), or better known as radial shockwaves. These 2 technologies differ in their generation devices, physical characteristics, and mechanism of action, but they share several indications.

The following 3 shockwave-generation principles are used for F-ESWT:

Electrohydraulic sources produce a plasma bubble by high-voltage discharge between 2 electrodes in water at the focus closest to a Para ellipsoidal reflector. The plasma expansion generates a shock front, which is reflected off the reflector and focused on a second focus at the target tissue.

Electromagnetic sources with flat or cylindrical coils are used. In the first system, a high-voltage pulse is sent through a coil, which is opposite a metallic membrane. The coil produces a magnetic field, resulting in a sudden deflection of the membrane and the generation of pressure waves in a fluid. The waves are focused by a lens that rise into a shockwave near the focus. The second electromagnetic generation source consists of a cylindrical coil and metallic membrane that is arranged inside a fluid-filled parabolic reflector. The membrane is accelerated away from the coil by a magnetic field. An acoustic pulse emerges radially and is concentrated onto the focus of the system after reflection off the reflector.

Piezoelectric sources produce shockwaves by a high-voltage discharge across piezoelectric elements mounted on the inner surface of a spherical backing that is placed inside a fluid-filled cavity. Each element expands, generating a pressure pulse that targets the focal region of the arrangement. Superposition of all pressure pulses and nonlinear effects produce a shockwave at the focal region(140).

In RPW generators, compressed air accelerates a projectile inside a cylindrical guiding tube. When the projectile hits an applicator at the end of the tube, a pressure wave is produced that radially expands into the target tissue. These devices do not emit shockwaves (148) because the rise times of the pressure pulses are too long, and the pressure outputs are too low. Nevertheless, RPW may induce acoustic cavitation(149).

The modes of action and the effects of RPW on living tissue may differ from those of focused shockwaves because bioeffects are related to the pressure waveform. F-ESWT and RPW may complement each other. While RPW is suitable for treating large areas, focused shockwaves can be concentrated at a much greater depth inside the body(141).

Mechanisms of action:

Despite the clinical success of the treatment, the mechanism of action of ESWT remains unknown. In 1997, Haupt proposed the following 4 possible mechanisms of reaction phases of ESWT on tissue(151).

Physical phase: This phase indicates that the shockwave causes a positive pressure to generate absorption, reflection, refraction, and transmission of energy to tissues and cells(152). Additional studies demonstrated that ESWT produces a tensile force by the negative pressure to induce the physical effects, such as cavitation, increasing the permeability of cell membranes and ionization of biological molecules. Meanwhile, many signal transduction pathways are activated, including the mechanotransduction signaling pathway, the extracellular signal-regulated kinase (ERK) signaling pathway, focal adhesion kinase (FAK) signaling pathway, and Toll-like receptor 3 (TLR3) signaling pathway, to regulate gene expressions (144,146,153,154,155).

Physicochemical phase: ESWT stimulates cells to release biomolecules, such as adenosine triphosphate (ATP), to activate cell signal pathways(156,157)

Chemical phase: In this phase, shockwaves alter the functions of ion channels in the cell membrane and the calcium mobilization in cells(158,159).

Biological phase: Previous studies have shown that ESWT modulates angiogenesis (von Willebrand factor), vascular endothelial growth factor, endothelial nitric oxide synthase, and proliferating cell nuclear antigen, anti-inflammatory effects (soluble intercellular adhesion molecule 1) and soluble vascular cell adhesion molecule 1, wound-healing (Wnt3, Wnt5a, and beta-catenin), and bone-healing (bone morphogenetic protein-2), osteocalcin, alkaline phosphatase, dickkopf-related protein 1, and insulin-like growth factor 1)(159-163).

The effects of ESWT are, with new functional proteins induced by ESWT, promoting a chondroprotective effect, neovascularization, anti-inflammation, anti-apoptosis, and tissue and nerve regeneration (143,153-157,157,160,163-193).
Furthermore, ESWT stimulates a shift in the macrophage phenotype from M1 to M2 and increases T-cell proliferation in the effect of immunomodulation (168,169).

ESWT activates the TLR3 signaling pathway to modulate inflammation by controlling the expression of interleukin-6 and IL-10 as well as improves the treatment of ischemic muscle(153,154).

It appears that ESWT plays a role in mechanotransduction, producing biological responses through mechanical stimulation on tissues (143,145,148,167).

Clinical Indications:
ESWT is indicated in chronic tendinopathies in which conventional conservative treatment is considered unsatisfactory after a prolonged and comprehensive management or as an alternative to surgery in patients with nonunion. ESWT is a noninvasive alternative in select cases when the indication for surgical treatment arises.

Tendinopathies:
Gerdesmeyer et al(199), in a multicenter randomized controlled trial (RCT) that included 144 patients, reported significantly better results in patients treated with F-ESWT, both low and high energy, compared with placebo, resulting in improvement with respect to pain, shoulder function, and calcium resorption in 86% in the high-energy group at 1 year compared with 37% in the low-energy group and 25% in the placebo ESWT group.

Cosentino et al(200), in a single-blind trial using F-ESWT, reported a significant increase in shoulder function, a decrease in pain compared with placebo, and calcium resorption of 71% by using F-ESWT, at 6 months. Hsu et al (201) in an RCT, achieved good or excellent results in 87.9% of patients treated with high-energy F-ESWT.

Cacchio et al(198). obtained a surprisingly high rate of reabsorption using RPW (86.6% complete and 13.4% partial resorption) at the 6-month follow-up; however, most studies have considered that high-energy F-ESWT is more likely to result in better radiographic and clinical outcomes(196-206)

Several systematic reviews and meta-analyses have demonstrated that high-energy F-ESWT is a safe, effective treatment for calcific tendinopathies(206-207).

Assuming that the mechanism of action is similar or the same in dogs, it stands to reason that the same results are achievable in canines as in people.

There have been numerous human studies that have shown that ESWT is efficient and helpful when treating patella (90,91,96-100) and achilles (108;110) tendinopathies, greater trochanteric pain syndrome (88,89) and lateral epicondylitis (74-79;81-83).The most well-known and common treatment performed is for plantar fasciitis (121-124) and in bone disorders.

Bone Disorders

Haupt (151) in 1997, recognized the dynamic interaction between ESWT and bone. It was initially hypothesized that shockwaves created microlesions in treated bone. This hypothesis changed when Wang et al.(160,161) demonstrated that shockwaves generate upregulation and expression of various pro-angiogenic and pro-osteogenic growth factors, stimulating bone-healing.

Basic research has shown that because of mechanical forces delivered by shockwaves to the cells and to the extracellular matrix, messengers are liberated and activate different genes and groups of genes in the cell nucleus (191,277-281). This biological conversion from a mechanical stimulus into electrochemical activity is called "mechanotransduction." (281)

The use of ESWT for nonhealing fractures was first reported, to our knowledge, in 1991 by Valchanou and Michailov (282) Since then, several observations and trials have supported the efficacy of ESWT for nonunion and delayed fracture-healing(283-298).

Cacchio et al.(293) in a Level-I RCT, compared different ESWT high-energy levels (0.4 mJ/mm^2 [Group 1] and 0.7 mJ/mm^2 [Group 2]) and surgery (Group 3) for the treatment of hypertrophic long-bone nonunion and obtained success rates of 70%, 71%, and 73%, respectively, at 6 months. No adverse effects occurred in the ESWT groups compared with a 7% rate of complications in the surgical group.

Furia et al.(295) had similar results. High-energy F-ESWT was observed to be as effective as intramedullary screw fixation in the treatment of nonunion of a fracture of the fifth metatarsal; however, screw fixation was more often associated with complications that frequently resulted in additional surgery.

Notarnicola et al (296) found that the results of ESWT were comparable with those of surgical stabilization and bone graft for the treatment of carpal scaphoid pseudarthrosis.

Kuo et al.(299) reported that the success rate of ESWT was 63.6% in the treatment of atrophic nonunion of the femoral shaft and could be as high as 100% if applied within 12 months after the initial treatment. Poor results were associated with instability, a gap at the nonunion site of >5 mm, and atrophic nonunion.

As some Level-I and II evidence has demonstrated that the efficacy of ESWT is comparable with that of surgery for the treatment of nonunion (293-296) and ESWT is practically free of adverse effects and more economic, it may progressively be considered as the first choice in the treatment of stable nonunions with a gap of <5 mm in long bones

For bone treatment, the basic principles of acute fracture management should be implemented after F-ESWT (immobilization, casting, and weight-bearing restrictions).

After ESWT, a comprehensive post-treatment schedule, individualized for each pathology and each patient's clinical status, should be given to the owner including avoidance of the use of the anatomic structure, a specific exercise program, and instructions to avoid overload.

ESWT is considered to be an alternative to surgery for several chronic tendinopathies and non-unions because of its efficacy, safety, and noninvasiveness. The best evidence supporting the use of ESWT was obtained with low to medium levels of energy for tendon disorders as well as with a high energy level for tendon calcification and bone pathologies in a comprehensive rehabilitation framework.

Myofascial trigger point eradication:

The acoustic energy used to treat a MFTP can also be used to identify both latent and active MFTPs. Certain ESWT systems have a scan or a diagnostic ultrasound that allows the practitioner to virtually locate a tender, painful, irritable, or pre-irritable area. It does this by directing energy, of lower power densities than treatment dosages, to the painful region. The patient with a MFTP will feel the acoustic energy as soreness. Even latent tender MFTPs can be identified and treated as part of that session. There is a post treatment-related pain which generally dissipates within 48 hours of treatment.

It has been hypothesized but not proven that patients treated for MFTPs using shock wave acoustic energy appear to have a longer remission period. The time between successive treatments is considerably longer when patients have been treated with acoustic compression. This might be explained purely as a treatment effect, or possibly by other confounding factors such as co-interventions (medications/therapies, etc.), inherent differences between subjects (severity, gender, age, comorbidities), or exposures to perpetuating and maintaining factors such as activities/exercises (eccentric exercise) and postures (fatigue/static tension states) since the link between MFTPs and certain muscle states (ischemia/hypoxia) have been postulated(163).

There is some evidence to suggest that shock wave acoustic compression energy systems achieve their results from reducing the concentration of nociceptor-stimulating substances inherent in MFTPs, which would in turn eliminate the cycle leading to possible plastic changes in the spinal cord by averting the sensitization phenomenon(164).There are a multitude of possible biochemical pathways and substance cascades that could be operating through mechanotransduction, or how an outside mechanical force, such as acoustic energy applied at the tissue can initiate a complex series of cellular signaling events that lead to changes in the cellular environment manifesting, in this case, as analgesia.

Contraindications:

Immune mediated joint disease
Infectious arthritis
Neoplastic disease
Diskospondylitis
Unstable fractures
Neurological deficits
Be cautious shock waving over lung fields, heart, brain, major blood vessels and nerves.

Extracorporeal Shock Wave Therapy

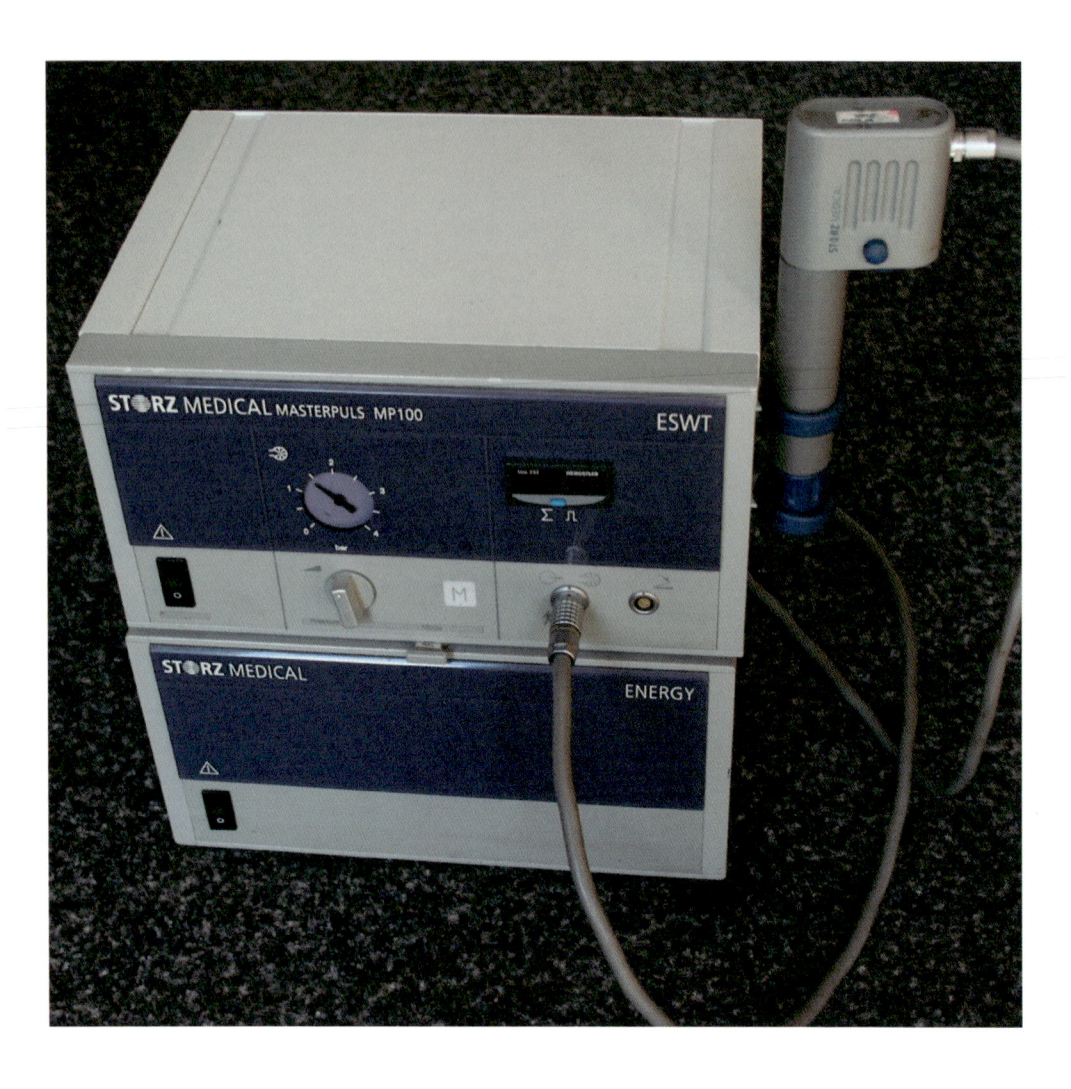

Extracorporeal Shock Wave Therapy

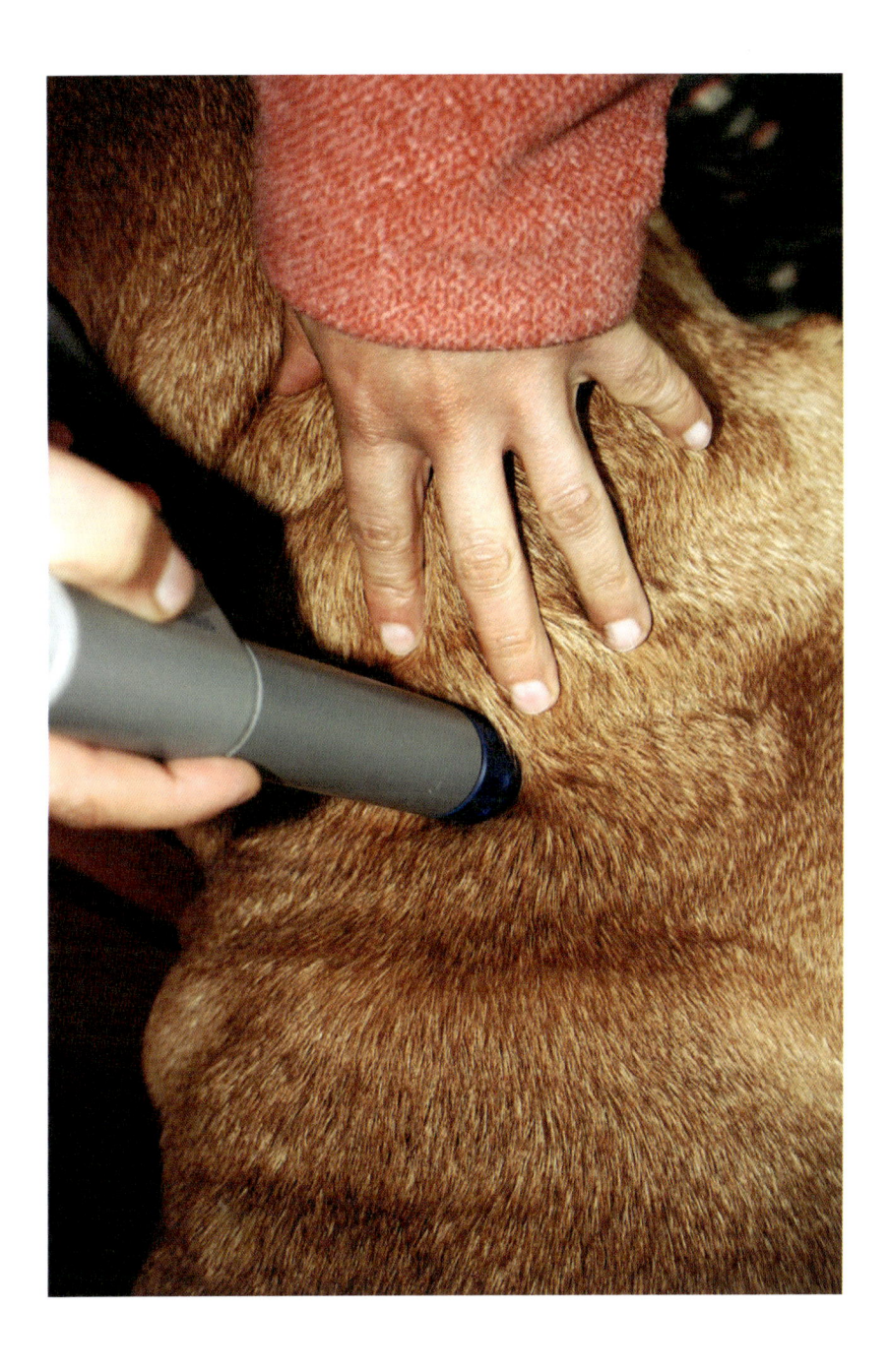

Extracorporeal Shock Wave Therapy

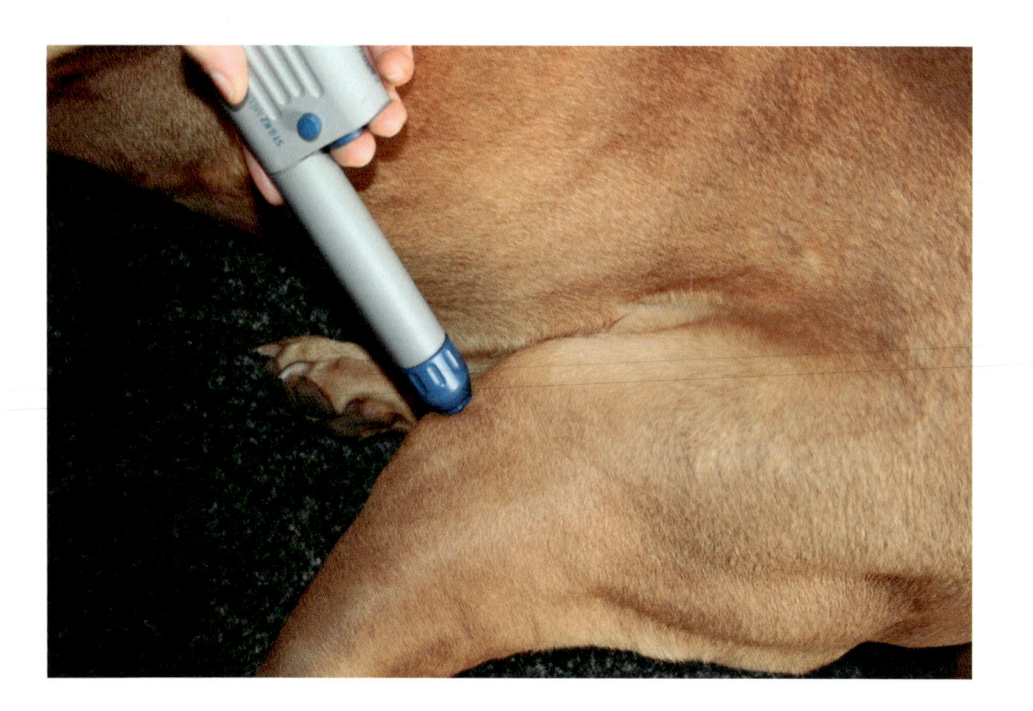

LASER THERAPY

Photo biomodulation (PBMT) is defined as "nonthermal interaction of monochromatic radiation with a target site." There is much controversy surrounding the term photo biomodulation, cold laser and low-level laser. For the purposes of this chapter we will call it laser therapy.
Rehabilitation is slowly becoming a standard of care in veterinary medicine. As this field grows and owners' expectations for fast return to function and activity expand, there's a need to offer better and faster options. Laser therapy is a vital and practical cog in the wheel of rehabilitative options.
It can be utilized for a large variety of cases, making it a feasible and profitable part of practice. With very few exceptions, cases can be treated with laser therapy as opposed to other modalities that may be limited by a patient's other medical conditions.

How does it work?
Studies of successful use of laser therapy for promoting tissue repair and pain reduction are well-established (321). Even though it is still rather new to animal rehabilitation, and more studies are needed here's what the studies show so far:

Laser therapy works at a cellular level to activate cytokines and other mediators along various cascades in the tissue. Chromophores and respiratory chain enzymes within the mitochondria and at the cell membrane absorb the photons. Oxygen production and adenosine triphosphate (ATP) production can be enhanced. ATP may also act as a signaling molecule to enhance cell-to-cell communication(322). ATP then binds with a cell receptor to allow sodium and calcium to enter, resulting in cascades or intracellular activities. This increased intracellular calcium increases mitochondrial function. ATP is thought to be a neurotransmitter, and this explains some of the effects of laser therapy in pain management (323).

Laser therapy stimulates collagen synthesis (324) and fibroblast development(325).It increases new blood vessel formation, allowing for repair of injured tissues(326). Additional studies have shown that laser therapy can lead to increased tensile strength (327)and faster closure of wounds (328).

Laser therapy has anti-inflammatory effects, and therefore can, as a result, act as an analgesic. Studies have indicated that inflammation can be reduced by laser therapy decreasing prostaglandin E2 (PGE2) and cyclooxygenase-2 (COX-2) concentration (329,330). This gives this therapy the same potential treatment pathway as corticosteroids and nonsteroidal anti-inflammatory drugs (NSAIDs). For patients that cannot take these systemic medications, and for owners looking for alternative treatment, laser therapy has been proven to be beneficial.

Reduction in inflammation and pain in both acute and chronic conditions will increase the patient's quality of life. By improving analgesia, laser therapy can be preemptive in preventing or minimizing chronic pain or wind-up and help reduce dependence on medications. By reducing the intake of pharmacological medications, we are improving the health of the animal in the most holistic way possible.

Veterinary rehabilitation focuses on holism. One of the main goals of rehabilitation is a return to normal or as near-normal function as possible. The benefits of photo biomodulation for rehabilitation patients focus on two main areas: increasing healing times through faster, stronger tissue repair, and the analgesic effect of the laser.
These combine to allow the patient as a whole to feel better and lead to the ability to exercise correctly, to gain strength and to return to function with an improved quality of life.

Role of lasers in rehabilitation
A practical approach is also needed, accounting for many factors including patient need, patient cooperation, cost, efficacy, and frequency and duration of treatment. It's critically important for the therapist to prescribe practical and realistic treatment plans for each individual patient.
Lasers are a popular modality that has been heavily marketed for the treatment of pain and wounds in the veterinary patient. Class IIIa lasers

Laser Therapy

provide a maximum output power of 5 milliwatts (mW), class IIIb lasers provide output power up to 500 mW, and Class IV lasers provide output power greater than 500 mW. Various Class IV lasers are marketed for veterinary use with power output ranging from 1 watt to 15 watts. The amount of laser energy delivered during a treatment session is reported in Joules (J), and one Joule is equal to 1 watt per second. The dose is reported as the energy per session in Joules divided by the area (cm2) where the energy is directed; therefore, the therapeutic laser dose is indicated in Joules/cm2.

For the below reasons, studies in people, regarding myofascial pain, are limited to Class IIIs.
Accurate therapeutic dose delivery is only possible with Class IIIa and IIIb but not for Class IVs. The later must be continually moved over the treatment area to prevent thermal injury, therefore, the joules delivered per cm2 is only an estimate. Total laser energy delivered to the target tissue within the patient becomes even more uncertain due to beam reflection and back-scatter (collectively referred to as remittance).

Treatment with Class IIIa and Class IIIb lasers is more commonly referred to as low-level laser therapy (LLT). Low-level laser therapy has been widely used in the treatment of MFTPs in people. Several double-blind placebo-controlled studies report positive effects of LLT on MFTPs.(331,332,333) However, other studies report no therapeutic benefit.(334,335). One systemic review did conclude that LLT could be effective in the treatment of MFTPs associated with lateral epicondylitis in people.(336)Proper therapeutic dosages for treatment are not known, and conflicting information exists in humans and in animal models. It has been suggested that inadequate dosage may be the cause of the unpredictability in the reported efficacy of laser therapy, especially by those marketing Class IV lasers.(332) However, two studies have reported efficacy with a lower dosage.(332,336) The later study, using the rabbit as an animal model, reported better treatment outcomes with energy of 5.4J per session versus 14.4J per session (total energy for 5 sessions was 32.4J and 86.4J, respectively).

Laser Therapy

Treatable conditions

Examples of conditions that could benefit from laser therapy treatment as a sole treatment modality include surgical incisions, wounds, lick granulomas, osteoarthritis and tail pull injuries.
Application to every surgical incision at the end of the anesthetic period can reduce postoperative pain and swelling.

Wounds can benefit from laser therapy in the late inflammatory or early proliferative phase, and laser therapy provides continued benefit in chronic or slow-healing wounds as healing progresses.

Lick granulomas can arise due to various causes. Addressing pain relief, improved circulation and antimicrobial pathways via laser therapy can provide improvement where other treatment modalities have either failed or address only a single potential cause of the granuloma.
Palliative management of chronic conditions can be achieved with laser therapy.

End-stage otitis externa in cases that are not candidates for surgical resection will benefit from reducing bacterial load and reducing inflammation and pain.

Laser therapy is a useful agent if other osteoarthritis management modalities have to be discontinued due to gastritis, liver or kidney disease as a result of NSAIDS.

Laser therapy can be used to stimulate acupuncture and dry needling points. In MFTP areas, laser therapy improves the local microcirculation, thus increasing the supply of oxygen to hypoxic cells, and helping to remove cellular metabolic by-products. Once stabilized, the microcirculation breaks the vicious cycle of pain-spasm-pain (339).

Laser Therapy

The most suitable laser wavelengths for deactivation of MFTPs are within the range 780-904 nm, corresponding to the infrared, since they have higher tissue penetration (338), as was seen in the present investigation. However, Ilbuldu et al. (337) used an electromagnetic spectrum below what is usually recommended (632.8 nm and 730 nm, respectively), achieving satisfactory results, which suggests that a suitable dosage is important for successful therapy. In fact, application of an optimal dose directly to the target area is even more important than the wave- length of the device, since under- or over-irradiation may be ineffective or even exert an inhibitory effect (339).

This may help to explain the better result obtained in the laser group with a dose of 4 J/cm2 than with 8 J/cm2. The dose should also be adjusted according to the type of tissue. For darker toned skin, a 50% increase over the usual dose is recommended, since melanin absorption is greater on the surface, thus reducing the dose at the target depth. For patients with substantial subcutaneous fat, the dose should also be increased accordingly because the fat may cause reflection, leading to lower absorption of radiation by the tissue (339,340).

On the basis of the present results, we recommend that laser therapy be applied two to three times a week, in agreement with Simunovic (341, 339), and since this is a chronic disorder (> 6 months), a lower dose of about 4 J/ cm2 is advisable. Although four sessions yielded satisfactory results, Venancio et al. (338) recommended a greater number of sessions (> 30 sessions).

635 NM (RED):
This laser is used anytime you would normally tonify a meridian.
Great for CHRONIC conditions
Very useful for treating scar tissue

450 NM (BLUE):
This laser is used anytime you would normally sedate a meridian.
Any time there is inflammation or heat.
Great for ACUTE conditions
Excellent for pain.

Laser Therapy

Neurological patients often need a comprehensive rehabilitation program that includes laser therapy to achieve favorable results. Patients suffering chronic pain from tail docking will benefit from laser therapy.

Laser therapy represents only one modality that can be included in an integrated rehabilitation program. It is important to prioritize the sequence of application with other modalities.

The release of endogenous opioids stimulated by this therapy has applications throughout both acute and chronic conditions in injury rehabilitation. Applying photo biomodulation to painful muscles, tendons, ligaments or joints before having the patient do therapeutic exercises makes sense.

It's important for the clinician to incorporate this therapy as one part of a complete rehabilitation program. An example is incorporating laser therapy during the first few weeks of rehabilitation for a dog with tendonitis. This results in a reduction of pain and stimulating cytokines and growth factors to achieve better tendon tissue healing. Laser therapy may be phased out of the rehabilitation program once initial goals have been achieved and the patient progresses to strength training and maintenance.

Osteoarthritis may initially require a high frequency of treatment through an induction phase. Then, as pain and inflammation are reduced, the frequency of treatments can be reduced through a transition phase, until a maintenance phase protocol is achieved.

Neurological patients, such as those with brachial plexus avulsion or intervertebral disk disease, may benefit from photo biomodulation throughout their entire rehabilitation process. Initially, it may be used for management of pain at the injury site or in inflamed muscles. Management of neuropathic pain is the primary use of laser therapy in these cases.

Laser Therapy

Laser therapy represents an exciting field in both human and veterinary medicine. While we need to learn more with regards to dosing and frequency, it has already proven to be a good component to the multifaceted approach to pain management.

Other therapies at a glance:

Electrotherapies: Several references exist that discuss the use of transcutaneous electrical nerve stimulation (TENS) in the management of pain in dogs; however, no specific mention of its use in myofascial pain was found.(341,342,343) TENS combined with other physical modalities appeared to have an immediate effect with regard to decreasing myofascial pain in people.(344) However, others concluded that insufficient evidence is available to determine the effectiveness of TENS in myofascial pain.(345)

Therapeutic Ultrasound: One randomized controlled study reported an immediate reduction in MFTP sensitivity with therapeutic ultrasound in humans.(346) Therapeutic ultrasound has been used to decrease stiffness of latent MFTPs in the trapezius muscle in people.(347) In that study, a 3 MHz therapeutic ultrasound was used at 1.4 Watts/cm2 for 5 minutes in a circular motion on an area twice the size of the 7cm2 ultrasound sound head. This is in contrast to previous studies that reported therapeutic ultrasound was no more effective than placebo.(348,349) Gam et al, surveyed patients up to 6 months after treatment by means of a patient questionnaire, while studies reporting benefits from therapeutic ultrasound were based on immediate patient response only.

Physical/Manual Therapies: Data is either inadequate or conflicting regarding most manual therapies for treatment of myofascial pain syndrome.(350) Current evidence regarding treatment of MFTPs with physical and manual therapies did not exceed the moderate level of evidence.(345) It was additionally asserted that most trials examined multimodal treatment programs, so positive effects cannot exclusively be credited to a particular therapy.

Ischemic compression, also known as trigger point pressure release, is a commonly described manual therapy for the treatment of MFTPs in people. Studies in people show that ischemic compression may be of benefit in treatment of MFTPs associated with shoulder pain, neck pain, headaches, and carpal tunnel syndrome.(344,351,352,353) Numerous descriptions of the technique can be found in the academic medical literature as well as in the lay literature regarding massage therapy. Digital compression of the MFTP for 60 to 90 seconds with increasing pressure is the most commonly described method. In dogs the tight band is identified and examined for the exquisitely tender MFTP then digital pressure is applied to the point of patient recognition. After 15 to 20 seconds pressure may gradually be increased in most patients. Providing a gentle stretch to the muscle while applying pressure may assist in release of the MFTP.

Laser Therapy

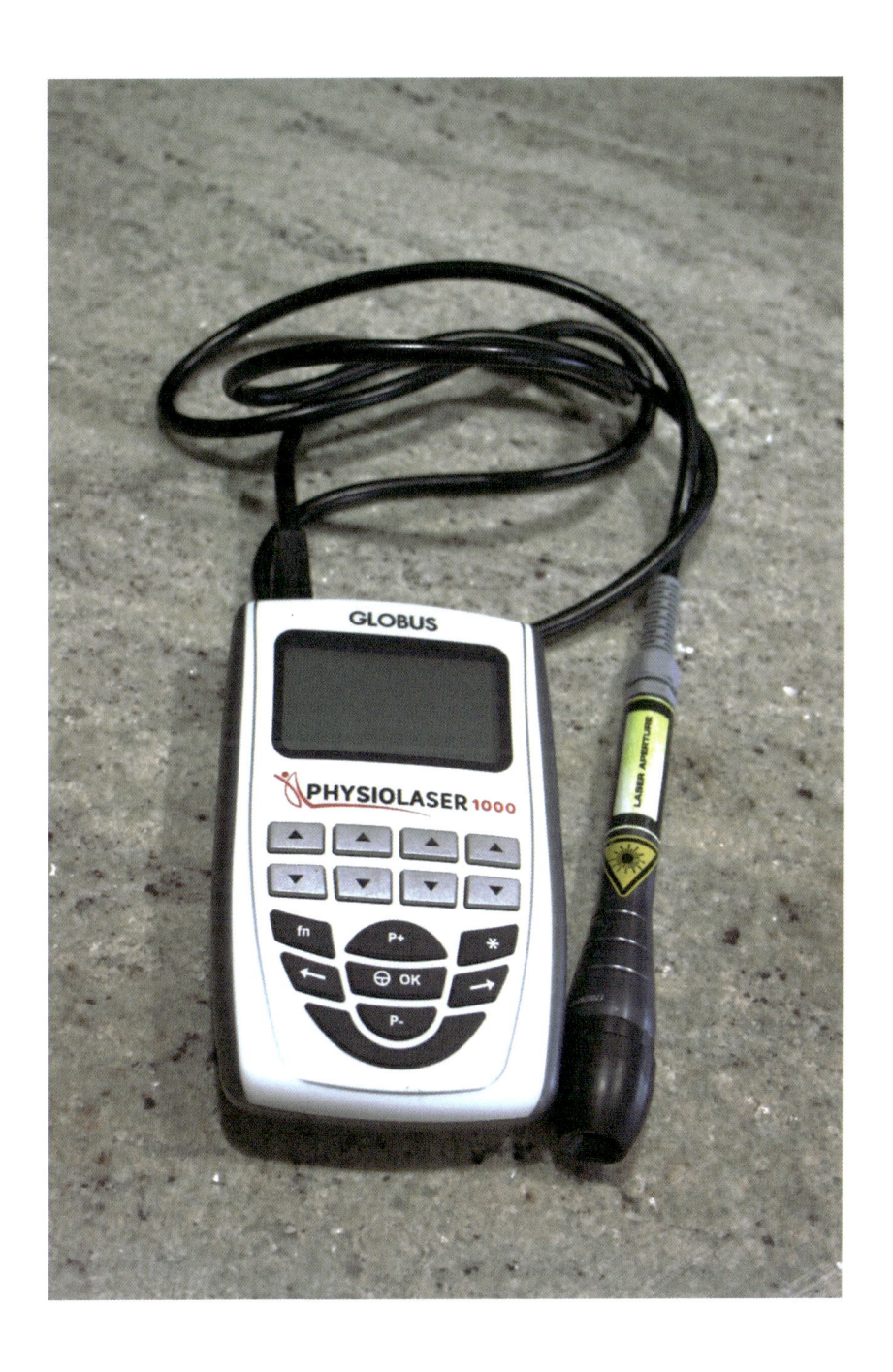

Laser Therapy

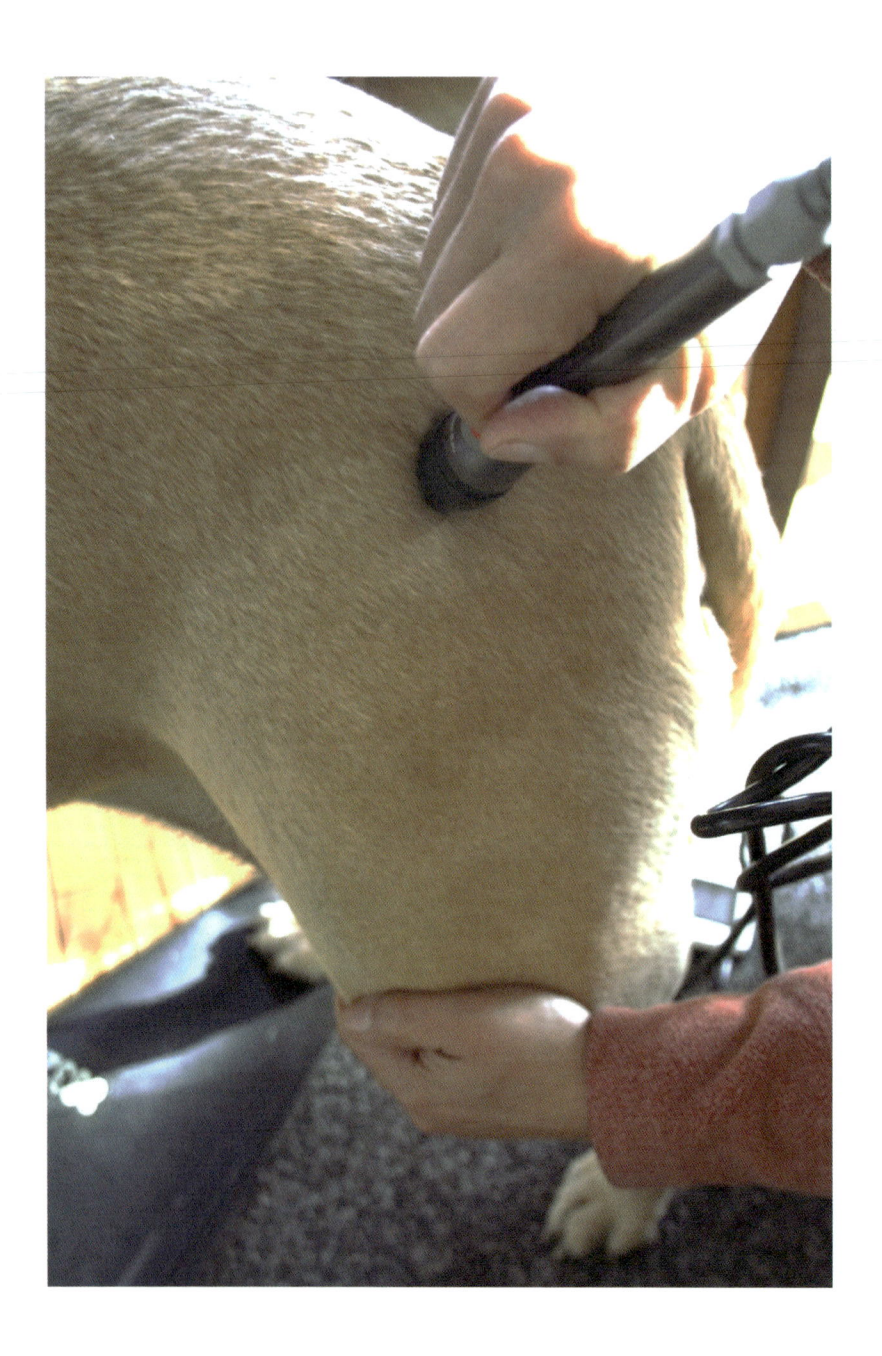

Laser Therapy

PRACTITIONER INTEGRATION AND LEGISLATION

"It takes a village to raise a child", is very applicable to animal rehabilitation and treating animals. Animal rehabilitation only started within the last 20 years. Most of the techniques used today were originally adapted from human practice. The CCRP program at University of Tennessee started in 1999 and the CCRT and CCRA programs in Florida and Colorado in 2003. The first comprehensive textbook on veterinary rehabilitation was written in 2004.

Veterinarians, physical therapists and veterinary technicians may pursue specialized training as Certified Canine Rehabilitation Practitioners (CCRP), Therapists (CCRT) and Assistants (CCRA). Veterinarians may also be board certified diplomates of the American College of Veterinary Sports Medicine and Rehabilitation (DACVSMR). Animal chiropractic courses and other physical therapy courses are expanding and becoming more popular.

As this is a cross disciplinary practice, veterinarians, physical therapists, chiropractors and technicians work in collaboration with each other, bringing a unique understanding to this field that combines the science of veterinary medicine with the manual skills and knowledge of physical therapy.

As you can see there are many avenues that one can get involved in the veterinary rehabilitation world. Some are more widely accepted than others. The most important thing that I have learned over the last 16 years is that integration in key. Stay in your lane. That is not to say that you shouldn't voice a well thought out opinion but let people with the knowledge and expertise in an area do what they do best. Veterinarians (depending on where they study) have approximately 6 years to study a wide range of species and pathologies, with very little exposure to the neuromusculoskeletal system unless they specialize further. The most successful scenario is realized for the patient when the veterinarian and the rehabilitative or non-veterinary practitioner work together to ensure a positive outcome. Egos and bombastic personalities generally result

Practice Integration and legislation

in failure as the focus on the patient is lost. Create working relationships with other practitioners and building a tribe whereby the patient's best interest is served is a win for everyone.

Myofascial dry needling is very new to the veterinary world and as such still falls under the rules of acupuncture. Please ensure that you know the rules and laws of your state and country before embarking on treating animals with dry needling.

NEEDLE SAFETY AND CONSIDERATIONS

Clean Needle Technique (CNT) is the standard by which acupuncturists and dry needling practitioners prevent occupational exposure to healthcare associated pathogens, including bloodborne pathogens and surface pathogens, and reduce the risk for some other adverse events associated with dry needling and acupuncture. CNT consists of the following components:

1. Hand sanitation.
2. Establishing and maintaining a clean field.
3. Skin preparation.
4. Isolation of contaminated sharps.
5. Standard precautions.
6. The use of sterile single-use needles
7. In addition, as needed: Follow appropriate emergency procedures in the event of a needlestick incident or some other clinical accident in the course of a dry needling treatment.

It should be stated at the outset that a more comprehensive risk management protocol is beyond the scope of this chapter.

Clean Needle Technique (CNT) must be distinguished from sterile technique. Sterile or aseptic technique, which is used in surgical procedures and many laboratory procedures, involves procedures that are kept sterile by the appropriate use of sterile supplies and the maintenance of a sterile field. While dry needling involves the use of sterile acupuncture needles that must be maintained in a sterile condition prior to the procedure, CNT is a clean rather than sterile procedure.

The insertion site is clean rather than sterile. Hands are in a clean condition rather than covered with sterile gloves. Gloves do not need to be worn except under specific conditions where exposure of the practitioner to blood or other potentially infected body fluids is possible.

Gloves are worn:

1. When bleeding occurs or is likely to occur.

2. When needling in or near the genital region.
3. While palpating near an area where there are lesions on the patient's skin.
4. In the event that there are skin lesions or open wounds on the practitioner's hands.

5. When cleaning blood or other possible infective material from a surface.

Hand Sanitation

Handwashing is an essential component of the CNT protocol. Washing hands with soap and water is the best way to reduce the number of microbes on them in most situations. If soap and water are not available, use an alcohol-based hand sanitizer that contains at least 60% alcohol. (358) Make sure to use enough sanitizer that the hands are completely covered and wet. Wash hands rather than use hand sanitizer if hands are visibly dirty.

Preparing and Maintaining a Clean Field

A clean field is the area that has been prepared to contain the equipment necessary for dry needling in such a way as to reduce the possible contamination of sterile needles and other clean or sterile equipment. Select a clean dry hard surface if a treatment table is not suitable.

- Establish a new clean field for each patient.
- Place materials such as needles in blister packs on the clean field.

- Place clean cotton balls or unopened swabs on the field. If desired, these items may be kept in a clean jar near the clean field.
- Clean the surface used for the clean field with a low-level disinfectant after every patient.

Skin Preparation

Needles should be used only where the skin is clean and free of disease. Acupuncture needles should never be inserted through inflamed, irritated, diseased, or broken skin. Otherwise, infections can be carried directly into the body past the broken skin barrier. The areas to be needled should be clean prior to treatment. Alcohol swabbing is recommended but not essential before acupuncture needle insertion as long as an area is clean. If swabbing an area, 70% alcohol or ethanol is required. Skin can be cleaned with 70% isopropyl alcohol, soap and water, or other methods as determined by the practitioner or clinic administrator.

According to the World Health Organization, both soap and water and 60-70% isopropyl (or ethanol) alcohol is adequate for preparing a human patient's skin for procedures such as needle insertion. (360) Isopropyl alcohol at a concentration above 70% is unacceptable because it evaporates too quickly to have an antiseptic effect.

Skin that is currently inflamed, or which has an active lesion should not be used for needle insertion. These areas often carry higher risk for infection.

The evidence suggests that both the practitioner's hands and the patient's skin at the insertion point need to be clean prior to administration of a needle. Risk assessment of potentially contaminated skin should be conducted to ensure appropriate cleaning of the skin is undertaken where required. In other words, if soiled, the patient's skin should be cleaned prior to needle insertion. There is no clear evidence that skin cleansing with soap and water, alcohol swabs, or antibacterial substances like chlorhexidine is better or worse than the other options. Even if skin is visibly clean, mild disinfection may still be performed prior to needle insertion as all OPIM (other potentially infectious materials) are not necessarily visible to the naked eye.

If the insertion site is cleaned with an alcohol swab, it should be allowed to dry prior to needle insertion to prevent pain from alcohol being inserted under the skin along with the acupuncture needle.

Alcohol Swab Method

Swab the points and allow the alcohol on the skin to dry. The same swab may be used for several points. A new swab should be used if the swab begins to change color, becomes visibly dirty, becomes dry, or has come into contact with any skin break, lesion, inflammation or infection. The alcohol should be allowed to dry to reduce the potential for discomfort during needling. A separate swab should be used for areas of high bacterial load, such as the groin.

Isolation of Used Sharps

Another critical component of CNT is the isolation of used sharps. Sharps should be isolated in a sharps container specifically designed for this use. Sharps containers are made of a material impervious to needles and fluids, such as plastic, and are designed to receive contaminated sharps without being able to retrieve them after the sharps are placed in the container. These containers are labeled as to contents and bear the biohazard symbol. Appropriate containers are available commercially.

Laser Therapy

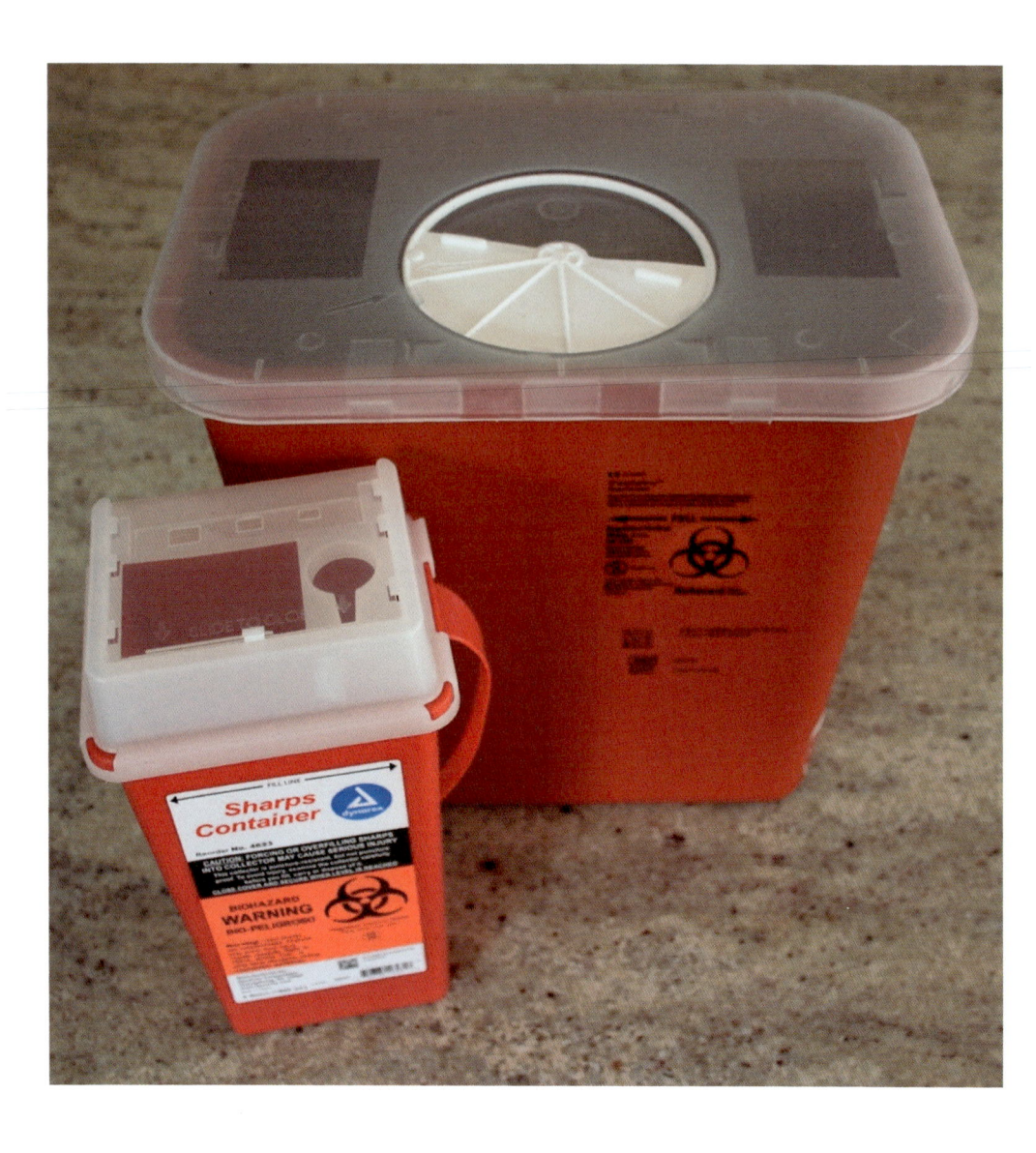

Basic Steps of the Clean Needle Technique for Dry Needling

1. The provider follows correct hand sanitation protocols.
2. A clean field is set up on a stable surface near the treatment table. The clean field may consist of a piece of paper toweling, table paper, a clean metal tray either prepared with a paper barrier or cleaned with an appropriate disinfectant between each patient visit, or a clean field purchased for this purpose.
3. Needles, in their original packaging, are placed on the center of the clean field. Non-sterile cotton balls and skin cleansing materials (e.g., alcohol swabs) are placed either nearby the treatment table in a clean container or on the periphery of the clean field.
4. Sharps and trash containers are placed away from the clean field.
5. The dry needling points on the patient's skin should be clean. For the purposes of Clean Needle Technique, skin can be cleaned with 70% isopropyl alcohol, soap and water, or another method but must be clean when inserting a needle.
6. If using alcohol to clean the skin, use a new swab/cotton ball whenever the alcohol swab becomes dirty or contaminated or is too dry to leave a thin layer of alcohol solution on the skin. The insertion point can then be palpated with the washed finger.
7. The needle should be inserted without touching its sterile shaft. Should the needle be long, the shaft may be held with sterile gauze or sterile cotton between the fingers and the needle shaft. Insert the needle only once. In the event that the needle location is changed, the needle should be withdrawn and placed in the sharp's container. A new needle must be used for each insertion.
8. The needle is then stimulated for therapeutic effect.
9. After the appropriate amount of time, the needle should be withdrawn and placed in a sharp's container. Do not place the needle in a tray for later transfer to the sharps container as this increases the risk of an accidental needlestick. Do not hand the

used needle to an assistant. This transfer also increases the risk of exposure by accidental needlestick.
10. At the end of treatment, the practitioner washes his or her hands and cleans up the clean field, including replacing or disposing of unused supplies. In the event that the practitioner has used some, but not all, of the needles in a multi-pack of acupuncture needles, all unused needles must also be disposed of in the sharp's container. Opened needle packs may not be used for a different patient or a treatment at a later time.

Palpating the Point

It is acceptable clean technique to palpate the MFTP after cleaning the skin, as long as the hands are clean and have not been contaminated. However, it is strongly recommended that before picking up the needle or palpating the point, the hands should be washed with soap and water or an alcohol-based hand sanitizer if they have been contaminated since the last handwashing by some activity such as arranging clothing or taking notes. After this second cleaning of the hands, nothing should be touched but the needle handle, guide tube, and the skin over the point. If anything, else is touched, the fingers should be cleaned again.

Inserting Needle to Correct Depth

While there is no absolute standard for the depth of needling, there are studies on methods of establishing safe depths (364) and recommendations from reliable practice textbooks. (361,362,365) Following are some general guidelines and recommendations:

1. Follow the suggested needle depths indicated in standard texts, being sure to allow for variation in body size, age, underlying disease and risk factors. For instance, in puncturing the MFTP in the triceps, a strong sensation and a LTR may be obtained when a depth of 0.5 inch is reached in a thin, muscular patient. On the other hand, sensation may only be induced when the

Needle Safety and Considerations

needle is inserted to a deeper level for an obese or heavily muscled patient.
2. Safe needling depth of the thoracic region to avoid pneumothorax and cardiac tamponade on most patients can be as little as 10-20 mm. Limiting the depth of needle insertion to the superficial muscular layer is critical and avoiding use of needles that are longer than the safe needling depth for a particular body area is strongly recommended.
3. Safe needling depth is recommended at 10-20 mm; less than the face width of a U.S. nickel, 20- cent Euro coin, Canadian 25-cent piece or English 20 pence. Rather than needling at a perpendicular angle, it is strongly recommended to needle at an oblique angle. This also ensures that needles will not travel deeper into the body.

Touching the needle during needle insertion

If you need to support the shaft of the needle during needle insertion, either because you are using a thin needle (e.g., 0.15 mm width) or a long needle (e.g., more than 25 mm length) or both, you must use a sterile barrier between your fingers and the shaft of the needle. While washing your hands removes most of the transient bacteria from the skin of the hands and fingers, it does not dislodge the resident bacteria. Any object that pierces the skin must be sterile. To support the shaft of the needle, when necessary, use sterile gauze or sterile cotton between your fingers and the needle shaft; then discard the gauze or cotton after completing the needle insertion. This will greatly reduce the possibility of cross infections from needling.

Needle Removal

There are no specific standards regarding needle removal techniques. While some will find using a one-handed method (use the same hand to withdraw the needle and cover the point with cotton) less likely to cause a needlestick than a 2-handed method (use different hands for needle removal and covering the point with a cotton ball), no specific studies have shown either method as being superior.

Needle Safety and Considerations

Similarly, there are no studies identifying the safest method for needle removal. While it is clear that removed needles need to be placed immediately into a sharp's container, there is no evidence indicating that needles must be removed and placed in a sharp's container one at a time. Limiting time and distance between removing the needle and placing used needles in a sharp's container is strongly recommended.

Always use a cotton ball or other clean, absorbent materials (swab, gauze) for covering the hole after needle removal; never use your hand or finger. Some blood may be present, a barrier between the practitioner's hands and the open area of skin is best to reduce the likelihood of transfer of pathogens.

Possible Complications:

Pneumothorax and Cardiac Tamponade

Pneumothorax is a complication of dry needling. This can be seen with the patient who suffers a pneumothorax during a demonstration of deep dry needling (DDN) to treat the muscles in the thoracic area. (374)

The primary areas associated with dry needling-induced pneumothorax are the regions of the thorax including the upper trapezius, thoracic paraspinal, medial scapular, and sub clavicular areas. (373)

Needling should be limited to superficial penetration over the chest, back, shoulder and lateral thoracic region, no deeper than the subcutaneous tissue. It is also strongly recommended to use needles that are not longer than safe needling depth at any thoracic region area.

In addition to depth, angle of insertion when needling the chest must be considered. Oblique or transverse needling on points located on the chest and avoiding an upward direction is critical to prevent heart injury.

Symptoms of cardiac tamponade include anxiety, restlessness, low blood pressure and weakness, chest pain radiating to the neck, shoulder, back or abdomen, chest pain that gets worse with deep breathing or coughing, problems breathing or rapid breathing, syncope, palpitations, drowsiness, and/or weak or absent peripheral pulses.

Infections

Infections may be local or systemic. *Staphylococcus aureus* and *Mycobacterium* may be part of common skin flora and the animal may be a carrier. A carrier may have no symptoms or indications they are a carrier unless they are tested, typically with swabs of the skin, nose or mouth. *S. aureus* can infect wounds and prevent healing, cause septicemia, or infect organs, bone, heart valve/lining or lung, and/or create an internal abscess. Patients can end up being hospitalized, may require surgery, months of IV antibiotics and may experience lifelong sequelae or even death.

A recent human study of acupuncture-related infection of skin and soft tissue such as mycobacterium including *Mycobacterium abscessus* and *Staphylococcus aureus* including MRSA was completed. Of the 239 cases reported for the period of 2000-2011, 193 were mycobacterium infection. The source of most of these infections was traced to reuse of improperly disinfected needles or therapeutic equipment or use of contaminated disinfectant or gel used for related procedures. (372)

While infections associated with needling are a rare occurrence, any disruption of the normal barriers to infection, such as puncturing through the skin and epidermal flora, can allow a pathogen to enter the body. Those with a reduction in normal immune function may then not respond adequately to the pathogen, allowing an infection to start.

Needle Safety and Considerations

Dry needling practitioners should take care to use Clean Needle Technique with all patients to prevent infections.

Stuck Needle

After a needle has been inserted, practitioners may find it difficult to rotate, lift or withdraw the needle. This is more common if a patient moves after the needle insertion, if the practitioner uses excessive rotation or twirling of the needle in a single direction, or if the needle is inserted to the depth that it gets stuck in the fascial layer. To manage a situation where the needle is stuck, reassure the patient and try to put them in a position so that their muscle relaxes. Then massage or lightly tap the skin around the point after which the needle should more easily be removed. If the needle is still difficult to withdraw, perform another needle insertion nearby so as to relax the muscles in the area of the stuck needle. If the needle is entangled in fibrous tissue, turn it in the opposite direction from the initial needle stimulation, twirling until it becomes loosened, then withdraw the needle.

Aggravation of Symptoms

Aggravation of symptoms occurs as a result of needling on an infrequent but consistent basis.(363, 364,365,366) Aggravation of symptoms is reported both as a potential adverse event and as an intended response to treatment, known as "Menken or Mengen phenomenon," or "healing crisis." (367) Many traditional medicine techniques include deliberate aggravation of symptoms (using a hot bath to bring about diaphoresis in the case of fever, etc.). Practitioners need to be clear about expected outcomes when speaking with clients prior to treating the patient.

Inflammation may be an expected response to a treatment. Inflammation, including cellular responses to stimuli, may increase

Needle Safety and Considerations

the inflammatory response that then brings about improvement of health. (368-371)

Within the tissues, inflammatory proteins transduce intracellular signals to define cellular responses essential to carrying out the healing processes.

Basic Principles for Needle Safety: A Summary

- Follow Clean Needle Technique
- Use only single-use sterile filiform needles.
- Clean hands immediately before any clinical procedure, including inserting needles, between patient visits, after contact with any bodily fluids or OPIM.
- Always establish a clean field ensuring the cleanliness of the practitioner's and patient's skin and the sterility of the shaft of the needle and other medical devices.
- Immediately isolate used needles and other sharps in an appropriate sharp's container.
- Do not needle or otherwise treat areas of the skin with active lesions.

MUSCLES OF THE NECK AND FORELIMB:

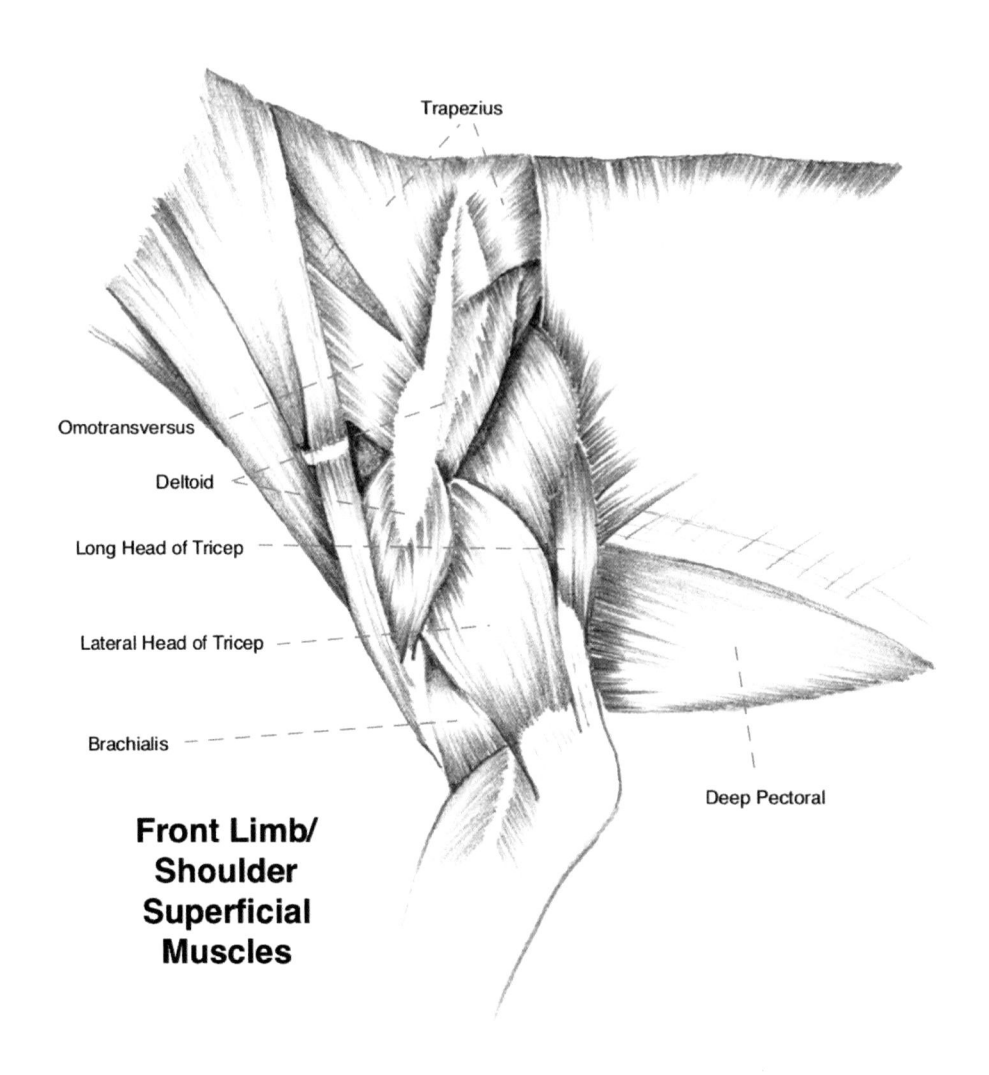

- Trapezius
- Omotransversus
- Deltoid
- Long Head of Tricep
- Lateral Head of Tricep
- Brachialis
- Deep Pectoral

Front Limb/ Shoulder Superficial Muscles

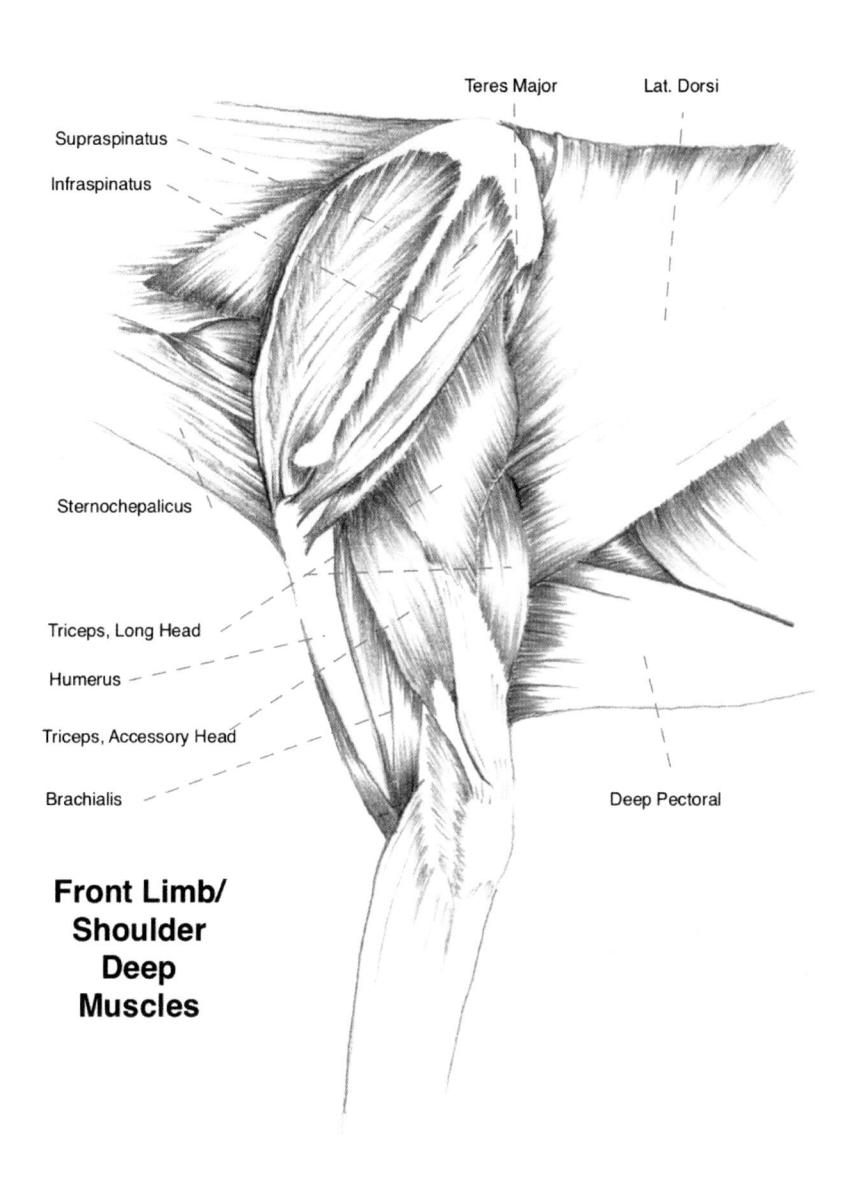

Labels on figure:
- Supraspinatus
- Infraspinatus
- Teres Major
- Lat. Dorsi
- Sternochepalicus
- Triceps, Long Head
- Humerus
- Triceps, Accessory Head
- Brachialis
- Deep Pectoral

Front Limb/ Shoulder Deep Muscles

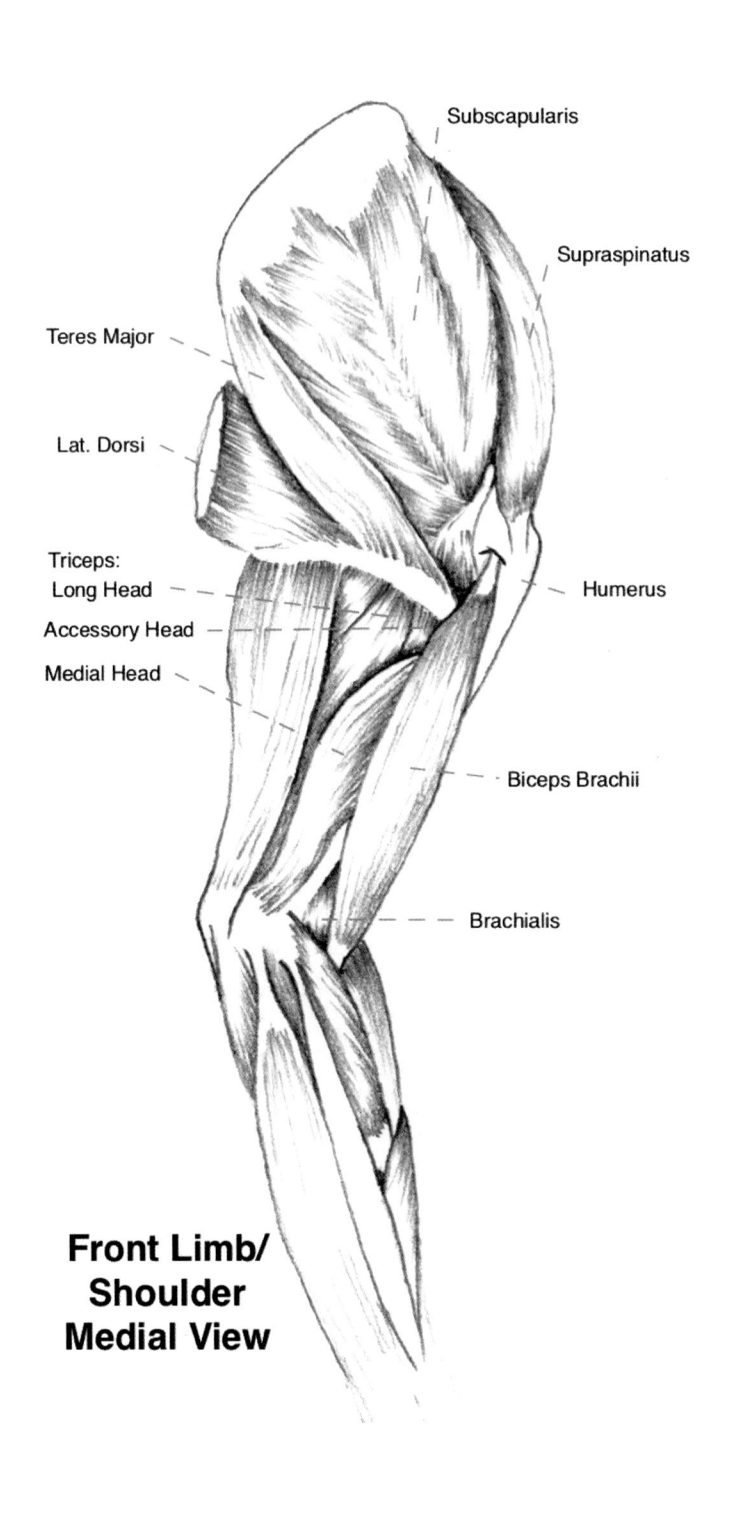

- Subscapularis
- Supraspinatus
- Teres Major
- Lat. Dorsi
- Triceps:
  - Long Head
  - Accessory Head
  - Medial Head
- Humerus
- Biceps Brachii
- Brachialis

Front Limb/ Shoulder Medial View

STERNOCLEIDOMASTOID MUSCLE (SCM)

This muscle is divided into two parts: The Brachiocephalic and Sternocephalic muscles. These are the most important muscles of the neck as they are essential for movement of the thoracic limb. In carnivores, the Sternocephalic muscle is divided into two portions, the Sternomastoid and the Sterno-occipital muscle. The Brachiocephalic muscle divides into the Cleidocervical and Cleidomastoid muscles. It has two origins and one insertion. The external jugular vein is wrapped by the superficial fascia so be careful when treating this area.

Origin:
Brachiocephalic: Cleidocervical: Median line of the nuchal ligament and occipital bone.
Cleidomastoid: Mastoid process of the temporal bone.

Sternocephalic: Sternomastoid: Manubrium of the sternum.
Sterno-Occipital: Manubrium of the sternum.

Insertion:
Brachiocephalic: Cleidocervical and Cleidomastoid insert as the Cleidobrachialis muscle between the vestigial clavicle and the humerus.
Sternocephalic: Sternocephalic inserts onto the mastoid process.
Sterno-Occipital inserts at the nuchal crest.

Action and function:
Brachiocephalic: Bilaterally: Pulls the head down and backwards.
Unilaterally: Neck flexion when shoulder is fixed, pulls the head, upper arm fascia and neck to one side and draws the forelimb forward during limb extension.

Sternocephalic: Bilaterally: Flexes the head and neck. Lateral flexion of the head and neck.
Unilaterally: Fixes the head during swallowing.

Sternocleidomastoid

Palpation and trigger point location: Put the patient in a seated or a lateral recumbent position, tilt the head up and to the opposite side to distinguish the muscle and make it visible. Palpate using the pads of the fingers, start at the superior nuchal line, move to the angle of the neck, to the lateral edge of the humerus and the first rib.
Be careful not to push too hard as the sternocephalic and brachiocephalic muscles can illicit symptoms such as nausea, imbalance, earache and deep aching pain. The sternocleidomastoid as a whole is one of the most prominent muscles for trigger points.

The sternocephalicus muscle has three MFTPs, one in the lower portion of the mid-muscle which refers pain to the sternum (s1), one in the mid portion of the muscle which refers pain to the maxilla, the eye, the TMJ and may have a part to play with difficulty swallowing due to referral to the tongue and pharynx (s2). The upper trigger point sends pain to the vertex of the head and may have some contribution to ear or eye pain (s3).

The brachiocephalic muscle has four-five MFTPs. The upper part has two trigger points that sit almost parallel to each other, TP2 is slightly caudal to TP1. Both these trigger points refer to the ear, and just behind the ear (b1+b2). The caudal MFTPS TP 3 and 4 refer to the caudolateral area of the neck and to the cranial portion of the shoulder and the humerus (b3+b4).

Sternocleidomastoid

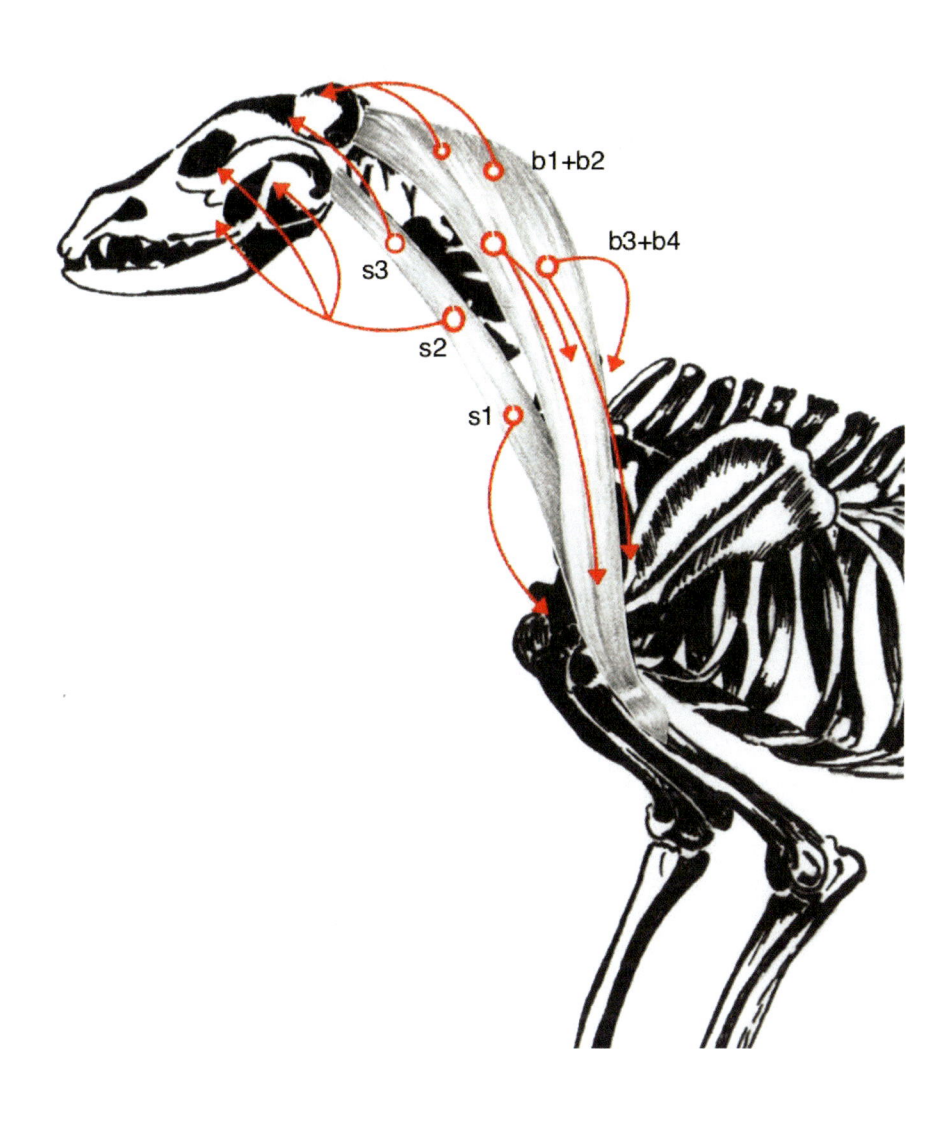

b1+b2

b3+b4

s3

s2

s1

Sternocleidomastoid

Pain Pattern: Neck pain-unilaterally or bilaterally depending on the symptomatic side. Frontal area, across the forehead to the opposite side. Upper trigger points: Temple pain, pain behind the ear, earache and caudo-lateral aspect of the neck.
Middle and lower fibers: Humeral, vertebral and cranial shoulder pain.

Symptoms include: Deep pain in the ear, neck pain, dizziness, and postural imbalance. Pain in the cheek, temple, maxilla.

Needling Technique: Preferably place the patient in a seated or lateral recumbent position, ensure that there is a slight lateral flexion of the cervical spine to approximately 10 to 20°, this will ensure that the muscle is in an appropriate position and angle to better palpate the trigger point and lock the muscle in place. By tilting the head toward the shoulder on the symptomatic side it allows the muscle to be under less tension. Grasp the muscle between the thumb, index and middle fingers, attempt to isolate the muscle belly where you perceive the trigger point to be with a "pincer" type grip. This is important for ensuring that you do not penetrate any vascular structures.

With some patients it is possible to almost separate the muscle from the other underlying muscles, and therefore isolate the trigger point more effectively. This is not possible in very heavy muscled dogs. While keeping your grip in this fashion, place the needle tube on the skin over the region where you would like the needle to be placed, tap the needle in with the guiding tube, and with the needling hand gently and slowly move the needle while visualizing the position of the trigger point in the muscle until the needling sensation is achieved. For greatest success in achieving the appropriate needling sensation and proper contact of the trigger point, imagine you are gripping and holding the trigger point between the fingers so that it will not move as you needle it. Always direct the needle in a manner so as to needle between the fingers and not toward the vertebra. The jugular vein is located here, so use a shallow needle insertion and be acutely aware of the course of the jugular vein and avoid it at all costs.

Sternocleidomastoid

Causative or perpetuating factors: overloading in lateral flexion and flexion of the neck and head. Heavy fore pullers, incorrect harness and collar fit, impact- dogs running into fences or each other. Falls in agility or heavy play. A leg length inequality or gait imbalance, any grade of lameness or hind limb abnormalities will cause the dog to strain the neck to maintain normal head position to level the eyes in compensation for a tilted biomechanical chain. A tight pectoral muscle increases tension on the SCM as it pulls on the brachiocephalic muscle. Cocking or tilting the head repeatedly can also activate MFTPs in this muscle.

Associated trigger points: Contra-lateral sternocephalic or brachiocephalic if unilateral.
- Omotransverse
- Mastoid
- Pectorals
- Temporalis

Stretches:
With a treat, turn the dogs head to the side, and look up, it will pull on the opposite muscle head.
Turn the head to the side and look down, and over the shoulder. Hold each of these positions for 10-20 seconds, do sets of 5 on each side, repeat 3 x a day.

Alternative stretch: stand over the standing dog and block their body with your legs, laterally flex the neck to the left, this will stretch the right brachiocephalicus muscle, hold for 15-30 seconds, repeat 5 times on each side.

OMOTRANSVERSARIUS (OMOTRANSVERSE)

The omotransverse muscle (Musculus omotransversarius) is a strong cord-like muscle between the wing of the atlas, the transverse process of the axis and the fascia covering the lateral aspect of the shoulder joint and the spine of the scapula. Its ventral border is fused to the cervical part of the trapezius muscle.

Location: lies adjacent to the brachiocephalicus and is not as thick.

Origin: Wing of the Atlas C1 or the transverse process of C2.

Insertion: distal end of the spine of the scapula.

Action: Bilateral and unilateral flexion and lateral flexion of the neck. Draws the scapula forward.

Innervation: Accessory nerve.

Pain pattern and trigger point location: There are three MFTPs in this muscle, one at the top, the middle and the bottom.
TP1 refers pain to the occiput and caudal cervical spine.
TP2 is found in the middle of the muscle and refers pain to the lower cervical vertebra and the scapula.
TP3 is found at the base of the muscle and refers pain locally and occasionally to the scapula.

Needling Technique: Preferably place the patient in a standing position as this will open up the upper thoracics and spread the scapula's, ensure that there is a slight flexion of the cervical spine to approximately 20°, this will ensure that the muscle is in an appropriate position and angled better to palpate the trigger point and lock the muscle in place. By tilting the head toward the shoulder on the symptomatic side it allows the muscle to be under less tension. Grasp the brachiocephalic muscle between the thumb, index and middle fingers, attempt to isolate the brachiocephalic muscle belly and pull it laterally to expose the

Omotransverse

omotransverse muscle at the scapula insertion. With most patients it is very difficult to separate the muscle from the other underlying muscles, and therefore isolate the trigger point more effectively.

This is not possible in very heavy muscled dogs. While keeping your grip in this fashion, place the needle tube on the skin over the region where you would like the needle to be placed, tap the needle in with the guiding tube, and with the needling hand gently and slowly move the needle while visualizing the position of the trigger point in the muscle until the needling sensation is achieved.

Causative and perpetuating factors: Mechanical overload in flexion- falling on their head, running into things headfirst. Playing violently with the rope or being yanked on a leash are common factors.

Associated trigger points: Sternocephalic
Brachiocephalic
Omotransverse opposite side if unilateral
Rhomboid
Pectorals

Stretches:
Turn the head to the side, and look up, it will pull on the opposite muscle head.
Turn the head to the side and look down, and over the shoulder. Hold each of these positions for 10-20 seconds, do sets of 5 on each side, repeat 3 x a day.

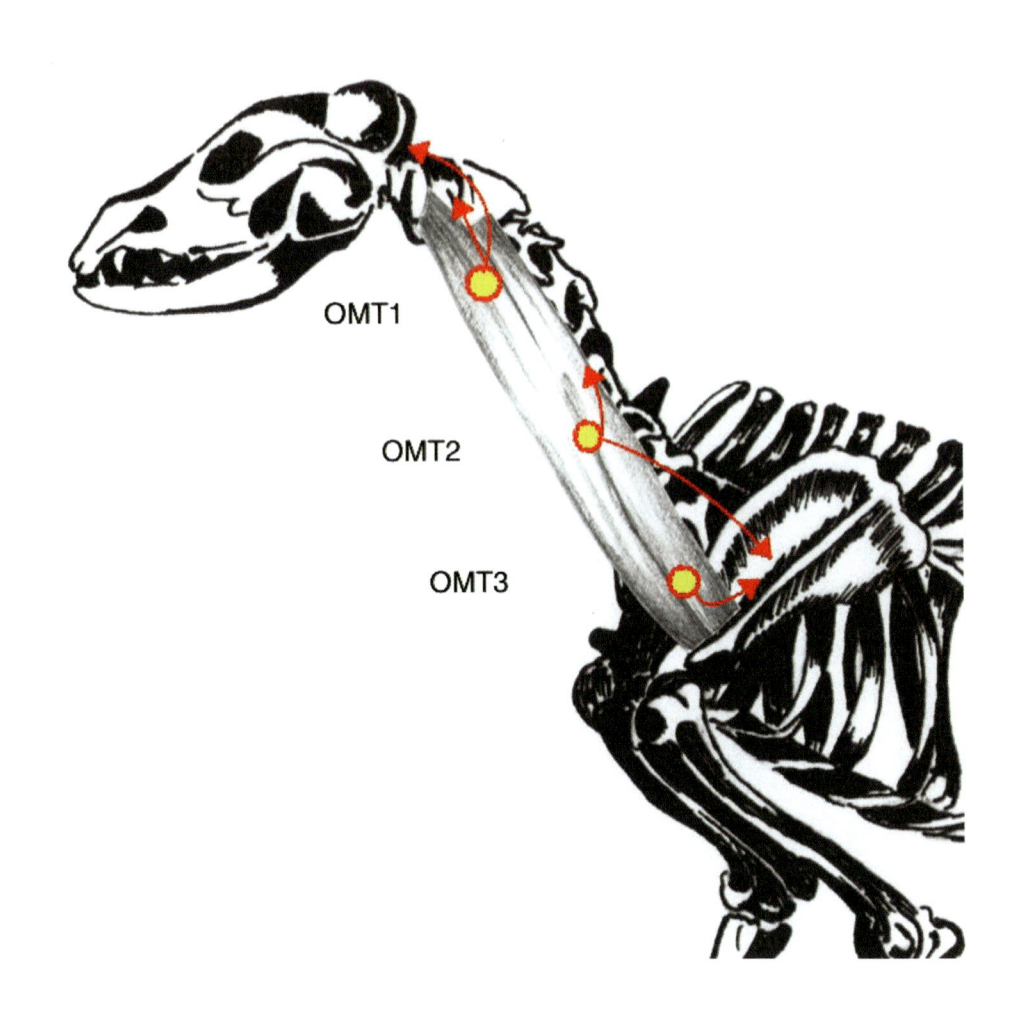

Omotransverse

OMT1

OMT2

OMT3

TRAPEZIUS

The trapezius is a broad, thin triangular, superficial muscle, that consists of a cervical and thoracic portion and lies over the shoulders.

Origin: Nuchal ligament C2-7 and the spinous processes of T1-8, supraspinous ligament.

Insertion: Both aspects of the spine of the scapula.

Actions: Elevates the scapula, protracts and retracts the scapula. Allows for abduction of the limb, the cervical portion draws the scapula forward while thoracic portion draws the scapula backwards.

Innervation: Dorsal branch of the accessory nerve.

Palpation: one of the most prominent muscles for trigger points. Using the pads of the fingers, start at the superior nuchal line, move to the angle of the neck, to the lateral edge of the clavicle, down to the spine of the scapula and inferiorly to T8.

Pain pattern:
Upper trigger points: Temple pain, pain behind the ear, and caudal-lateral aspect of the neck.
TP1 is located in the upper third of the cervical portion of the trapezius. This refers to the caudolateral aspect of the neck, the jaw and the mastoid.
TP2 is located caudal and lateral to TP1 and refers to the occiput.

Middle fibers: Scapula, vertebral and caudal shoulder pain.
TP 5 is found just above the scapula in the middle trapezius fibers. This trigger point refers pain to the lower cervical and upper thoracic dorsal spinous processes and vertebral bodies, as well as the scapula.

Lower fibers: supra or inter-scapula regions.

Trapezius

TP3: This is one of the most common trigger points, located in the mid-region near the lower border of the muscle near the scapula and refers pain to the high cervical region of the paraspinals, mastoid, acromion and suprascapular area.
TP4 is found slightly cranial to TP3 and refers to the medial aspect of the scapula.

Needling Technique: Patient is positioned in a down stay for needling the thoracic portion of the trapezius, however it will be easier to have the patient sitting when needling the cervical portion of the trapezius. Grasp the trapezius muscle between thumb and index/middle with a pincer grip. It is best to try and position the trigger point between the thumb and fingers therefore isolating and stopping movement of that small area of muscle, this allows the practitioner to isolate and accurately needle the area. Always direct the needle in a manner so as to needle between the fingers and not toward the lung apex.

Causative or perpetuating factors: overloading in lateral flexion of the neck and head. Falls, poor leash and harness choices, rope playing and yanking of the neck. Falling down off a height such as stairs or the couch. A cervical flexion/ extension injury. Sustained loads such as harnesses that stress the shoulders, or dogs that pull a cart.

Associated trigger points: Supraspinatus
Opposite Trapezius.

Stretch exercises: Neck rotations as far as possible towards the hind quarter, 5 -10 reps per side, sets of 3 twice a day.

Trapezius

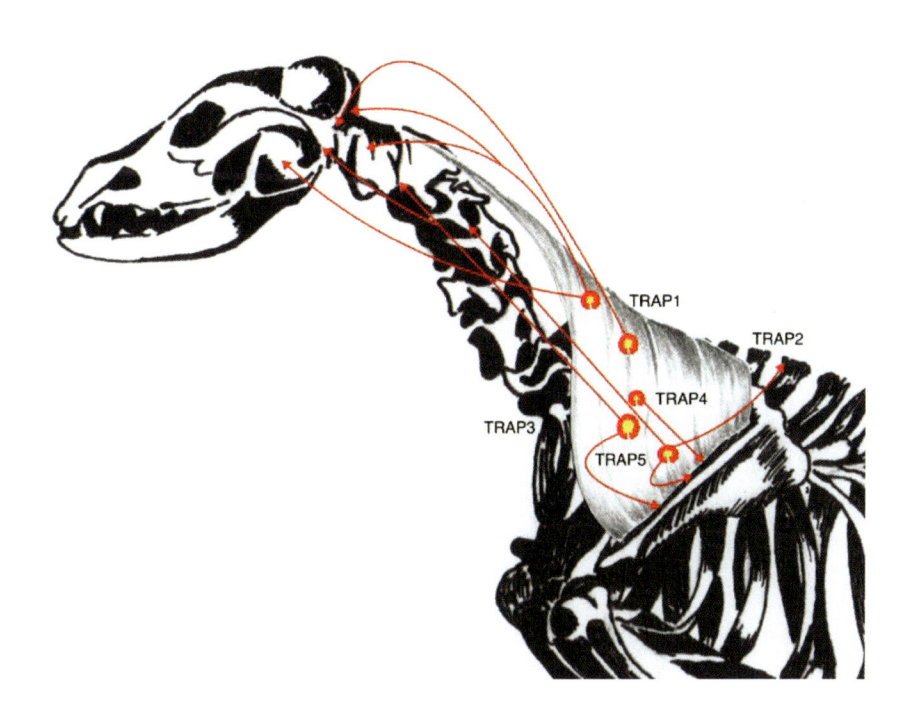

RHOMBOIDEUS (RHOMBOIDS)

Thick muscle lies along the back of the neck to the back of the withers and is deep to the trapezius. There are three portions to the rhomboid, a cervical, thoracic and capital portion.

Origin: Nuchal ligament and spinous processes of C2-6. Supraspinous ligament and the spinous processes of T1-7.

Insertion: Medial aspect of the base of the scapula and scapula cartilage.

Action: Elevation of the scapula. Bilateral extension of the head and neck. Unilateral flexion of the head and neck. Helps dog flex and look up and over the shoulder. Draws the limb forward and fixes scapula to the trunk.

Innervation: dorsal and ventral branches of the cervical and thoracic nerves.

Palpation: Locate the inferior aspect of the scapula at T7, medial spine of the scapula and the spinous processes of C2-T5. Place the patient in a lateral recumbent position with the affected side up and the head in neutral. Palpate the rhomboids from the medial spine of the scapula to the spinous processes of C2-T5.

Pain pattern and trigger point location: Supraspinous and medial scapula pain. Characterized as a deep aching pain and is unaffected by movement. There are two to three MFTPs in this muscle. They are located in the muscle along the medial border of the scapula and refer pain along the border of the scapula and the vertebra.

Needling Technique: With the patient in a down position or side lying, try to allow the patients forelimb to be off the edge of the treatment table or held in extension by a helper so as to open up the distance between the medial edge of the scapula and the spine, this will allow easier palpation of the rhomboid belly. Once you have identified the

Rhomboid

trigger point location, stabilize it between any two fingers and insert the needle so that the direction is from medial to lateral towards the medial edge of the scapula, the angle must be acute (approx. 5-10 degrees) so there is no chance of pierce the lung fields.

Causative or perpetuating factors: chronic overload from repetitive trotting and impact, doing weave poles, agility impact work, incorrect harness fit. Certain fore heavy breeds (staffies, pit bulls, certain terriers, bulldogs).TPLO surgery or any other biomechanical change that results in a leg length inequality activates these trigger point,

Associated myofascial trigger points: Pectoral
Brachiocephalicus
Infraspinatus

Stretch: With a treat get the dog to look up and over the shoulder, hold for 10 seconds, repeat on the other side, 5-10 reps, sets of 3.

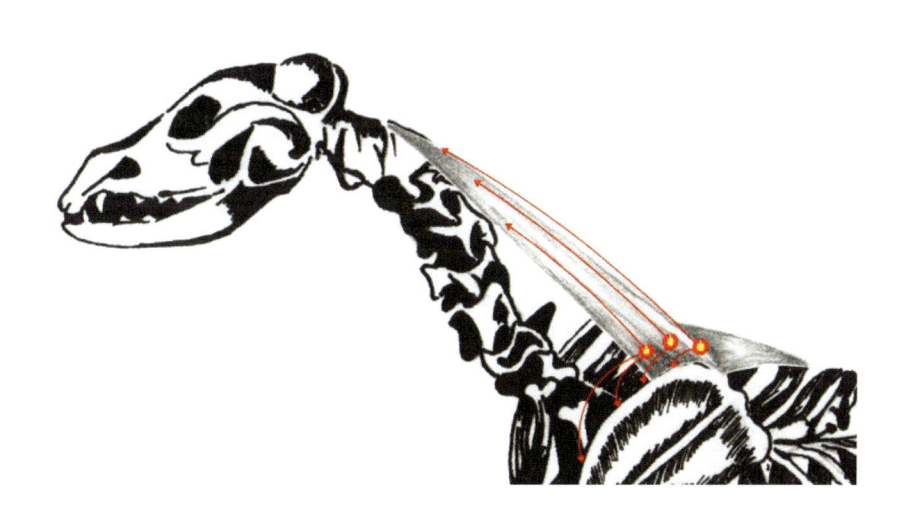

SUPRASPINATUS (SUPRASPINOUS)

Lies deep to the trapezius and brachiocephalicus. Creates the front aspect of the shoulder.

Origin: Supraspinous fossa of the scapula.

Insertion: Greater and lesser tubercles of the humerus.

Action: Extension and internal rotation of the shoulder (the lesser tubercle assists with the internal rotation), helps to stabilize the shoulder joint.

Innervation: Suprascapular nerve.

Palpation: Palpate deep into the supraspinatus fossa, move towards the acromion. Many trigger points are found all the way through the supraspinatus muscle, lateral to the medial scapula spine.

Pain pattern and MFTP location: There are two MFTPS.
TP1 is found in the medial portion of the muscle,
TP2 is found adjacent to TP1. Both trigger points refer pain to the middle deltoid region, lateral epicondyle and forelimb. Pain is felt on abduction of the shoulder and forelimb.

Needling technique: Palpate the muscle with patient side lying and using the index or middle finger isolate the trigger point under that finger and try to trap it against the scapula surface, this will help you direct the needle toward the scapula, this ensures that you will definitely not pierce through into any vessels or nerves.

Causative or perpetuating factors: Lunging hard at something, jumping, slipping with the leg out, falling onto the shoulder, breaking or pouncing hard, digging. Repetitive hard pulling on a leash perpetuates these MFTPS.

Supraspinatus

Associated trigger points: Subscapularis
Infraspinatus
Middle Trapezius
Deltoid
Latissimus Dorsi.

Stretch: Pull the asymptomatic fore across towards the back and pull up. Hold for 15 seconds for 5 reps 3 x a day.

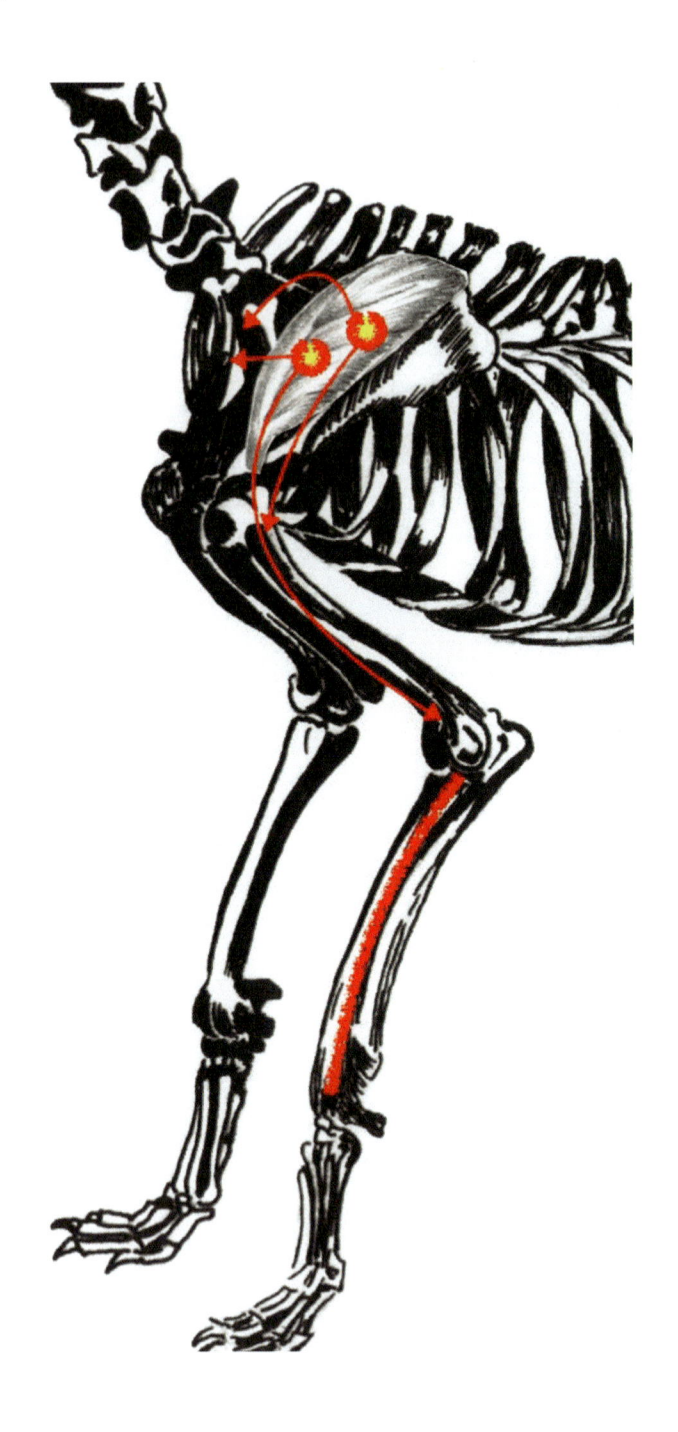

Supraspinatus

INFRASPINATUS (INFRASPINOUS)

Lies deep to the trapezius and deltoid. Contributes to the shoulders form and shape.

Origin: Infraspinous fossa of the scapula.

Insertion: Lateral tuberosity of the humerus- outer side of the greater tubercle of the humerus.

Action: Flexion, abduction and external rotation of the shoulder. Helps stabilize the shoulder joint.

Innervation: Suprascapular nerve.

Palpation: *Infraspinatus myofascial trigger points are one of the leading causes of shoulder pain.* Due to the fact that it is one of the rotator cuff muscles and is in the top three muscles, to produce shoulder pain, it is an essential muscle to check.
Infraspinatus is best felt with the leg in external rotation and is located in the infraspinatus fossa.
Use a flat digital palpation to locate myofascial trigger points.

Pain pattern:
Proximal trigger point TP1 is found in the top part of the muscle and refers pain deep in the anterior deltoid and shoulder joint, extending to the front and lateral aspect of the leg, forelimb and the radial distribution of the paw. Pain may refer to the caudal cervical and sub-occipital area of the neck.
Distal trigger point TP2 found in the middle of the muscle refers pain predominantly to the spine of the scapula. Patients are unable to weight bear without pain, cannot extend the front leg out to the same stretch as the unaffected limb, and will constantly want to flex the leg.

Needling technique: Patient is lying lateral recumbent, isolate the point with flat palpation using the index and middle fingers, trap the trigger

Infraspinatus

point under or between the fingers against the scapula. Needle to the appropriate depth and towards the scapula itself.

Causative and perpetuating factors: overload stress when the front leg is in flexion and extension. Infraspinatus is easily activated by unusual and transient movements that create an acute overload.

Associated trigger points: Deltoid
                         Biceps brachii
                         Supraspinous
                         Latissimus Dorsi.

Stretch: Hold the leg in an abducted and slightly externally rotated position for 20-30 seconds, sets of 3-5, 3 x a day

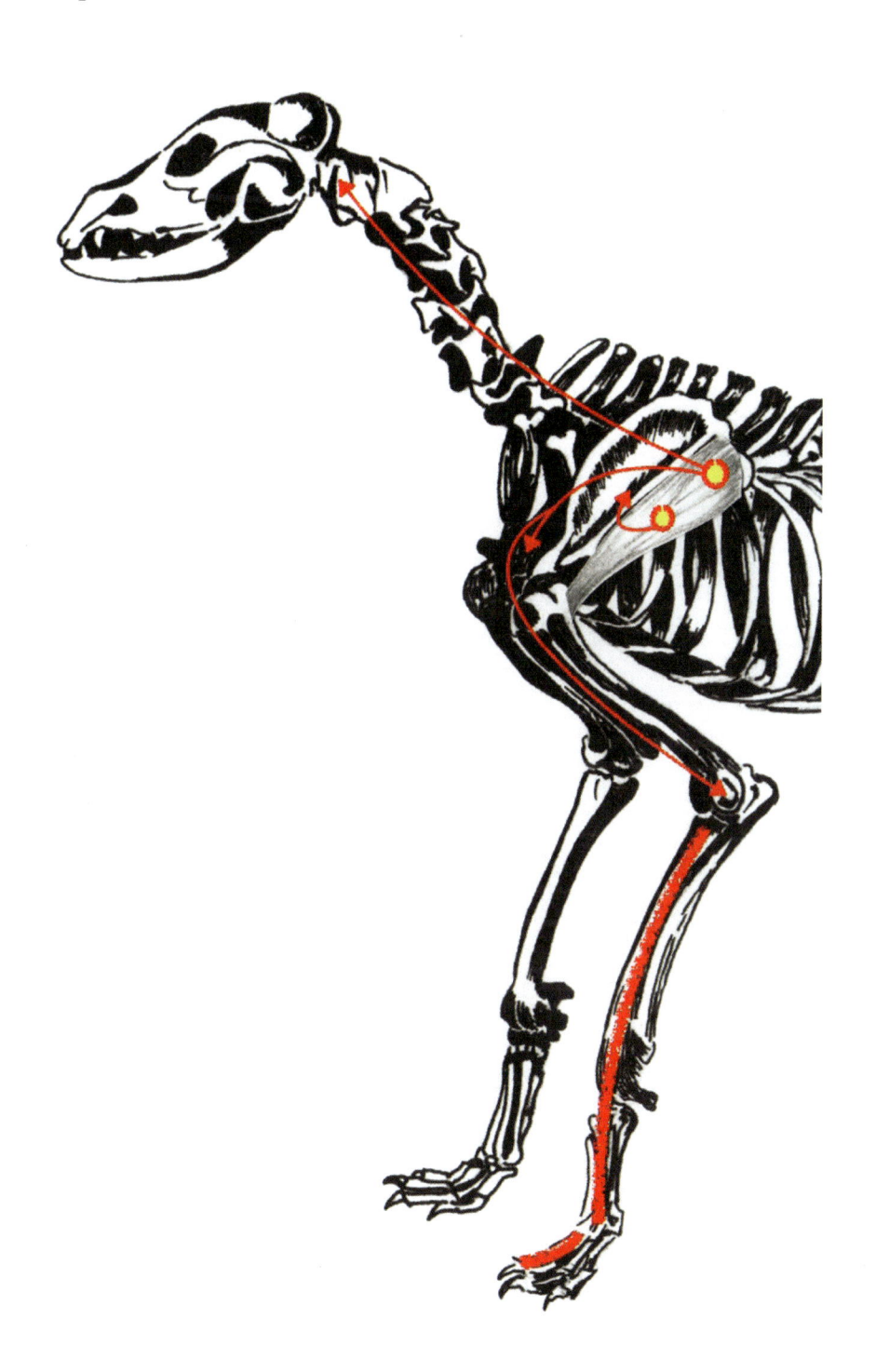

Infraspinatus

DELTOID

This muscle is a superficial muscle that has two portions. The dorsal portion is wider and is attached along the scapular spine and an acromial portion which is smaller and tapers at both ends.

Origin: Posterior spine of the scapula and the acromion process. Located at the bottom end of the spine of the scapula.

Insertion: Deltoid tuberosity of the humerus- located laterally along the humerus a third of the way down.

Action: Flexion, external rotation and abduction of the shoulder. Flexes the shoulder joint and pulls the forelimb away from the body.

Innervation: Axillary nerve.

Palpation: Look for the delto-pectoral groove that separates the pectoral muscle and deltoid. Palpate caudally and laterally. There are normally significant trigger points found in this muscle and can be very tender.

Pain pattern and MFTP location: MFTPs are found in the cranial, middle and caudal portion of the deltoid muscle. These are generally not named as they are numerous and only refer pain locally, therefore they do not need to be distinguished from each other. They generally refer pain in a localized pattern around the MFTP. Cranial and medial shoulder, there may be a reduction in abduction strength in external rotation. Caudal fibers cause a reduction in abduction strength in internal rotation.

Needle technique: When needling the deltoid, have the patient side lying/lateral recumbent. Begin by palpating with all the fingers so as to find the most active point, when the point is found, isolate the band of affected muscle with the index and middle fingers, press downwards with good pressure so that the trigger point is firmly held in place and

Deltoid

will not easily move. Direct the needle towards the trigger point between the fingers this will ensure 100 % success in needling that trigger point. Remember if you can't feel the trigger point with the fingers, you cannot needle it! Depth of insertion is in relation to the depth of the trigger point and muscle size.

Causative and perpetuating factors: acute or chronic forelimb overload. Slipping when jumping, digging and sharp stopping injuries. Loss of balance, overexertion and falling downstairs activates the cranial MFTPs. Over-exercising and intramuscular injections activate the caudal deltoid MFTPs. The middle MFTPS are activated by overload and vigorous jerky movements with the limb in abduction.

Associated trigger points: Pectoral
　　　　　　　　　　　　Biceps Brachii
　　　　　　　　　　　　Triceps brachii
　　　　　　　　　　　　Latissimus Dorsi.

Deltoid

BICEPS BRACHII

Runs ventrally to the shoulder joint and medial to the forearm to the radius.

Origin: Supraglenoid tubercle of the scapula.

Insertion: Radial tuberosity.

Action: Extension of the shoulder and flexes the elbow. Acts as a stabilizer of the shoulder and carpal joint.

Innervation: Musculocutaneous nerve.

Palpation: Flex the elbow to between 15-45 degrees to locate the bicep tendon in the bicipital groove. External rotation of the foreleg will make the tendon more palpable in the groove.

Pain Pattern and trigger point location: cranial leg and shoulder pain. There are two, sometimes three MFTPS in this muscle.
TP1 is found dorsally in the muscle near the origin. It refers to the cranial aspect of the shoulder.
TP2 is found in the middle of the muscle and refers locally and ventrally to the leg.
TP3 is found in the ventral portion of the muscle, close to the insertion at the radial tuberosity and refers down the leg to the carpus.

Needling technique: The patient is placed in a side lying position with the leg supported so that the bicep muscle is under no tension. Palpate the bicep and when finding the trigger point, isolate its position with a pincer grip or pushed down flat with the index and middle finger against the humerus. Needle directly toward the trigger point at the depth required. This muscle requires a fairly shallow needling technique.

Causative and perpetuating factors: sustained elbow flexion, stopping suddenly, digging, explosive take offs, deep sand running. Most trigger

Biceps Brachii

points are perpetuated by overuse and repetitive activity involving elbow flexion.

Associated trigger points: Supraspinous
                                    Triceps brachii.

Stretch: Hold onto the leg, flex it towards the back. Hold the stretch for 20 -30 seconds, sets of 3, 3 times a day.

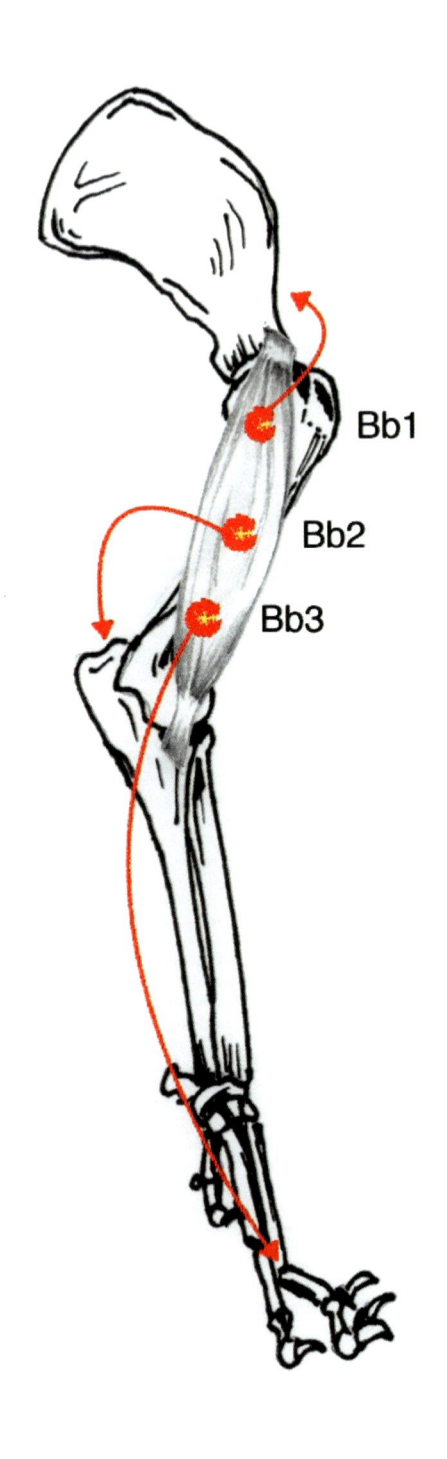

Biceps Brachii

Bb1
Bb2
Bb3

TRICEPS

This muscle is a fleshy superficial muscle that has four heads: a long head, a medial head and a lateral head. In the dog there is an additional accessory head.

Origin: Long head: Caudal distal boarder of the scapula to two thirds up the caudal border.
Lateral head: Caudal and lateral on humerus.
Medial head: Caudal and medial on humerus.
The Accessory head originates from the caudal part of the neck of the humerus and blends with the long and lateral heads.

Insertion: Long, lateral and medial head: Olecranon process of the ulna.

Action:
Long head: Flexes the shoulder joint and extends the elbow joint.
Lateral head: Extends the elbow joint.
Medial head: Extends the elbow joint.

Palpation: Move cranially from the olecranon process to the caudal aspect of the humerus. The long head is the most pronounced muscle, followed by the strong lateral head and followed by the much smaller medial head.

Pain pattern and trigger point location: caudal aspect of the front leg, lateral epicondyle, pain in the suprascapular region, ulna radiation into the paw.
TP1 is found in the middle of the long head of the tricep. It refers pain to the caudal aspect of the humerus and shoulder and down towards the carpus.
TP2 is found in the lateral portion of the medial head of the triceps. It refers pain to the lateral epicondyle and the ulna aspect of the arm.
TP3 is found in the middle of the lateral head of the triceps and refers to the caudal aspect of the arm down to the paw.

Triceps

Needling technique: Place the patient in a side lying position with the foreleg supported so that the weight of the leg does not place tension on the triceps musculature, localize the trigger point with the palmar surfaces of the fingers, when found, trap the point and needle to depth according to the size of the muscle.

Causative and perpetuating factors: Overload stress due to pushing off into ambulation. May be repetitive overload on a fatigued muscle or an explosive movement that injures the triceps. Repetitive pushing or rapid extension of the leg. Leg length inequalities activate triceps MFTPs due to gait abnormalities.

Associated trigger points: Latissimus Dorsi
         Biceps brachii
         Deltoid

Stretch: Place the leg in flexion and straighten the leg. Hold for 10-30 seconds, release and repeat for 5-10 reps and sets of 3

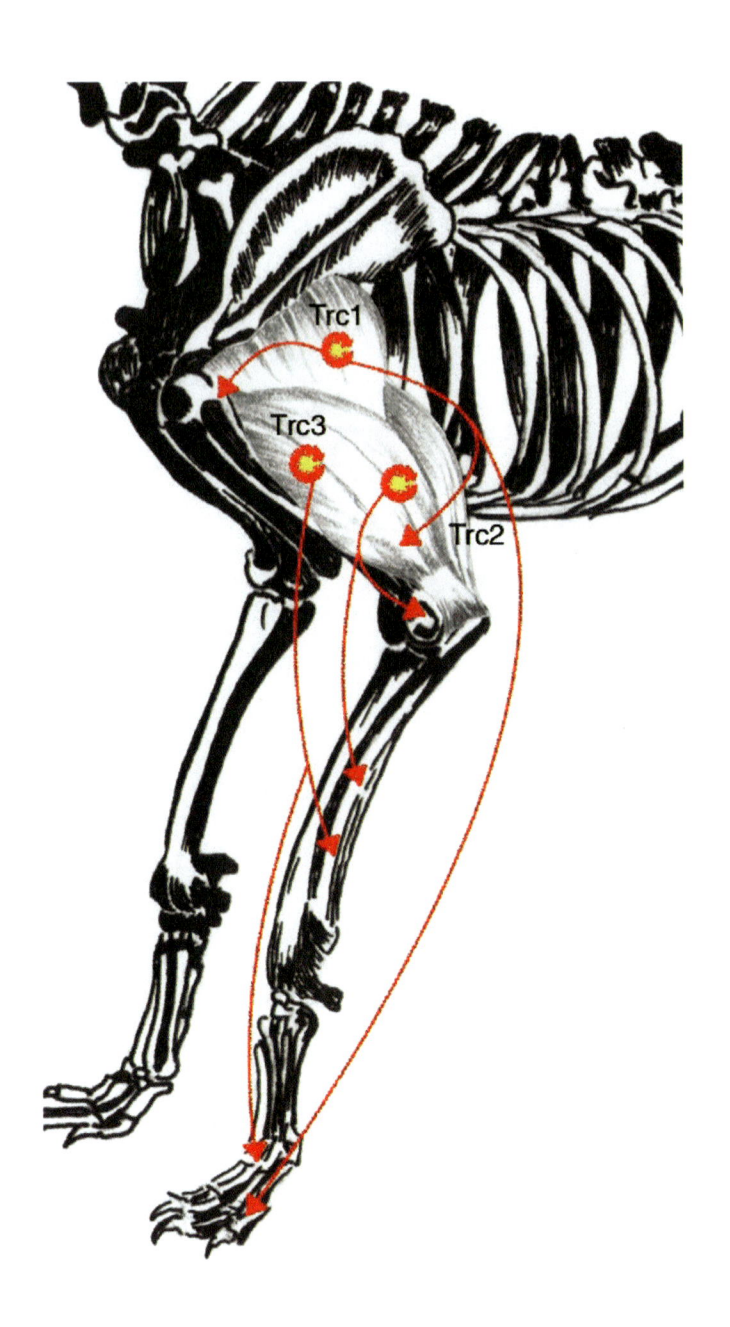

Triceps

TERES MINOR and MAJOR

Origin: Teres major and minor originates at the caudal border of the scapula.

Insertion: Teres minor and major tuberosity.

Action: Flexor of shoulder joint. Supports adduction of the limb.

Innervation: Axillary nerve.

Palpation:
Teres minor is round in carnivores and triangular in all other domestic species. Teres minor lies deep to the deltoid muscle. Most myofascial trigger points in the teres minor are found deep under the deltoid and can be exquisitely tender on palpation. Teres major is not a very large or defined muscle in dogs.

Pain pattern and trigger point location refers to the deltoid, extensor surface of the forearm.
Patient has difficulty and pain on flexion and extension of the shoulder and forelimb and presents as a very sensitive area on palpation. These trigger points are very difficult to feel as they are generally underneath the deltoid.

Needling technique: Needling is best done with the patient side lying with the leg in adduction across the chest. Using the index and middle finger isolate the active trigger point area and trap the trigger point between the fingers. Aim the point of the needle toward the trigger point between the fingers, needle depth is according to the muscle thickness.

Causative and perpetuating factors: overload under compression or concussion movements such as stopping suddenly from a sprint or repetitive running on uneven surfaces, slips and falls.

Associated trigger points: Triceps brachii

Teres Major and Minor

                    Latissimus Dorsi
                    Deltoid
                    Subscapular

Teres Major and Minor

LATISSIMUS DORSI

Latissimus dorsi is a superficial muscle which originates from the broad thoracolumbar fascia, lies caudal to the scapula on the lateral aspect of the thorax and trunk and inserts on the major teres tubercle of the humerus. In dogs this muscle attaches to the last thoracic vertebra, lumbar vertebra and ribs. It gives off a branch to the deep pectoral muscle and attaches on the greater tubercle.

Origin: Thoracolumbar fascia.

Insertion: Teres major tuberosity of the humerus.

Action: Draws the limb backwards and acts as an antagonist to the brachiocephalic muscle.

Palpation: place the patient in a side lying position, use a pincer grip to lift the posterior axillary fold away from the thoracic wall. Move caudally towards the iliac crest and then medially towards the spine. Alternate between a pincer grip cranially to a flat pad palpation caudally.

Pain pattern: There is a dorsal and ventral trigger point. The cranial trigger point TP1 is found just underneath the scapula on the lateral aspect near the axillary fold. This refers to the inferior angle of scapula, mid thoracic spine, cranial and caudal aspect of shoulder, down the medial aspect of the leg and into the lateral aspect of the paw.
TP2 is a caudal trigger point in the lower third of the muscle. The referral pattern for TP2 is the cranial aspect of the shoulder, the trunk and iliac crest.

Needling technique: Patient is placed in a down position with the affected leg hanging off the examination table. Palpate and isolate the points with the index and middle fingers, or with a pincer grip if the trigger point is located on the free portions of the muscle, this is possible

Latissimus Dorsi

only on certain dogs on the lateral borders of the muscle. The trigger points found over the rib regions need to be isolated and needled at a very acute angle and not deep toward a rib.

Causative and perpetuating factors: Slipping with the leg out, falls onto the back and ribs. Repetitive extension or shoulder weight bearing, when combined with adduction activates and perpetuates these trigger point. Dogs who are cage resting or are lying down a lot can activate these trigger points due to constant pressure on one side when sleeping.

Accessory trigger points: Triceps brachii
                                 Rectus abdominis
                                 Brachioradialis
                                 Deep Pectoral

Latissimus Dorsi

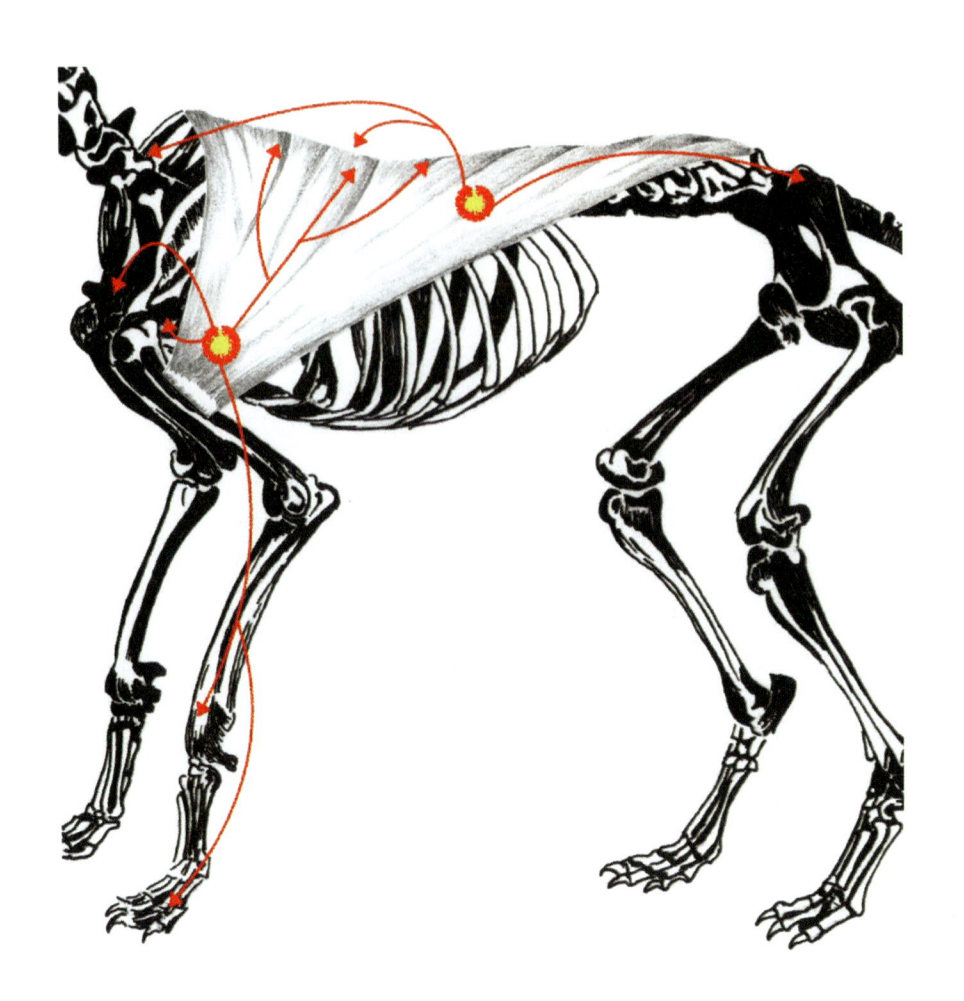

PECTORAL

Anterior chest area located in between the front legs. The Superficial Pectoral muscles occupy the space between the ventral part of the thoracic wall and the proximal part of the thoracic limb, forming the ventral aspect of the axilla. The superficial pectoral muscle is comprised of the descending and transverse pectoral muscle. The deep pectoral muscle is a very strong muscle that goes from the sternum, xiphoid and costal cartilage to the humerus.

Origin: Descending pectoral muscle originates from the manubrium of the sternum.
The transverse pectoral muscle arises caudal to the descending pectoral muscle and from the ventral aspect of the sternum from rib 1-6 rib cartilage and blends with the fascia of the forearm. In dogs the descending pectoral muscle is barely distinguishable from the thick transverse pectoral muscle.
The deep pectoral muscle originates from the sternum and from the 4th rib cartilage.

Insertion: Descending pectoral muscle inserts on the crest of the greater tubercle of the humerus. Transverse pectoral inserts onto the fascia of the arm. Deep pectoral muscle inserts onto the medial and lateral aspect of the proximal humerus, at the lesser tubercle.

Action: Forelimb adduction, movement towards the midline.
Superficial- draws the limb forward and backwards, draws the trunk side wards. Deep- draws the limb backward, supports the trunk cranially over the advanced limb. Deep is an extensor of the shoulder joint.

Innervation: Cranial and caudal thoracic nerves.

Palpation: have the patient side lying, start at the medial attachment at the sternum and palpate outwards with a flat palpation, move laterally to the bicipital groove and axilla. Use a pincer grip palpation on the

Pectoral

lateral aspect of the muscle. Do a light superficial sweep for trigger points then repeat deeper and with more pressure to elicit the deep pectoral muscle.

Pain pattern: There are two prominent trigger points here, TP1 is found adjacent to the lateral aspect of the sternum at approximately the 3rd rib. TP2 is found in at the level of the 5th rib and is more lateral than TP1. These trigger points present as shoulder pain, chest pain and pain that may refer to the ulna distribution of the forelimb and lateral digits.

Needling technique: Patient is side lying, allow the foreleg on the affected side to be supported, if the trigger point is located toward the lateral portion of the muscle you may use a pincer grip to isolate the trigger point, however if the trigger point is closer to the sternum one will use a flat two finger palpation and isolation technique. When the trigger point is found, it is imperative to trap the point either between the fingers or on top of a rib. It is very important to angle the needle toward the trigger point at an acute angle, never at 90 degrees! The safest way to ensure no penetration of the organs is to needle shallow and at an acute angle and toward solid anatomy such as a rib, this way if you needle too deep by accident you will hit bone and not the organs.

Causative and perpetuating factors: Limping on front or hind leg. Digging, falling with the leg flexed or abducted, loading the forelimb or shoulder as a result of hindlimb compensation. Dogs with elbow dysplasia. Incorrect harness fit that causes excessive rounding of the shoulders. Immobilization of the forelimb while the arm is cast or slung, especially if kept in adduction. Excessive exposure to cold (water, snow or air) can activate these MFTPs.

Associated trigger points: Deltoid
                                     Trapezius
                                     Rhomboids

Stretches: Place the dog on their side with the affected limb up, slowly and gently pull the leg into extension and hold for 10-20 seconds, repeat 5 times.

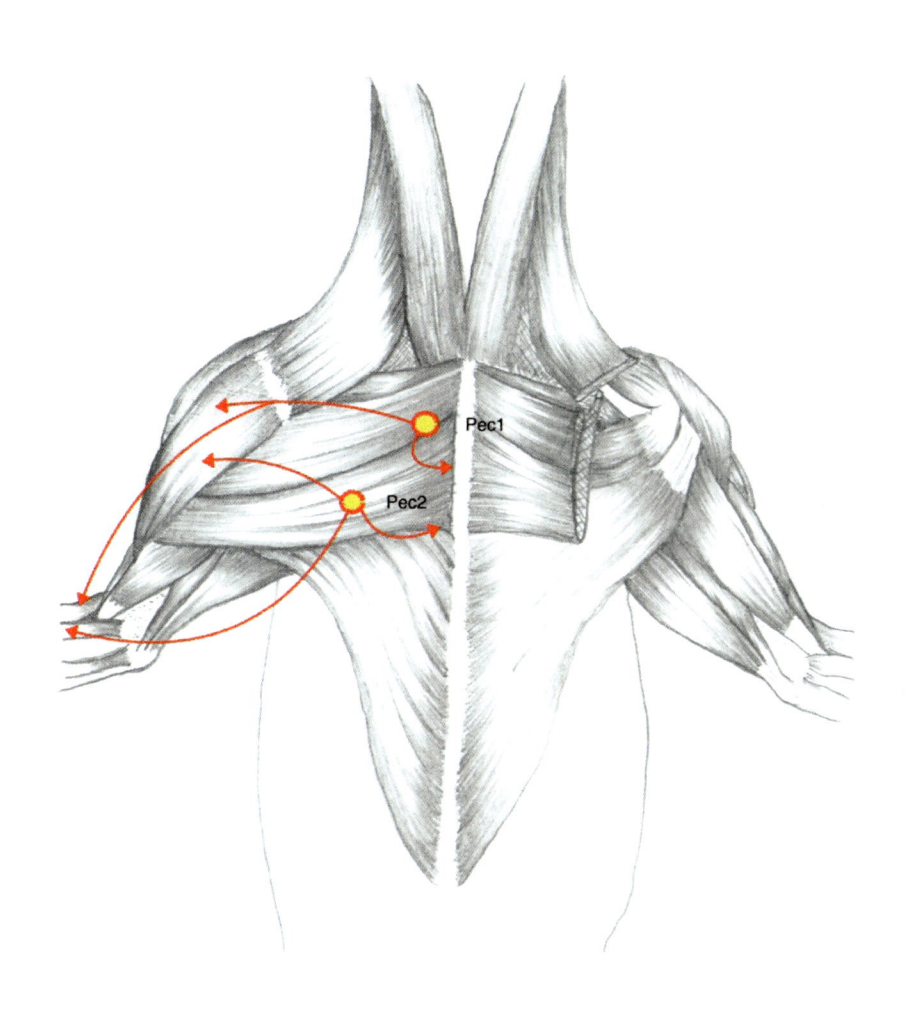

Pectoral

MUSCLES OF THE HINDLIMB:

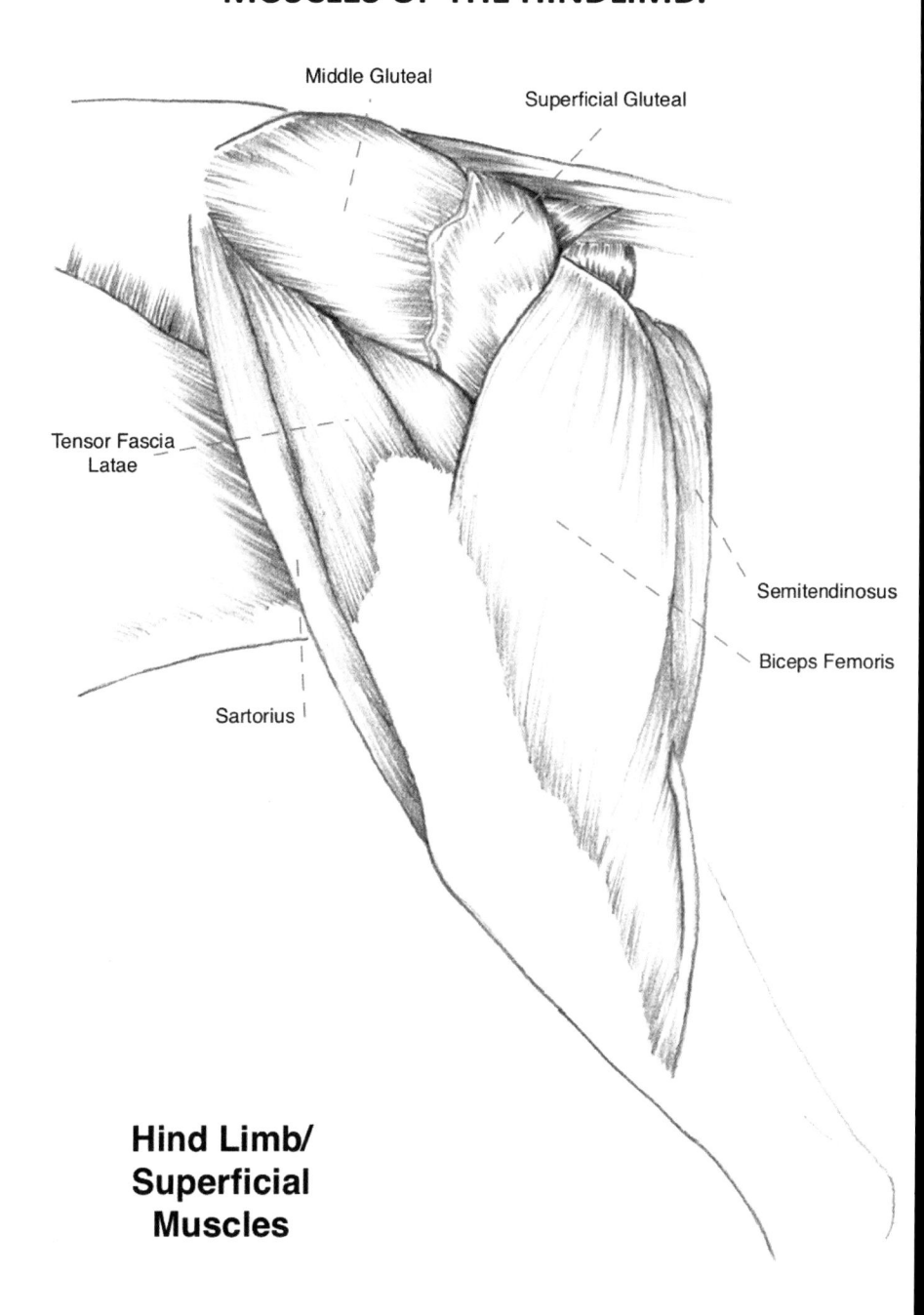

- Middle Gluteal
- Superficial Gluteal
- Tensor Fascia Latae
- Semitendinosus
- Biceps Femoris
- Sartorius

Hind Limb/ Superficial Muscles

Hind Limb/ Deep Muscles

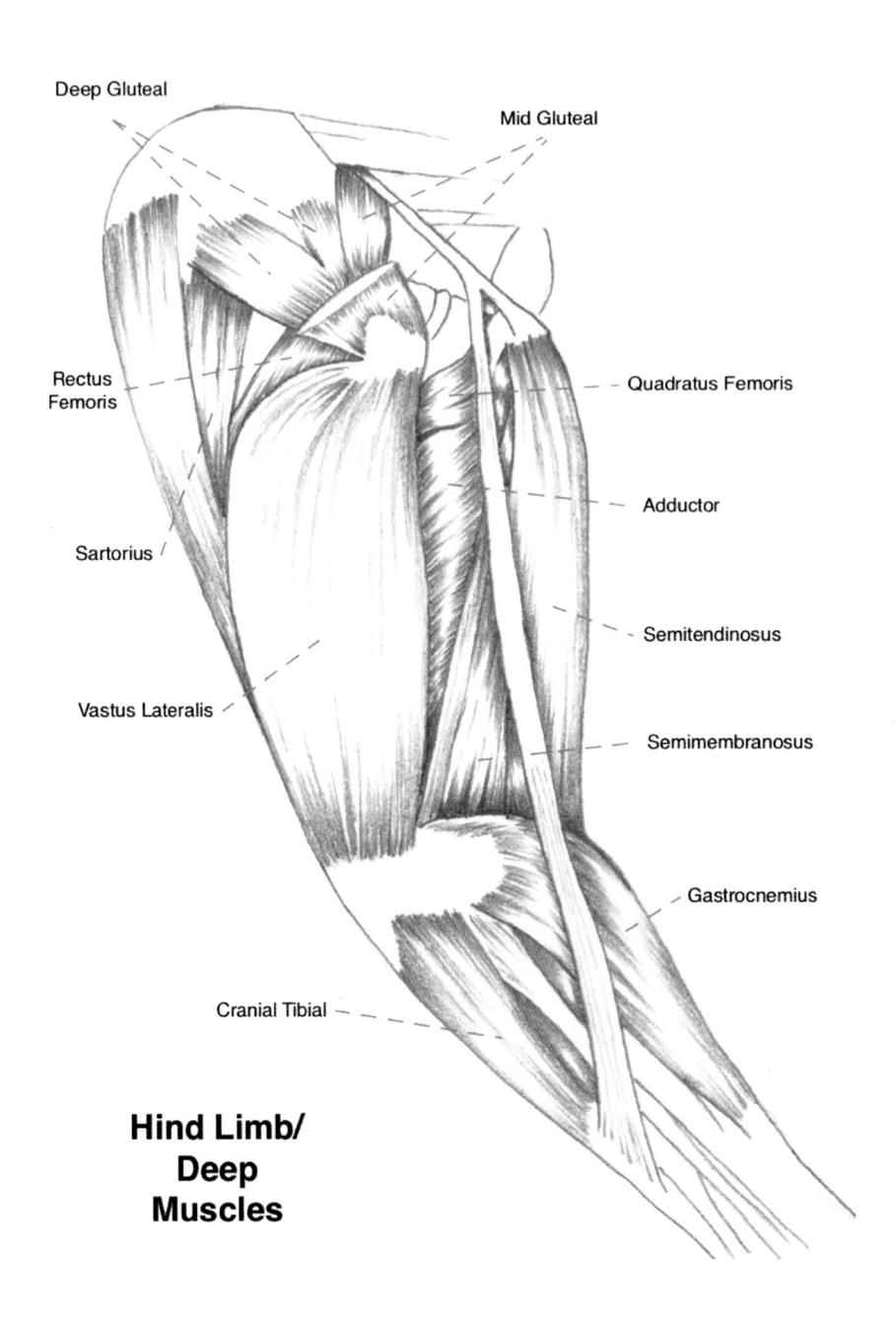

Labels:
- Deep Gluteal
- Mid Gluteal
- Rectus Femoris
- Quadratus Femoris
- Sartorius
- Adductor
- Semitendinosus
- Vastus Lateralis
- Semimembranosus
- Gastrocnemius
- Cranial Tibial

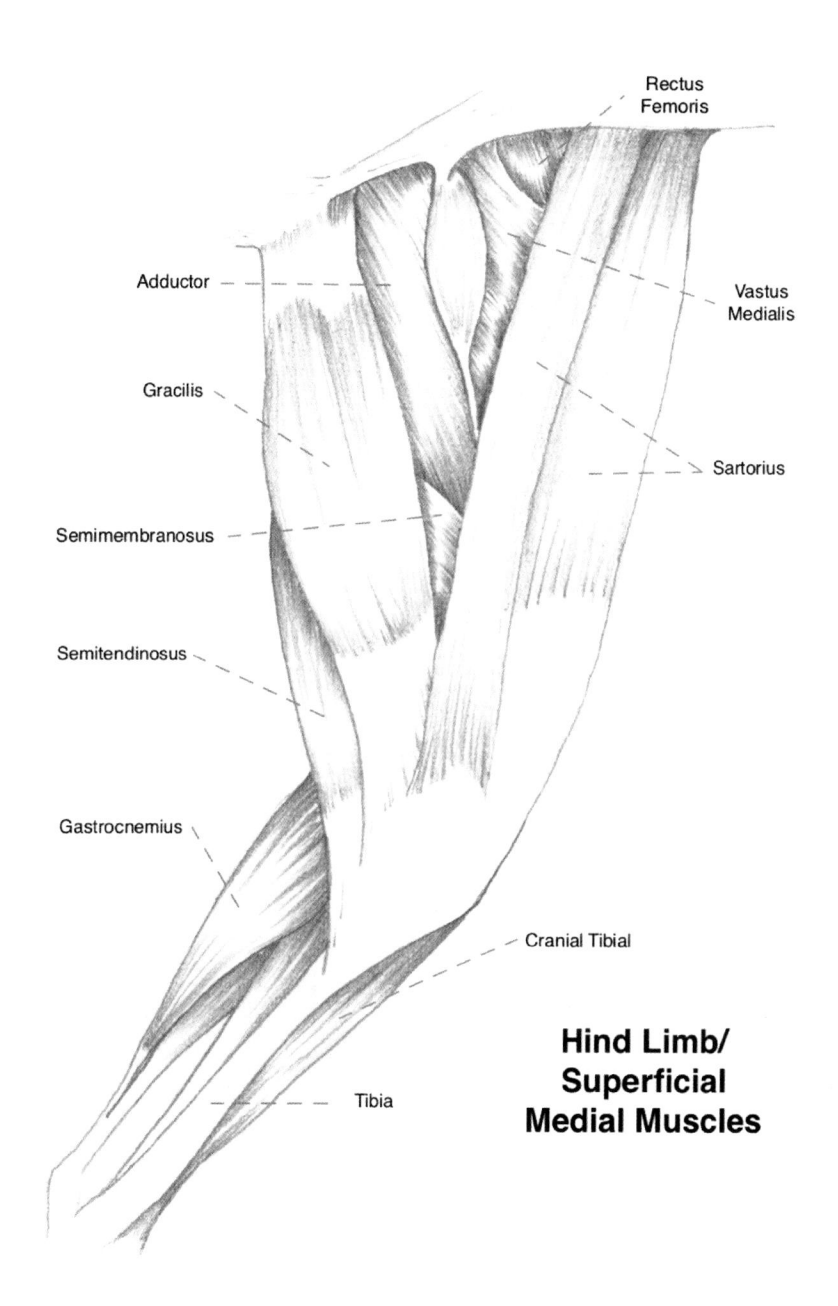

Hind Limb/ Superficial Medial Muscles

- Rectus Femoris
- Adductor
- Vastus Medialis
- Gracilis
- Sartorius
- Semimembranosus
- Semitendinosus
- Gastrocnemius
- Cranial Tibial
- Tibia

Hind Limb/ Deep Medial Muscles

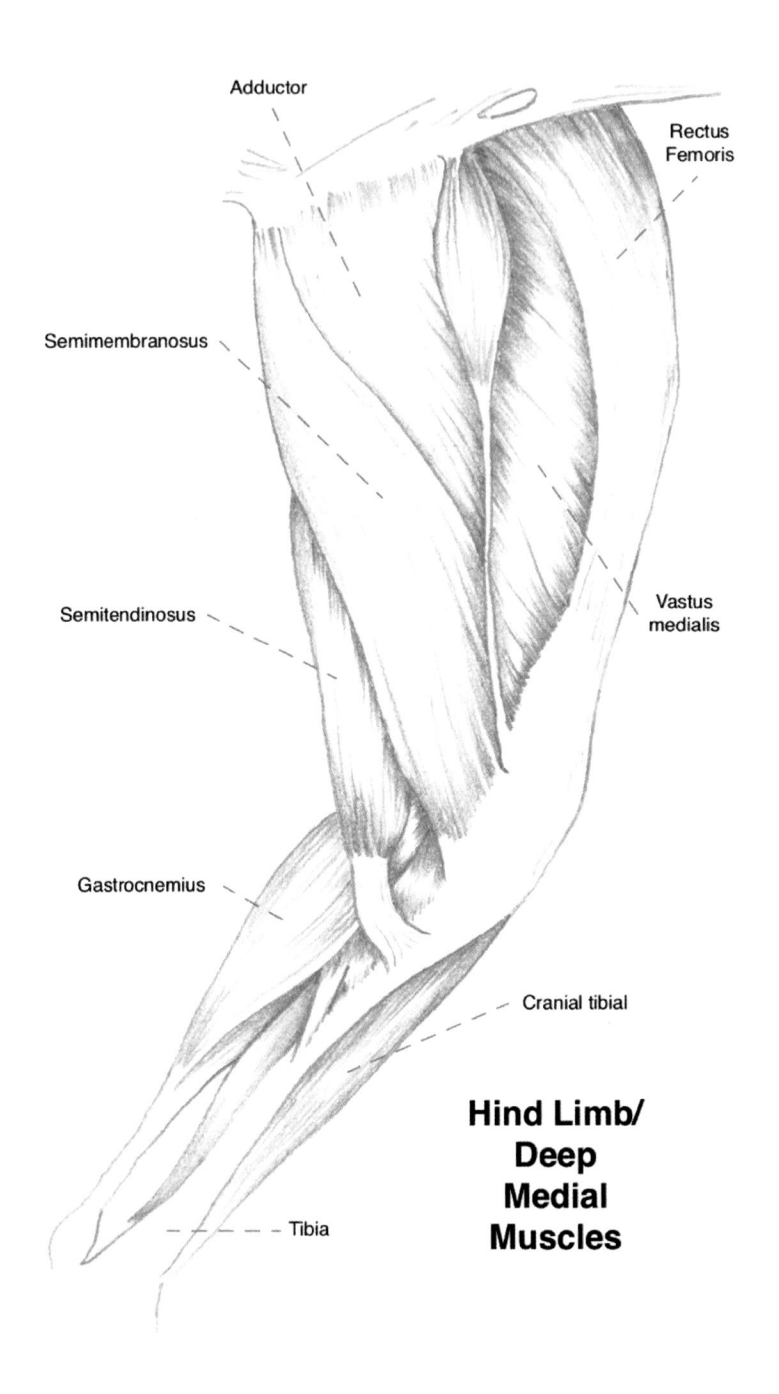

- Adductor
- Rectus Femoris
- Semimembranosus
- Semitendinosus
- Vastus medialis
- Gastrocnemius
- Cranial tibial
- Tibia

156

SUPERFICIAL GLUTEAL MUSCLE

Together with the middle gluteal it gives the dogs buttocks its form. It is a rectangular muscle extending between the sacrum, the first caudal vertebra, the ilium and the greater trochanter distally. It originates from the gluteal fascia, the lateral aspect of the sacrum, the sacroiliac, L7 and the sacrotuberous ligament.

Origin: Lateral border of the sacrum, 1st caudal vertebra via the sacrotuberous ligament. Cranial dorsal iliac spine via the deep gluteal fascia.

Insertion: Third trochanter.

Action: Hip extension and abduction of the limb.

Innervation: Caudal gluteal nerve.

Palpation and trigger point location: Side lying posture. Palpate from the lateral aspect of the sacrum, to the iliac crest, and to the hip joint. Finger pad palpation is best used for this area, and you will get a pain response from the dog when you find an active trigger point. There are three prominent trigger points in this muscle.

Trigger point 1 is found lateral to the sacrum and is located halfway down the muscle. This trigger point refers to the caudal aspect of the ilium, the sacroiliac joint and the sacrum on the ipsilateral side. There may be radiating pain into the buttock, lower back and the hip.

Trigger point 2 is found dorsal to the ischium. Pain from this trigger point radiates into the entire buttock and the sacrum. This may present as the dog not wanting to sit square and may be agitated when made to do so.

Superficial Gluteal

Trigger point 3 is found medially and ventrally close to the beginning of the coccygeal segments. Pain from this trigger point goes to the sacrum and coccyx.

Pain pattern: Crest of the ilium, sacroiliac, sacrum, buttock and posterior thigh. Symptoms include pain when walking, stair climbing, climbing hills, getting up from a seated position. Any ambulatory movement or changing position that requires pelvic flexion or extension.

Needling technique: Place the patient in a down stay or lateral recumbent posture. Trap the point between index and middle finger, direct the needle between the fingers toward the trigger point.

Causative and perpetuating factors: Overload and overuse injuries, chronic overload due to flexion of the hip, leg length inequality, sacroiliac joint dysfunction. Hip dysplasia, degenerative or injured stifles, limping.

Associated trigger points: Longissimus
                            Middle gluteus
                            Piriformis
                            Tensor fasciae latae.

Stretches: Cross affected leg behind the unaffected leg, shift weight to the affected hip, weight shift back and forth between affected and unaffected limb hold for 10 seconds, 5 sets.

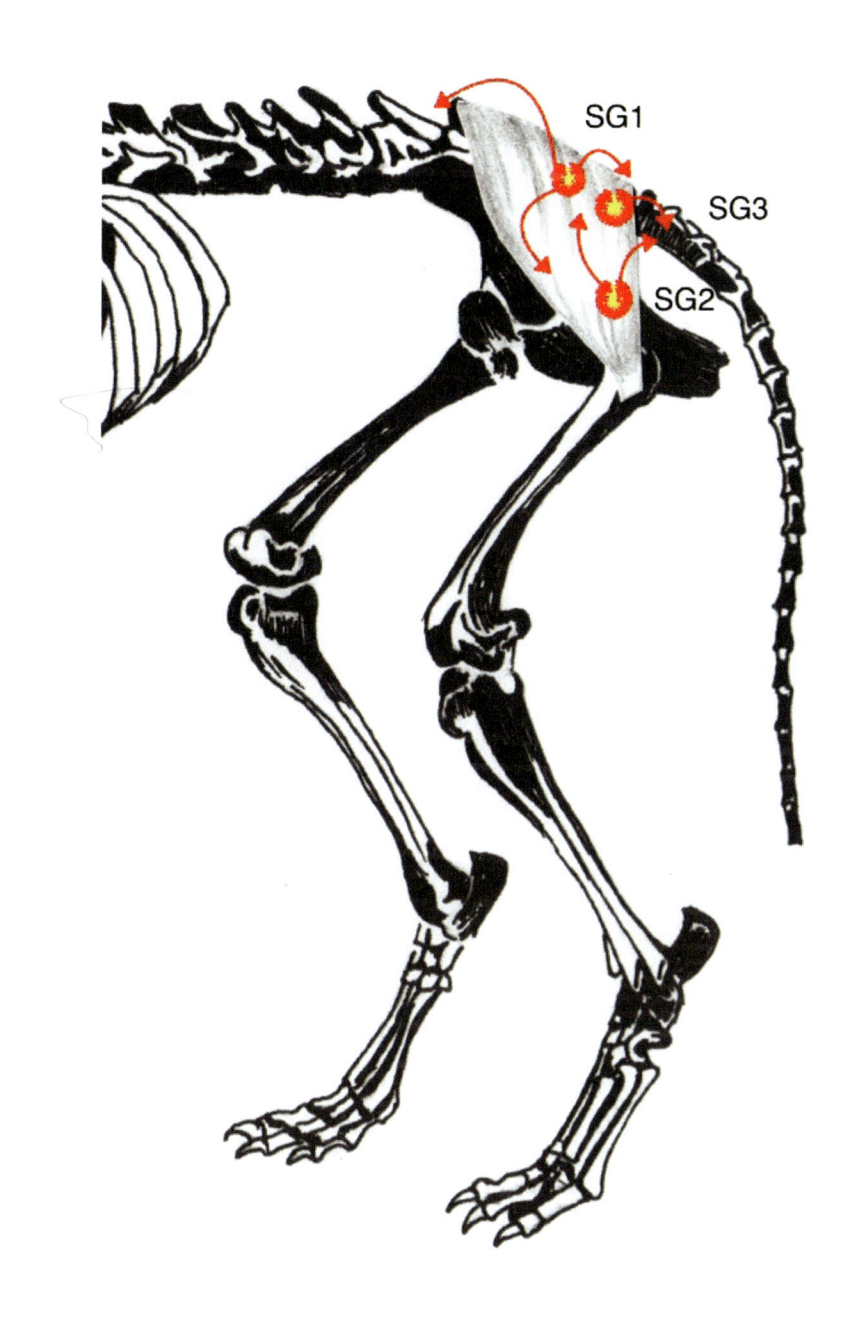

Superficial Gluteal

MIDDLE GLUTEAL MUSCLE

The middle gluteal muscle is the biggest of the gluteal muscles and give the dogs buttocks its form. The deep caudal portion of the middle gluteal is called the piriformis muscle. The middle gluteal sits between the TFL and the superficial gluteal muscle.

Origin: Gluteal surface of the ilium, between the iliac crest and the gluteal line. Iliac crest.

Insertion: Greater trochanter.

Action: Hip extension. Draws the limb into abduction and extension. It rotates the pelvic limb medially.

Innervation: Cranial gluteal nerve.

Palpation and trigger point location: Side lying posture. Palpate from the lateral aspect of the sacrum, to the iliac crest, and to the hip joint. Finger pad palpation is best used this area, and you will get a pain response from the dog when you find an active trigger point.

Trigger point 1 is closest to the iliac crest and the sacroiliac. This trigger point refers to the caudal aspect of the ilium, the sacroiliac joint and the sacrum on the ipsilateral side. There may be radiating pain into the buttock and the hip.

Trigger point 2 is found ventral to the iliac crest and is centered along the iliac crest. Pain from this trigger point radiates more laterally and into the mid-gluteal region and the upper thigh.

Trigger point 3 is found below the iliac crest near to tuber ischium. Pain from this trigger point goes to the lumbar spine and over the sacrum bilaterally.

Middle Gluteal

Pain pattern: Crest of the ilium, sacroiliac and sacrum. Buttock and posterior thigh pain. Symptoms include pain when walking, stair climbing, climbing hills, getting up from a seated position. Any ambulatory movement or changing position that requires pelvic flexion or extension.

Needling technique: Place the patient in a lateral recumbent posture. Trap the point between index and middle finger, direct the needle between the fingers toward the trigger point.

Causative and perpetuating factors: Overload and overuse injuries, chronic overload due to flexion of the hip, leg length inequality, sacroiliac joint dysfunction, hip dysplasia, degenerative or injured knees, limping.

Associated trigger points: Longissimus
　　　　　　　　　　　　　Piriformis
　　　　　　　　　　　　　Tensor fasciae latae
　　　　　　　　　　　　　Superficial gluteal
　　　　　　　　　　　　　Hamstring

Stretches: Cross affected leg behind the unaffected leg, shift weight to the affected hip, weight shift back and forth between affected and unaffected limb hold for 10 seconds, 5 sets.

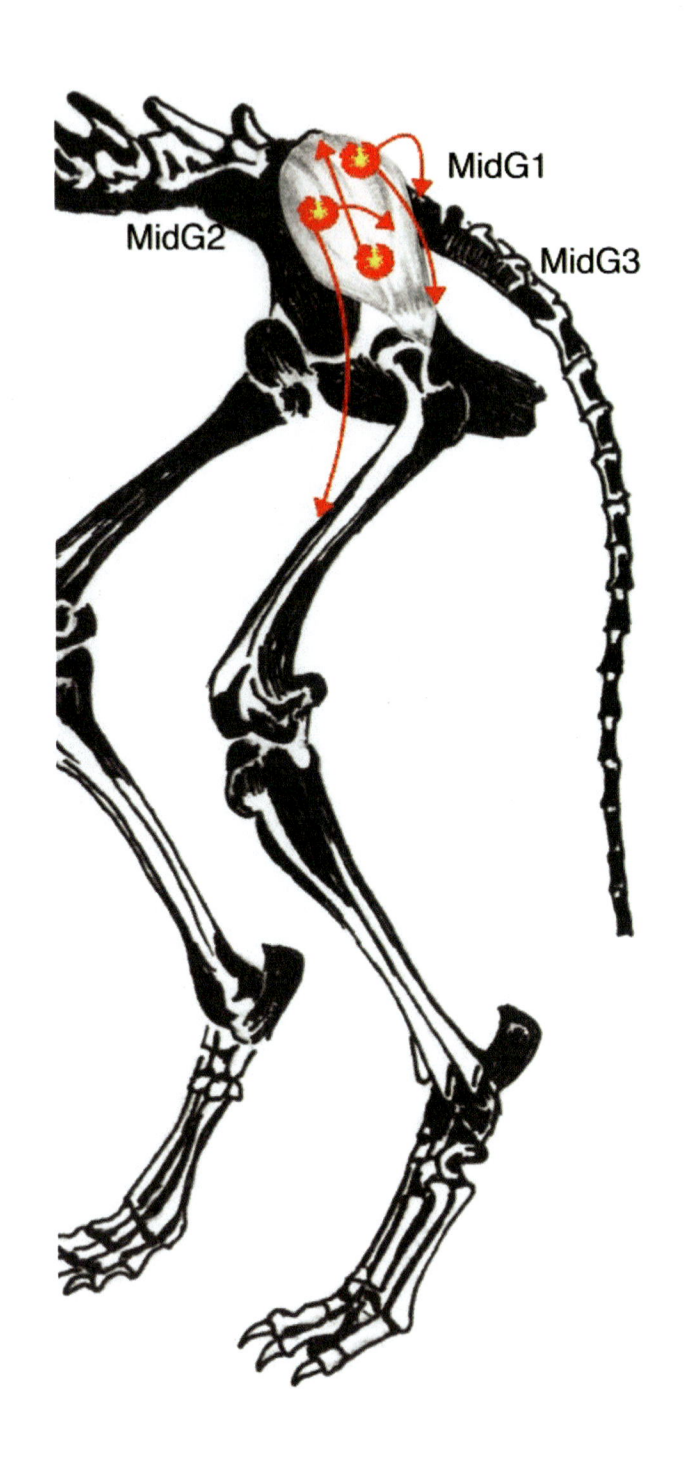

Middle Gluteal

TENSOR FASCIAE LATAE (TFL)

The tensor fasciae latae is the most cranial muscle in the rump. It fills the triangle between the lateral angle of the ilium and the stifle joint, then it wraps around the cranial aspect of the thigh.

Origin: Ventral portion of the iliac spine and aponeurosis of the middle gluteal muscle. From there it fans out into three parts until it reaches just distal to the patella. It is bordered by the middle gluteal and sartorius muscle.

Insertion: Fasciae latae of the lateral leg just distal to the patella.

Innervation: Cranial gluteal nerve.

Action: Assists in flexion of the hip, extension of the stifle and helps to advance the limb in the swing phase of locomotion. In addition to this it stabilizes the pelvis when walking.

Palpation and trigger point location: Dog lies lateral recumbent with the affected side up. Internal rotation of the thigh against resistance makes the muscle present.
From the tuber coxae, palpate laterally till you reach the greater trochanter of the femur. Continue to palpate caudally until just below the stifle.

Pain pattern and trigger point location: Deep in the hip, down the lateral aspect of the thigh to the knee. *Mimics hip pathology.* Patient can't walk quickly or lie on the affected side.

There is one major trigger point in the TFL that is located in the cranial aspect of the TFL close to the iliac spine. This trigger point refers to the hip and the cranio-lateral aspect of the leg to the knee.

Tensor Fascia Latae

There are generally multiple small satellite trigger points in this muscle and in the fascia itself. Be sure to palpate the whole extent of the muscle and treat accordingly.

Needling technique: Patient must be placed lateral recumbent. Palpate and isolate with the index and middle fingers, trapping the points with gentle pressure and needle gently and superficially, as often these points will not be deep. You can needle these at any angle.

Causative and perpetuating factors: Walking or running on uneven surfaces or on cambered roads, immobilization of the limb or disuse atrophy of the muscles of the knee. Acute trauma such as landing awkwardly after jumping may initiate trigger points in this muscle.

Poor conditioning and inadequate warm up before sprinting and immobilization of the limb may perpetuate these MFTPs.

Associated trigger points: Superficial gluteal
Middle gluteal
Rectus femoris
Iliopsoas.

Tensor Fascia Latae

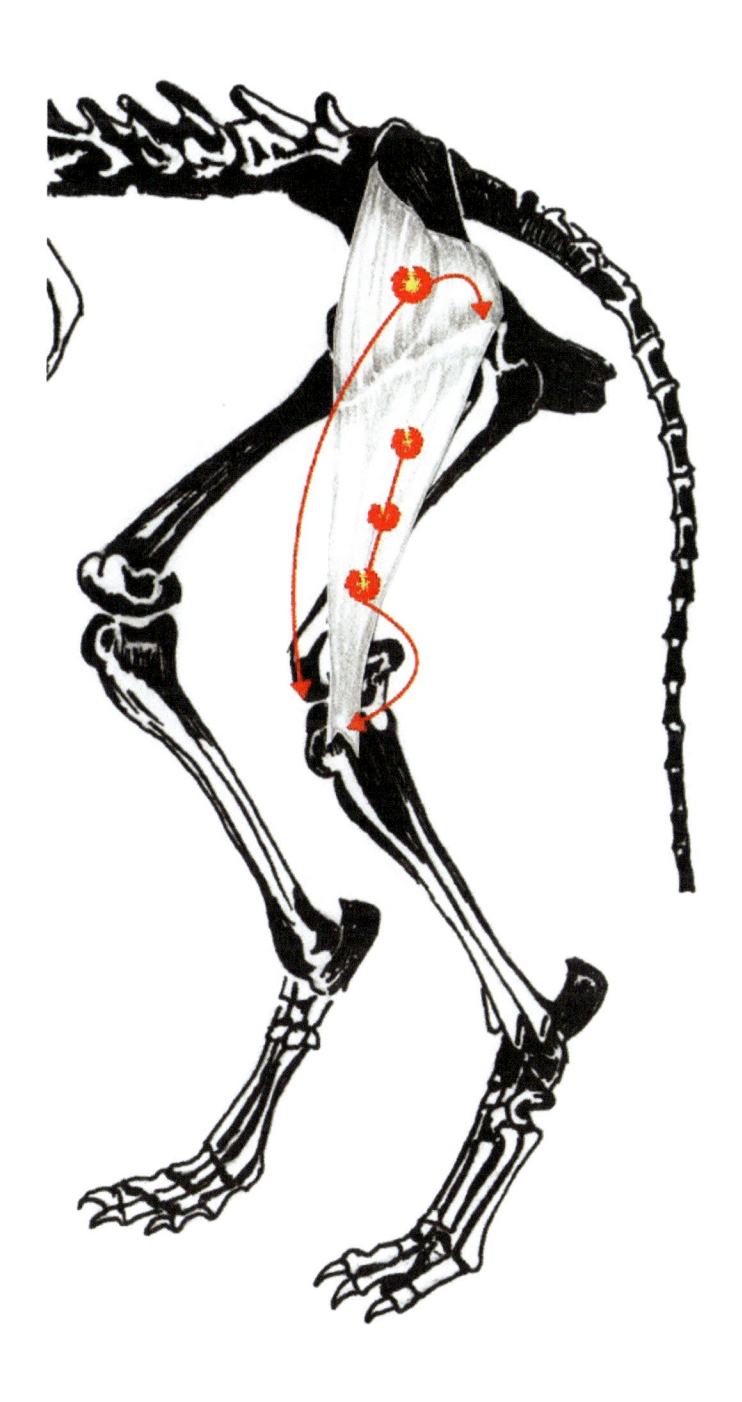

PIRIFORMIS

The piriformis lies caudal and medial to the middle gluteal muscle and is covered by the superficial gluteal muscle.

Piriformis syndrome can be a debilitating issue and was not diagnosed until recently in canines.
Most dogs are diagnosed with dysplasia or possibly nerve damage. Piriformis syndrome was never really thought of in dogs until recently. Maja Guldberg, DVM, did a study on a dog named Iris. In the initial stages of the study, there was little to no information documented about the piriformis. Since the pelvis region on dogs is similar to humans this vet started with what was available regarding this syndrome in humans. Many diagnostics were run to rule out other possibilities in Iris, and they came to a preliminary conclusion that it was probably a sciatica issue. The overall cause of Iris' sciatica was constriction of the piriformis muscle causing entrapment of the sciatica nerve. The study concluded that sciatica and piriformis syndrome does exist in dogs and this was causing lameness and pain for Iris. This is obviously not a peer reviewed study as the sample was too small, with many holes in the standard "study" process etc., but purely a clinical representation of what was found and treated, therefore opening our eyes to another differential in practice.

Piriformis Syndrome is described as entrapment of the sciatic nerve at the greater sciatic notch due to abnormalities in the piriformis, resulting in spasm, edema and contracture of the muscle causing entrapment of the sciatic nerve.

Origin: Last sacral vertebra (S3), the first caudal vertebra and the sacrotuberous ligament.

Distal attachment: Greater trochanter of the femur.

Action: Extension of the hip. Draws the hip and leg into extension and aids in external rotation of the thigh and abduction of the leg when in a

Piriformis

neutral position. When flexed, the piriformis internally rotates and abducts the hip.

Innervation: Sacral nerve 1 and 2.

Palpation and trigger point location: Patient is lying lateral recumbent. Palpate from the posterior superior iliac spine to the greater trochanter of the femur and the entire lateral aspect of the sacrum. This is a difficult muscle to feel as one needs to palpate through the superficial gluteal muscle to feel it.
Trigger points are located at the cranial aspect and the middle of the muscle and refer to the buttock and the hip on the ipsilateral side.

Pain pattern: sacroiliac and buttock pain, caudal aspect of the hip, dorsal 2/3 of the caudal aspect of the thigh.

Needling technique: Patient must be placed in a lateral recumbent position. Palpate and isolate the trigger points with the index and middle fingers, trapping the points with gentle pressure and needle gently and very superficially. Avoid needling the deep trigger points at all costs. Needling the sciatic nerve is not something you want a patient to experience. Rather stretch the muscle if you are unsure.

Causative and perpetuating factors: Acute/chronic overload, Hip arthritis and dysplasia. Falling on the pelvis or running may activate these trigger points. Perpetuating factors are immobilization of the limb, chronic infections or a foot injury causing a change in gait.

Associated trigger points: Superficial and middle gluteal muscles.

Piriformis

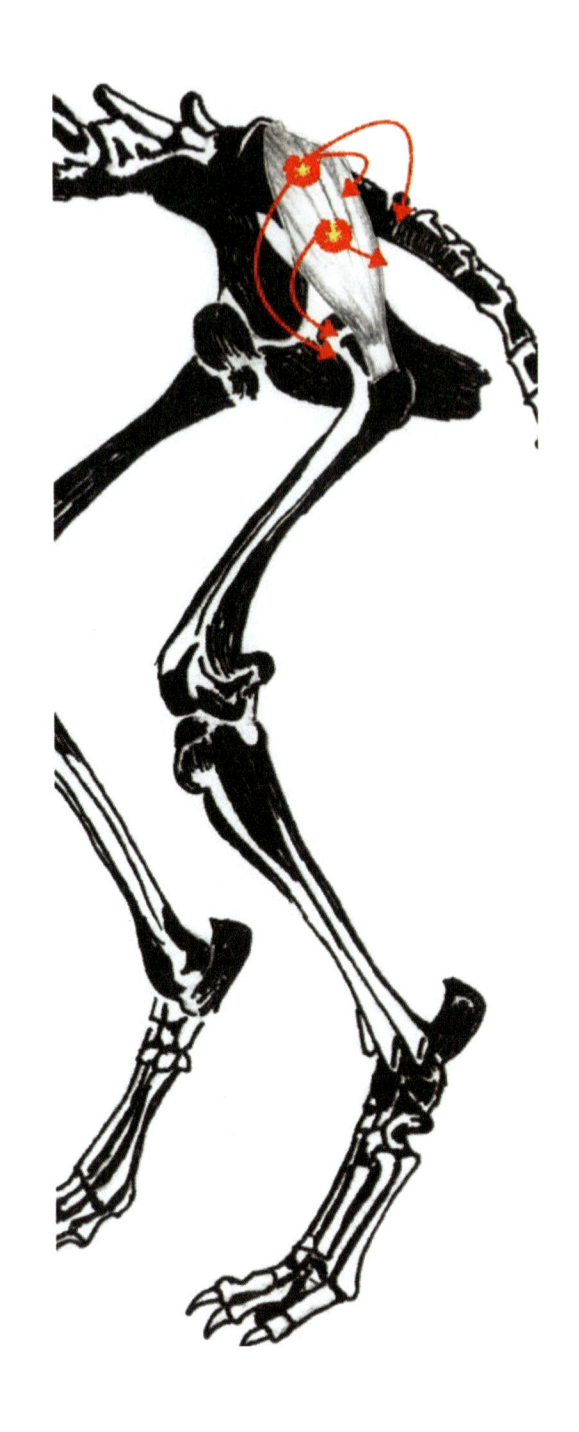

HAMSTRING

Biceps Femoris, Semitendinosus and Semimembranosus.

Biceps femoris is the largest and most lateral muscle of the thigh. It is superficial and covered by fascia and the skin. There is a strong cranial part which arises from the sacrum and the sacrotuberous ligament and a smaller caudal part which arises from the ischium. The biceps femoris splits into two tendons and then unite again via an aponeurosis with the crural fascia and the stifle fascia. This fascia then inserts onto the patella, patella ligament and tibial tuberosity. The sciatic nerve is interposed between the biceps femoris and the underlying muscles so be careful of needling too deep and hitting this nerve.

Semitendinosus is a large muscle that forms the largest part of the caudal aspect of the thigh. It runs from the ischial tuberosity to the tibia and forms the common calcaneal tendon.

The semimembranosus is the most medial muscle and is entirely fleshy unlike in humans. It originates from the ischium and attaches on the medial condyle of the femur and tibia.

Origin:
Biceps femoris: The vertebral head arises from the sacrum and the sacrotuberous ligament. The pelvic head is smaller and caudal and arises from the ischiatic tuberosity. The united muscle belly splits into two tendons.

Semitendinosus: Pelvic head originates from the ventral surface of the ischial tuberosity. There is no vertebral head in canines. The semitendinosus arises between the pelvic heads of biceps femoris and the semimembranosus muscle.

Semimembranosus: Pelvic head originates from the ventral aspect of the ischium, the ischiatic tuberosity. Distally the muscle splits into two parts.

Hamstring

Insertion:
Biceps femoris: Both muscle bellies broaden distally and unite via an aponeurosis with the crural fascia and the fascia of the stifle. Through this fascia they insert to the patella, the patella ligament and the tuberosity of the tibia.

Semitendinosus: The pelvic head unites with the tendons of the sartorius and gracilis muscle and inserts on the cranial aspect of the tibia and with a separate tendon insertion on the calcaneal tuberosity.

Semimembranosus: From the split the one part runs along the caudal aspect of the adductor muscle, then inserts into the medial femoral condyle. The longer tendon inserts on the medial tibial condyle.

Action:
Bicep femoris: extension of the thigh and hip, flexion of the leg, external rotation of the flexed leg.

Semitendinosus: When weight bearing, the semitendinosus is responsible for extension of the hip, stifle and tarsus, which propels the trunk forward. On non- weight bearing it flexes the stifle, rotates the leg outwards and moves it backwards.

Semimembranosus: When weight bearing, the semimembranosus is responsible for extension of the hip and stifle, which propels the trunk forward. On non-weight bearing it is responsible for adduction and retraction of the limb.

Innervation:
Biceps femoris, semimembranosus and semitendinosus: Sciatic nerve.

Palpation and trigger point location:
Patient is standing or lying recumbent. Flex the leg against resistance. Both bicep femoris heads will become evident on the lateral aspect. Palpate from the ischial tuberosity to the head of the tibia and the patella.

Hamstring

Medial to the biceps femoris is the semitendinosus. This is palpated from the ischial tuberosity to the proximal tibia.

Semimembranosus lies on the medial aspect of the femur and extends to the medial femoral condyle and the tibia. Flat palpation is most effective here. When this muscle is injured it has a tendency to fibrillate and flutter a lot. It fatigues very fast and weight bearing is a challenge.

The number of trigger points in each of these muscles varies, but the locations are consistent. MFTPs in the semimembranosus, semitendinosus and biceps femoris are all located in the middle of the muscle and refer pain up to the gluteal area and medial and lateral aspect of the caudal surface of the hind leg respectively. There are on average 3-5 MFTPs per muscle group.

Pain pattern:
Biceps femoris: posterior and lateral knee, from the posterior lateral thigh to the gluteal fold.

Semitendinosus and semimembranosus: lower buttock, upper thigh, posterior medial thigh and knee.

Needling technique: Needling of the hamstring more often than not requires deep needling, it can be difficult to trap the trigger point easily and some deep pressure is required. Direct the needle towards the trigger point once it has been trapped in place. Needling can be done standing or lateral recumbent.

Causative and perpetuating factors: Any action where the muscles are overloaded (acute or chronic) in hip extension or stifle flexion/extension. Common causes of injury are running in deep sand and quick changes in direction when sprinting. This is very common in agility dogs.

Associated trigger points: Adductors
Paraspinals-longissimus

Hamstring

        Iliopsoas
        Quadriceps
        Gluteal muscles
        Rectus abdominis.

Hamstring

Semimembranosus Muscle

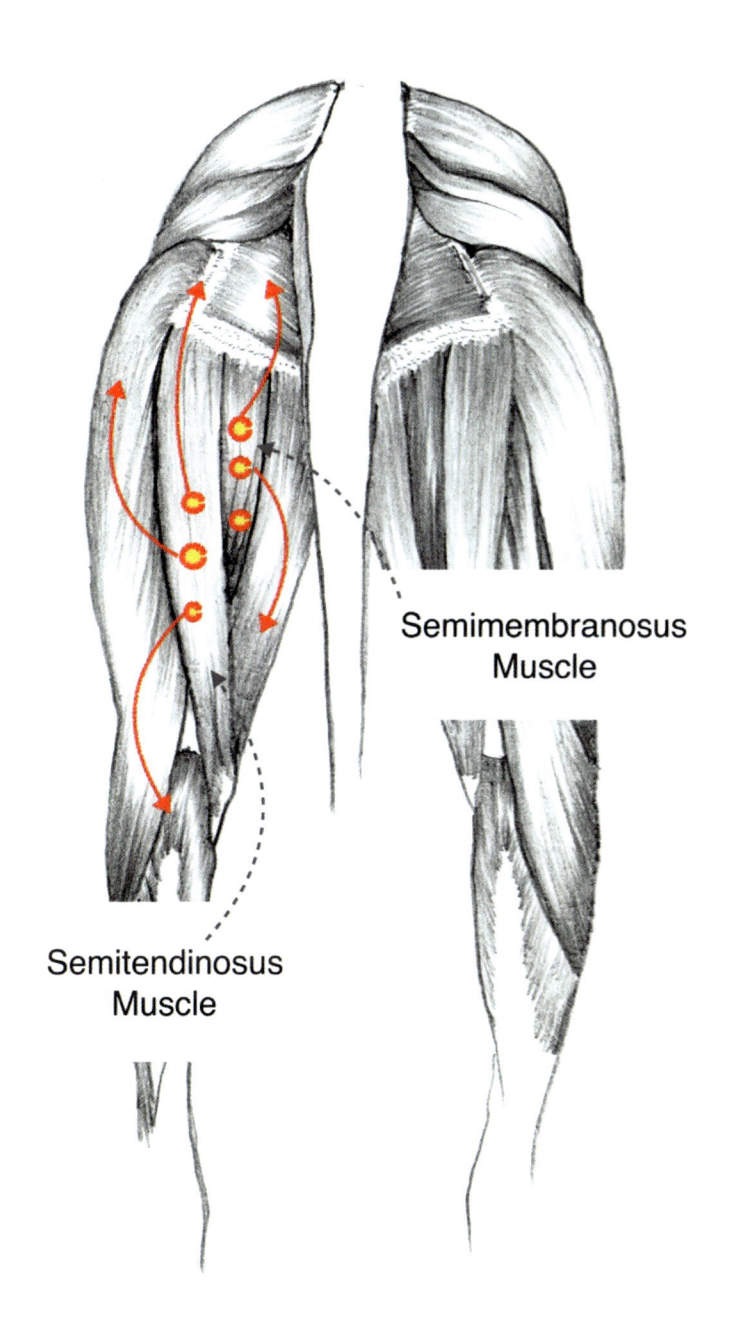

Semitendinosus Muscle

Hamstring

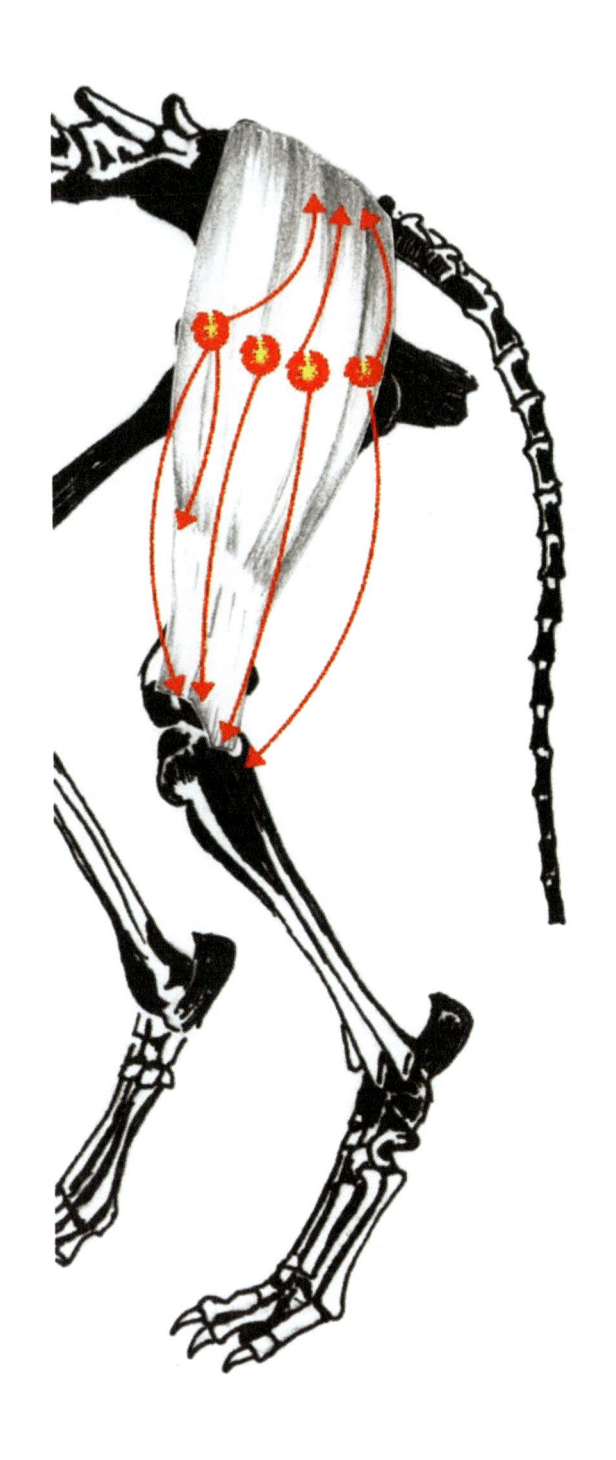

HIP ADDUCTORS

There are two adductor muscle. Adductor longus, adductor magnus et brevis. These muscles are found in the deep layer of the muscles. This muscle group is pyramidal in shape and sits between the semimembranosus and pectineus. It extends from the pubic symphysis to the caudal aspect of the femur.

Origin: They all originate on the pelvis via the symphyseal tendon. They are situated near the ischiatic arch, the ventral surface of the pubis and ventral surface of the ischium. The adductor longus is fused to the pectineal muscle.

Insertion: Inserts into the whole lateral lip of the caudal rough face of the femur.

Action: Adduct limb and extends the hip and stabilizes the hind leg. It aids in moving the rump forwards and sideways.

Innervation: Obturator nerve.

Palpation and trigger point location: Adductor magnus and longus – patient is side lying on the affected side with the top leg pulled away.

Adductor Magnus: flex the leg of the thigh to be palpated, externally rotate and abduct the thigh. Place the leg on a pillow. Palpate adductor magnus, posterior to the adductor longus and brevis, from the ischial tuberosity to the medial aspect of
the femur.

Adductor longus: Adductor longus is anterior to adductor magnus. Palpate adductor longus from the pubis to the distal 1/3 of the femur. Adductor brevis cannot be palpated as it lies deep to adductor longus, pectineus.

Hip Adductors

Adductor longus has 2 MFTPs that are located in the dorsal portion of the muscle, near the attachment. These trigger points refer to the medial aspect of the stifle and presents as stiffness. Pain in the medial and cranial portion of the thigh and occasionally down to the medial side of the foot is a common referral pattern for these MFTPs.

Adductor Magnus MFTPs. There are generally 2-3 MFTPs found here. TP1 is found in the middle of the muscle and refers pain to the groin, and over the cranio-medial portion of the thigh to the knee.
TP2 is found dorsal to TP1 and refers to the pelvis, pubic bone, rectum and vagina.

Pain pattern: Adductor magnus: Dorsal trigger points create deep pelvic pain, pubic bone, vagina, rectal, and bladder pain. Middle trigger points refer to the craniomedial aspect of the thigh from groin to above the knee.

Adductor longus: pain in the groin and hip during activity. Reduced abduction and external rotation of the thigh. Pain deep in the groin, and craniomedial part of the upper thigh. Pain above the medial aspect of the knee.

Needling technique: With the patient lying lateral recumbent on the affected side, flex, externally rotate and abduct the top leg and have a handler hold it. The leg to be treated is now exposed. Flex the treating leg and palpate with any two fingers of the palpating hand. When found trap the trigger point and laser the trigger point. I would caution against needling this area due to all the sensitive structures found in that quadrant, especially arteries and veins.

Causative and perpetuating factors: Overload due to misstep and a fall. Hip arthritis or dysplasia, compensation due to cranial cruciate dysfunction or any other knee pathology. Running uphill or downhill can perpetuate these trigger points, as well as having the hip in a fixed flexed position for a period of time.

Associated trigger points: Vastus medialis

Hip Adductors

        Gracilis (very occasionally)
        Sartorius.

Stretches: Lie on the back with legs extended into the air and separate the legs to the widest stretch the inner thighs can tolerate. 30 secs for 3-5 sets.

Hip Adductors

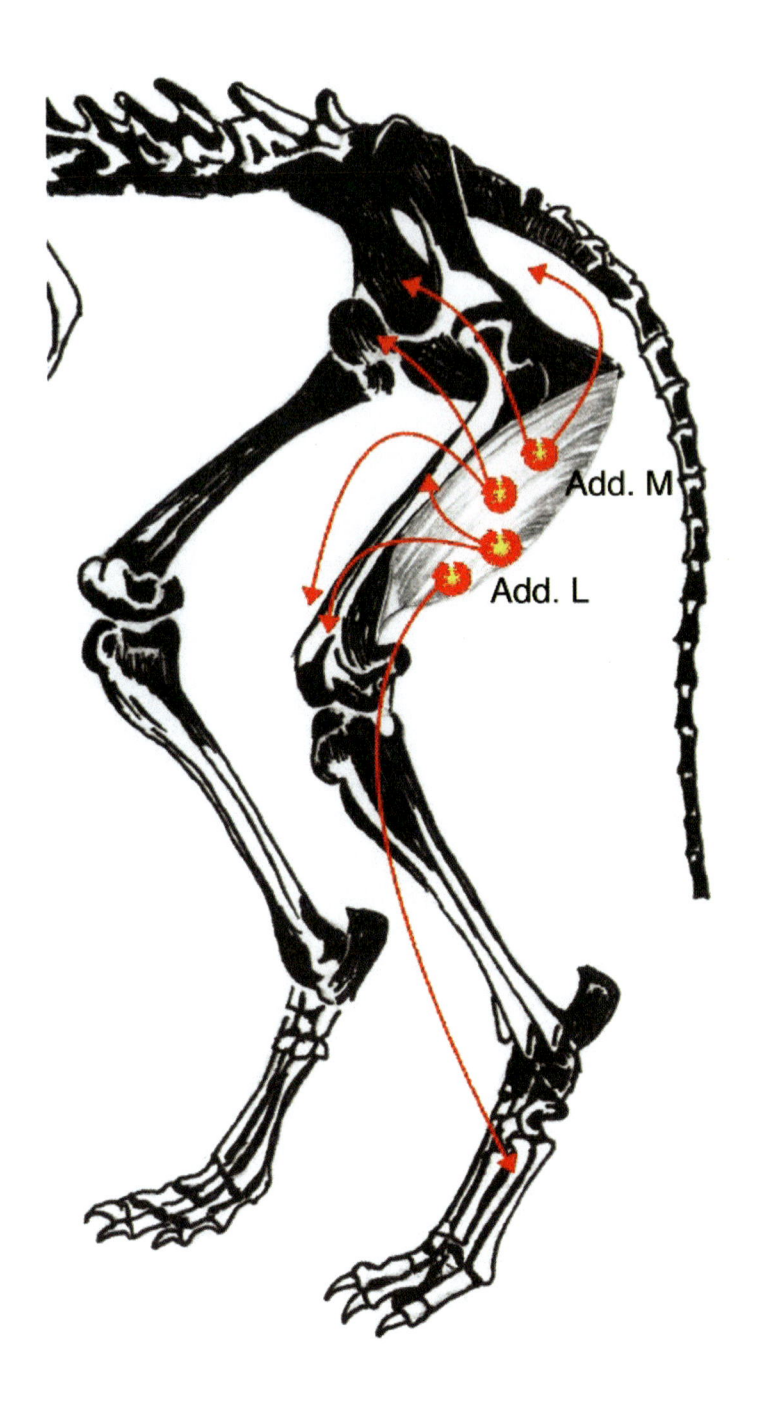

178

THE FEMORAL TRIANGLE

The femoral triangle is an area that one should avoid at all costs with respect to dry needling and here is why:
This is the shallow triangle that allows a pathway for the femoral vessels that run to and from the pelvic limb.

The triangle is made up of the sartorius cranially, pectineus and adductor caudally, iliopsoas proximal laterally and vastus medialis distal laterally.

The triangle contains the femoral artery and vein. The vein lies caudal to the artery. The saphenous nerve is also found in this triangle. The saphenous nerve arises from the cranial side of the femoral nerve and innervates the sartorius muscle. The cutaneous portion of the saphenous nerve innervates the skin on the medial side of the thigh, stifle, leg, tarsus and paw.

I highly recommend avoiding needling around this area. The risk of hitting a vein, artery or nerve are far too high and the same effect can be achieved by using the piezo electric or the laser.

QUADRICEPS

Rectus Femoris, Vastus Lateralis, Vastus Medialis and Vastus Intermedius

The quadratus muscle forms the bulk of the muscle cranial to the femur. There are four portions to the muscle that are not as distinct in canines as other species. All four unite to form a single tendon that includes the patella as a sesamoid bone within it and inserts at the tibial tuberosity as the straight ligament of the patella.
The rectus femoris muscle is also known as the straight muscle of the thigh.

Origin:
Rectus Femoris: The shaft of the ilium, cranial to the acetabulum.
Vastus Lateralis: lateral side of the upper ¾ of posterior femur and linea aspera of the posterior femur.
Vastus Medialis: posteromedial aspect of the shaft of the femur.
Vastus intermedius: cranial and lateral surfaces of the upper 2/3 of the shaft of the femur. This muscle is completely covered by the other heads of the quadratus muscles.

Insertion:
Rectus Femoris, Vastus Lateralis, Vastus Medialis and Vastus Intermedius: All converge to form a single tendon which includes the patella as a sesamoid bone and ends at the tibial tuberosity as the straight ligament of the patella.

Action:
Rectus femoris: extension of the stifle, flexion of the thigh and hip on the pelvis when the pelvis is flexed.
Vastus lateralis, medialis and intermedius: extension of the leg at the knee (stifle).
Vastus lateralis and medialis work together to ensure correct patella tracking.

Quadriceps

Innervation: Femoral nerve.

Palpation and trigger point location:
Rectus femoris covers both the hip and knee joint. Palpate the rectus femoris from the anterior superior iliac spine to the tibial tuberosity.

The most common trigger point is found in the upper portion of the muscle and refers to the lower cranial thigh and the cranial aspect of the stifle. These trigger points are often overlooked and are a common cause of weakness and lameness.

The Vastus Lateralis is palpated on the craniolateral aspect of the thigh, cranial to the Iliotibial band, from the greater trochanter to the common tendon.

Vastus lateralis develops MFTPS along the lateral aspect of the muscle. There are four common areas for MFTPS. TP1 is found dorsal to the patella, in the lower medial aspect of the muscle. Pain refers to the knee, and upwards over the thigh.

TP2 is found lateral to TP1. Pain refers up the lateral aspect of the thigh and down towards the hock.

TP3 is found in the middle of the muscle and refers to the entire length of the lateral thigh, towards the pelvis and down to the stifle.

TP4 is found in the upper most portion of the muscle and refers pain locally.

The Vastus Medialis is palpated on the craniomedial aspect of the thigh at the common tendon. Trigger points are often missed here due to the tautness of the muscle which causes a restriction in movement of the stifle.

TP1 is found on the medial aspect of the muscle just above the knee and refers pain to the knee.

Quadriceps

TP2 refers pain to the mid-thigh and refers pain from the middle of the muscle to the knee

Vastus Intermedius lies deep to rectus femoris and can only be accessed when the rectus femoris is soft and pliable. It is hard to identify and treat MFTPs here.

Pain pattern:
Rectus femoris: cranial aspect of the knee, deep to the joint. Pain after activity, walking downstairs is painful.

Vastus Lateralis: caudolateral aspect of the knee. Pain can be felt from the iliac crest down the caudolateral thigh to the stifle.

Vastus Medialis: craniomedial stifle pain, pain down the ventral ½ of the medial thigh, may cause buckling of the stifle.

Vastus Intermedius: cranial thigh, craniolateral upper thigh, stair climbing is difficult, and straightening a flexed stifle after sitting is challenging.

Needling technique: Place the patient in a lateral recumbent position with the leg to be treated as the top leg so that the quadratus is accessible. Due to the thickness of the quadricep muscle deep needling is required, isolate the point and needle as required with direct perpendicular direction.

Causative and perpetuating factors: There are various causative factors, such as chronic overload caused by tight hamstrings, acute overload from a vigorous eccentric contraction such as mis-stepping in a hole, falling or stumbling off steps or a curb and direct trauma from impact against the femur can activate MFTPs in the head of the quads.

Excessive stifle flexion or having the limb immobilized for long periods of time may perpetuate these MFTPs (e.g.: ehmer sling). Post hip fracture and or surgery often results in rectus femoris MFTPs.

Quadriceps

Abnormal hip biomechanics and the resulting overload perpetuates rectus femoris MFTPs and causes compensation in the vastus lateralis.

An unstable hock or foot exacerbates vastus medialis MFTPs. Laxity in the foot also results in hyper pronation which may perpetuate MFTPs in this muscle.

Vastus lateralis MFTPs are exacerbated by limb immobilization and by the muscle being kept in a shortened position for a long period of time. Direct trauma such as a sideways slip may create overload in this muscle resulting in MFTPs.

Associated trigger points: Hamstring muscles- these shorten (especially biceps femoris) due to the antagonist relationship with the quadratus group.
 TFL and vastus medialis have a direct relationship, so if there are MFTPs in either muscle, check the other one. Iliopsoas compensation may occur when rectus femoris is not functioning correctly.

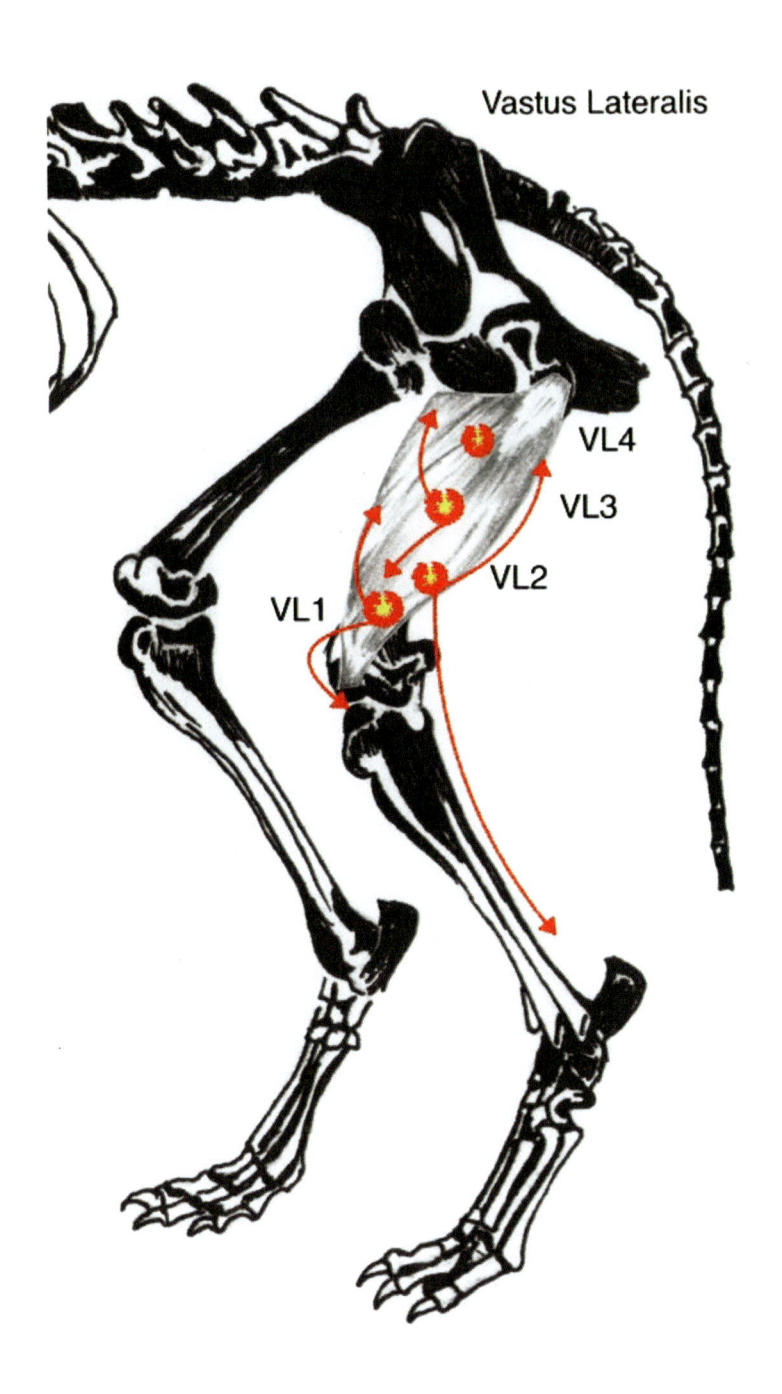

Quadriceps

Vastus Lateralis

VL4
VL3
VL2
VL1

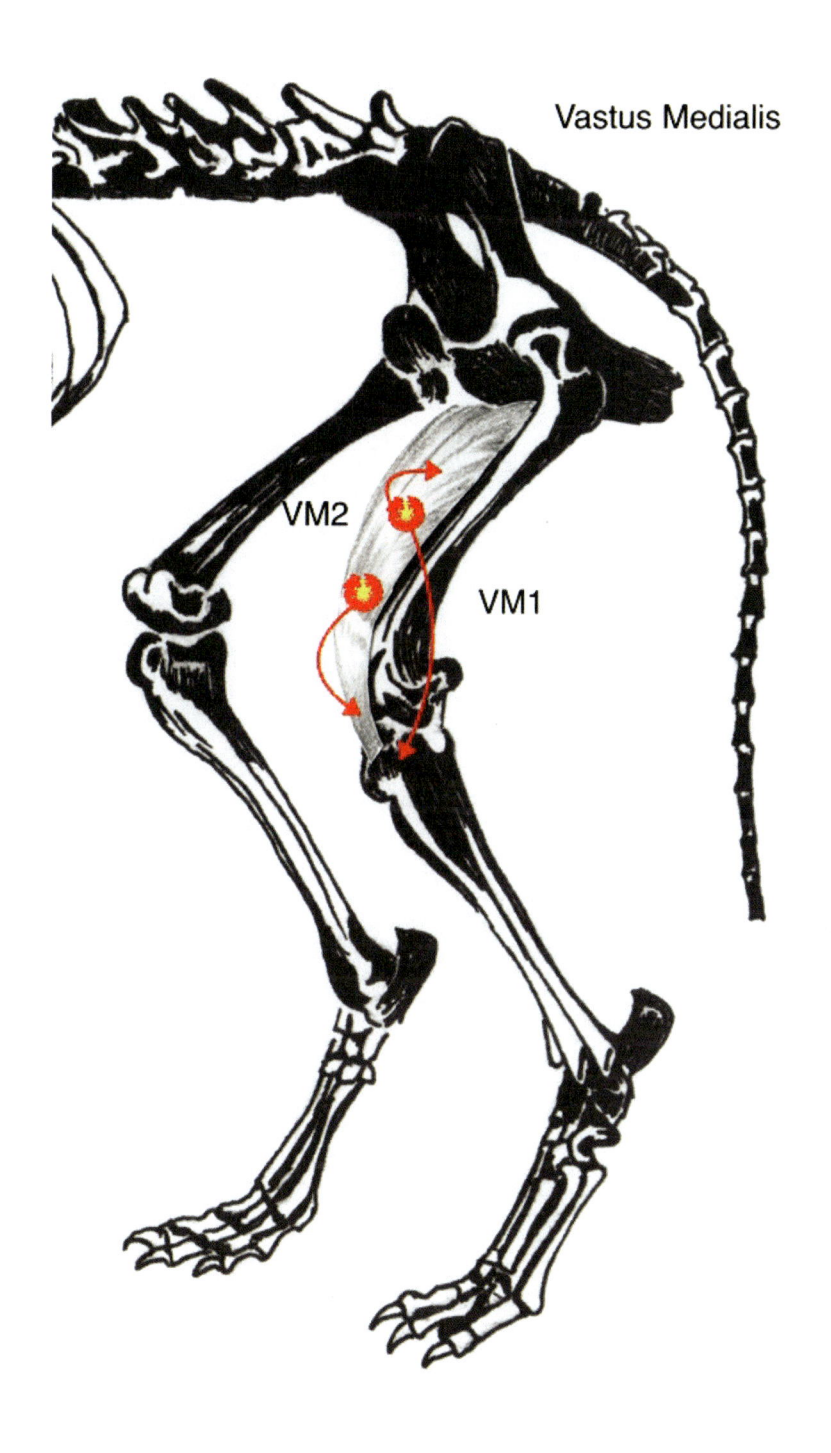

Quadriceps

Vastus Medialis

VM2

VM1

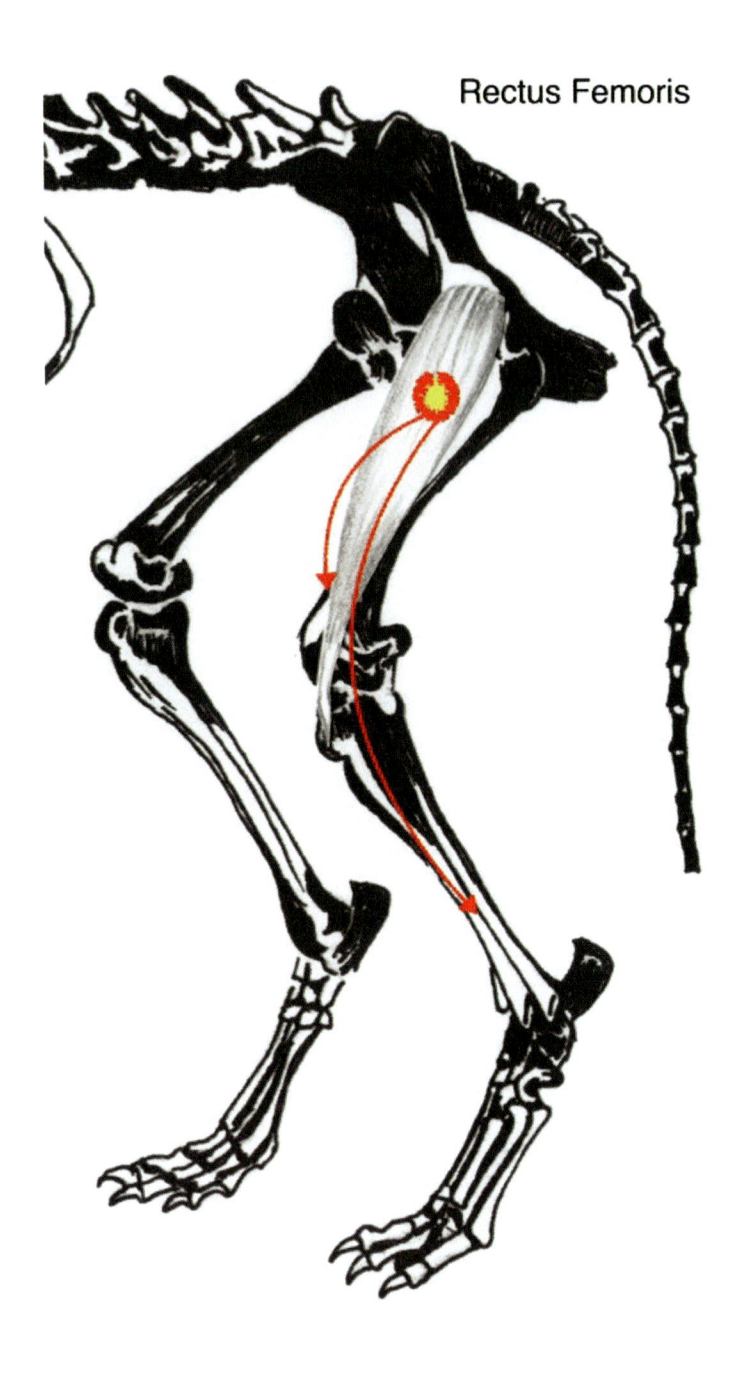

Quadriceps

Rectus Femoris

SARTORIUS

The sartorius muscle consists of two parts that lie on the cranial and craniomedial surfaces of the thigh. These parts extend from the ilium to the tibia. The cranial part forms the cranial contour of the thigh. The caudal part is on the medial side of the thigh and is significantly thinner, wider and longer than the cranial part. Both muscle parts are found predominantly on the medial side of the quadriceps femoris.

Origin: Cranial- crest of the ilium and thoracolumbar fascia
Caudal- cranial ventral iliac spine and adjacent ventral border of the ilium.

Distal attachment: Cranial- patella via the rectus femoris muscle.
Caudal- cranial border of tibia.

Action: Flexion of the hip. The cranial part extends the stifle, caudal part flexes the stifle.

Innervation: Femoral nerve

Palpation: Patient is lying lateral recumbent with the affected side down. Move the top leg out of the way and support with a pillow or a roller. Palpate from the cranial ventral iliac spine to the patella and cranial border of the tibia. This is a sensitive area to palpate and the patient may be reactive. A superficial, light, flat palpation is advised.

Pain pattern and trigger point location: There are three palpable trigger points in the cranial part of the sartorius.

TP1 is found in the upper third of the muscle near the crest of the ilium, approximately 1/6 away from the insertion. Referral from TP1 is into the upper portion of the muscle and leg.
TP2 is found in the middle portion of the muscle and refers to the middle and lower portion of the leg.

Sartorius

TP3 is found in the lower third of the muscle and refers to the stifle, the patella and the lower portion of the leg.

There are two palpable trigger points in the caudal part of the sartorius. TP1 is found in the upper third of the muscle near the ilium insertion. Referral from TP1 is into the upper portion of the muscle and leg.
TP2 is found in the middle portion of the muscle and refers to the middle and lower portion of the leg.

Laser technique: Patient must be placed in a lateral recumbent position. Palpate and isolate the trigger points with the index and middle fingers, trapping the points with gentle pressure and laser. *Avoid needling these trigger points at all costs.* Needling these trigger points due to the area that they are found in can be dangerous.

Causative and perpetuating factors: Acute/chronic overload, Hip arthritis and dysplasia. Sartorius MFTPs are generally found in conjunction with other muscle dysfunctions and are part of a multiple-muscle syndrome.

Associated trigger points: Quadriceps-particularly rectus femoris.
Gluteals may be contributors as primary trigger points, with sartorius compensating for their dysfunction and resulting in the formation of secondary trigger points in the sartorius.
Iliopsoas
Pectineus
Tensor fasciae latae

Note: The patient may present with signs and symptoms of stifle pain. After ruling out structural pathology of the stifle, examine for MFTPs in this area.

Sartorius

Sartorius / Cranial part

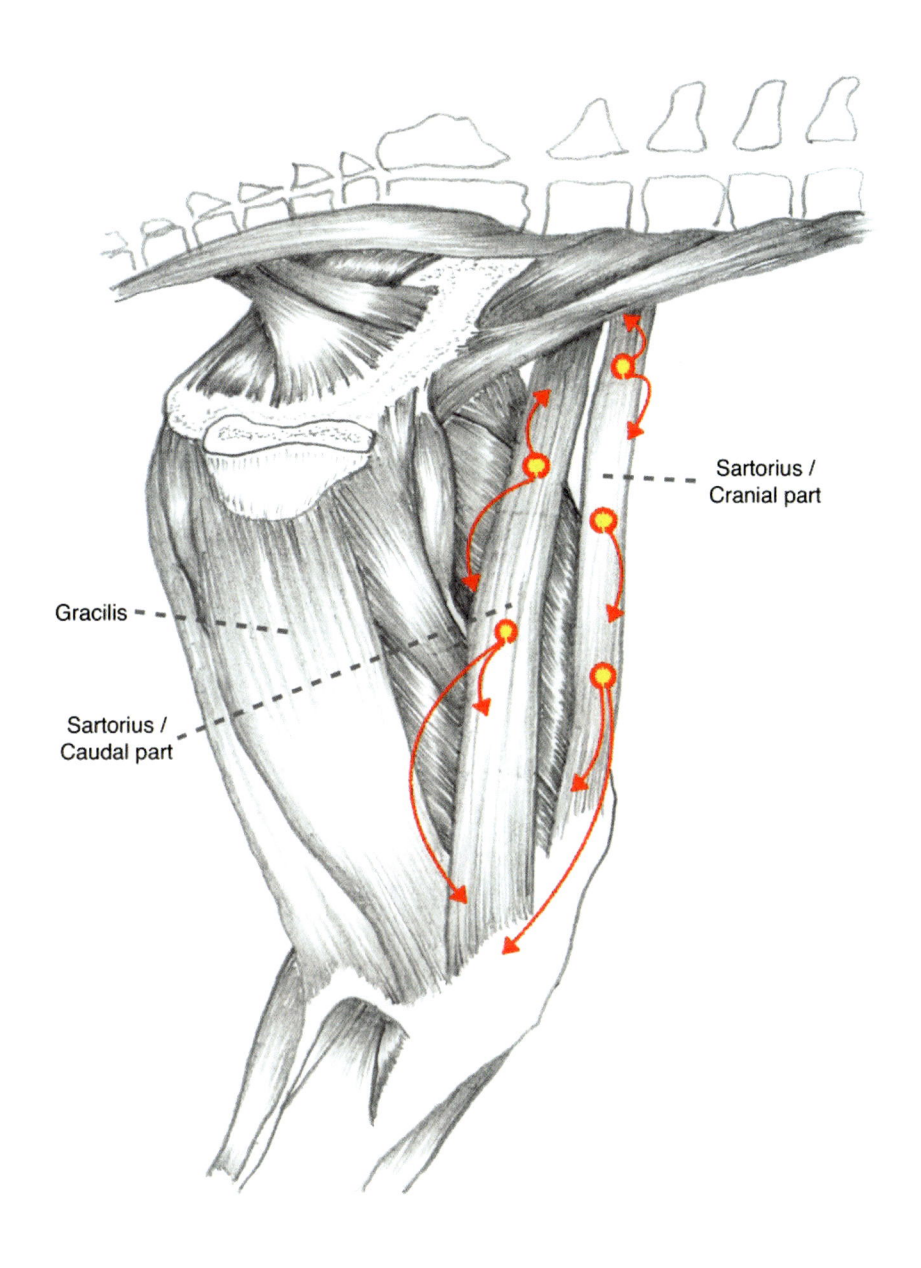

Gracilis

Sartorius / Caudal part

GRACILIS

The gracilis muscle arises from the symphysial tendon, a thick flat tendon attached ventrally to the symphysis pelvis. The gracilis aponeurosis covers the adductor.

Origin: Pelvic symphysis by means of the symphysial tendon

Distal attachment: Cranial border of tibia. Together with semitendinosus, the tuber calcanei.

Action: Adduction of the limb, flexion of the stifle, extension of the hock and hip.

Innervation: Obturator nerve.

Palpation and trigger point location: Patient is lying lateral recumbent with the affected side down. Flex the leg that is to be palpated, externally rotate and abduct the thigh. Place the leg on a pillow.

Palpate from the pelvic symphysis along the medial aspect of the leg all the way to the tibial border. This is a thick fleshy muscle that covers the adductors. There are a lot of trigger points in this muscle.

There are three distinct trigger points here, TP1 is found in the upper ¼ of the muscle in the muscle belly.
TP2 is found in the middle of the muscle.
TP3 is found in the lower 1/3 of the muscle. All of these points refer locally as well as to the medial aspect of the leg and up into the pelvis and genital region.

Pain pattern: Dorsal trigger points create deep pelvic pain, pubic bone, vagina, rectal, and bladder pain. Middle and ventral trigger points refer to the craniomedial aspect of the thigh from groin to above the stifle.

Gracilis

Laser technique: Patient must be placed in a lateral recumbent position with the affected side down. Flex the leg that is to be palpated, externally rotate and abduct the thigh. Place the leg on a pillow.

Palpate and isolate the trigger points with the index and middle fingers, trapping the points with gentle to moderate pressure. Avoid needling the trigger points at all costs due to the femoral triangle. Needling these trigger points due to the area that they are found in can be dangerous. I would not advocate needling this area. Piezo electric or laser is a better choice here.

Causative and perpetuating factors: Acute overload, Hip arthritis and dysplasia. Slipping and abducting the leg. These muscles may be perpetuated by running up or down hills. MFTPs here are generally not insidious but are acute in onset.

Associated trigger points: Semimembranosus
Sartorius
Iliopsoas
Adductors
Rectus femoris.

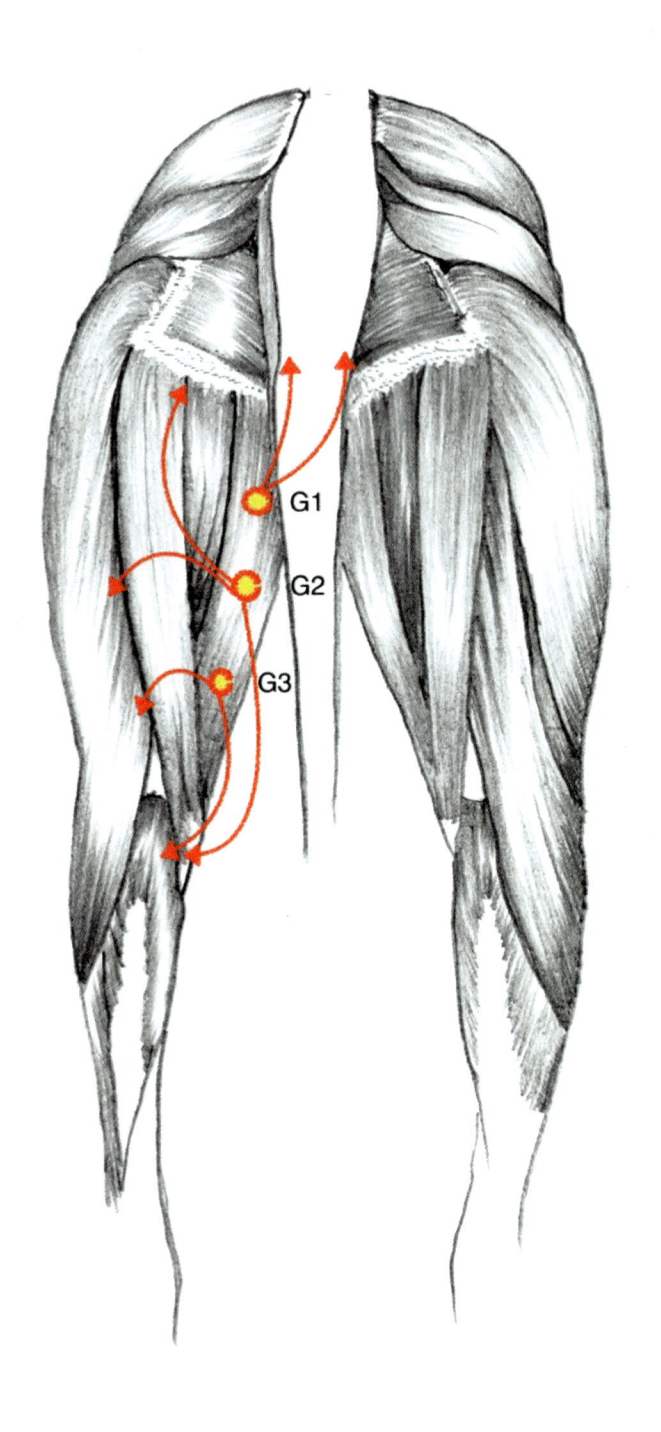

Gracilis

QUADRATUS LUMBORUM (QL)

One of the most common source of lower back pain.
This muscle is very strong in canines and has a thoracic and lumbar spine portion.

Origin:
Thoracic: Bodies of the last three thoracic vertebra.
Lumbar: Proximal ends of the ribs and the transverse processes of the lumbar vertebra.

Insertion:
Thoracic: The transverse processes of the cranial lumbar vertebra.
Lumbar: The ventral border of the sacrum and the wing of the ilium.

Action:
Unilaterally: stabilizes the lumbar spine. Acts as a hip hiker and aids in flexion of the sacroiliac joint.
Bilaterally: extends the lumbar spine, fixes the last ribs, helps with contraction of the diaphragm.

Palpation: and trigger point location: Depress the area between the iliac crest and the thirteenth rib, press medially and obliquely toward the transverse processes of the lumbar spine. Start superiorly at T13 and then palpate caudally toward the iliac crest. These trigger points are easy to feel and will feel like pebbles in the muscle.

There are two superficial MFTPS that are found in the lateral portion of the muscle and two deep MFTPs that are found medially.

TP1 is found in the cranial lateral portion of the muscle and is a superficial MFTP. This refers pain to the ilium and the iliac crest as well as the caudal aspect of the abdomen.
TP2 is found slightly below TP1 on the lateral aspect of the muscle just above the iliac crest. This MFTP refers pain to the hip, upper and outer thigh and there may be tenderness when touching the greater trochanter.

Quadratus Lumborum

Patient may present with pain on palpation of the femoral head, pain when lying on the affected side and may be lame on the affected leg. TP3 is located caudal and medial to TP1 at the level of the L4/5 vertebra. TP4 is located in the medial aspect of the muscle, parallel to TP2, just above the iliac crest. These MFTPs refers pain to the sacroiliac joint, the sacrum and the buttock area.

Dogs are very reactive to palpation over these active MFTPs, so caution is advised.

Pain pattern: Lateral border of the iliac crest and the greater trochanter. Deep trigger points refer to the sacroiliac joint and deep in the buttock. Inability to stand from a seated position and walk, can't roll over. These trigger points may also mimic kidney or hip issues and are very painful. Dogs with MFTPs in the QL often can't stand stacked and will lilt to the short leg side.

Needling technique: This can be needled with the patient lateral recumbent or if a small thin dog, in a down position. On certain dogs a decent amount of pressure is required from the non-needling palpating hand, when the trigger point has been located, press down firmly with the index and middle finger trapping the point. Aim the needle in the direction of the point between the fingers, the depth of the point varies therefore the length of the needle will need to be estimated accordingly. If the patient is lying on their left side, move their right hip into extension. This makes the trigger points easier to palpate and trap, making it easier to needle them. You will then needle their right quadrate lumbar muscle.

Causative and perpetuating factors: Overload stress from compensating with any lameness, front or back. Fatigue- acute or chronic from overloading the muscle when running, jumping, repetitive twisting or any sustained and repetitive strain. Leg length inequality, weak core and abdominals and chondrodystrophic dogs are perpetuating factors for these MFTPs.

Associated trigger points: Gluteal muscles

Quadratus Lumborum

Thoracolumbar paraspinals
Piriformis.

Quadratus Lumborum

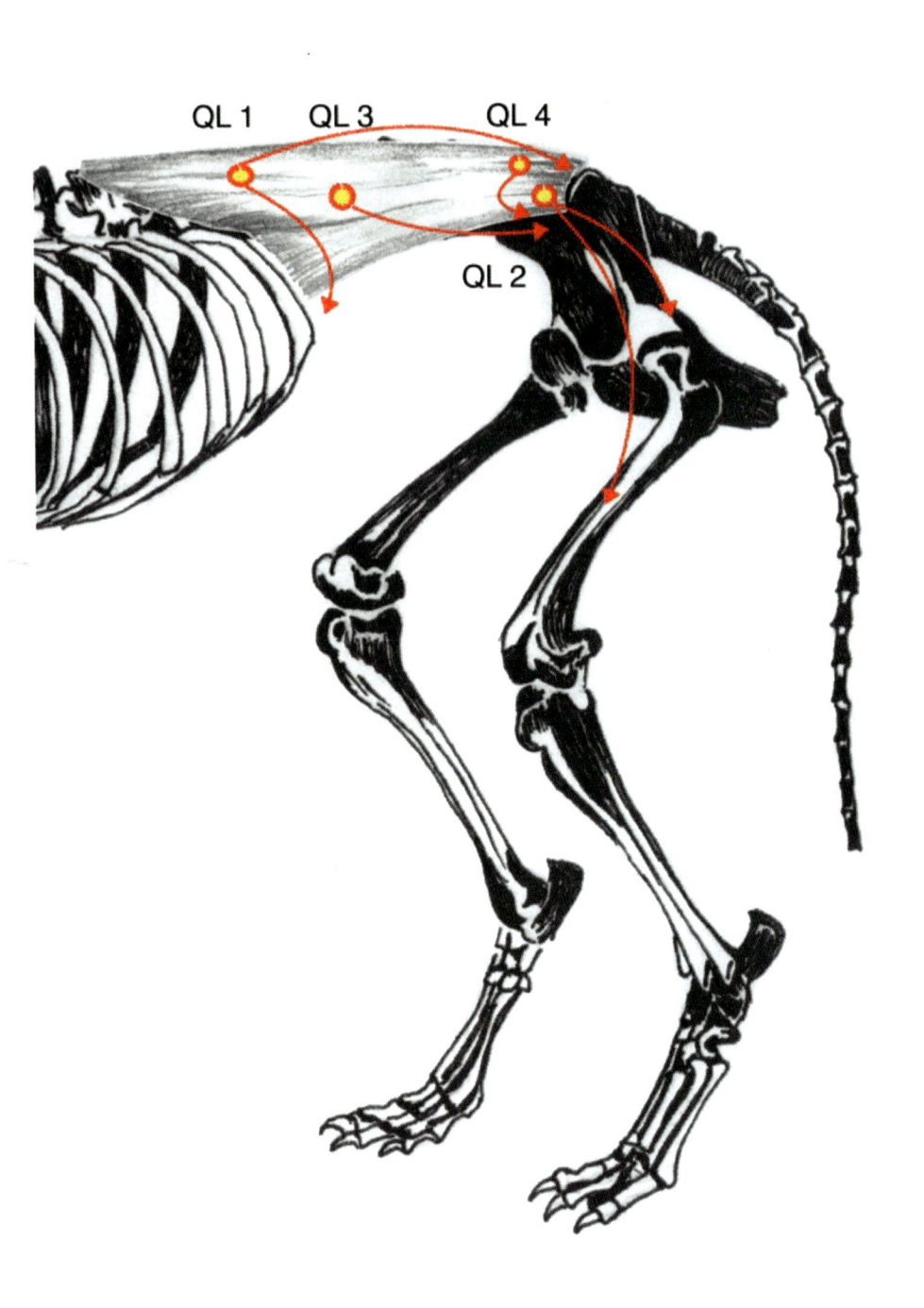

ERECTOR SPINAE or PARASPINALS

Iliocostalis Thoracis and Lumborum,
Longissimus Thoracis and Lumborum
Spinalis

Topographically the iliocostalis can be divided into a thoracic and lumbar portion. The fibers run cranioventrally and span several vertebral segments. It originates from the iliac crest, transverse processes of the lumbar vertebra and the fascial sheet that separates the longissimus from the iliocostalis. It then extends cranially as iliocostalis thoracis and runs from the 12th rib, next to the broadest muscle of the back on the dorsal side of the rib angle and ends with a common tendon insertion on the last cervical vertebra-C7.

The longissimus muscle is the most pronounced muscle of the paraspinals and extends from C7 at the neck, all the way along the back to the pelvis. It is the longest muscle of the body. It is thickest in the lumbar portion and gradually narrows as it navigates to the thoracic region. The longissimus muscle of the atlas and the head originate from the transverse processes of T2 and T3 and C3-7. These run cranially and insert on the wing of the atlas and the mastoid process of the occiput.

Spinalis is the least prominent of these muscles and is medially situated. It originates from the spinous processes and transverse processes of the first six lumbar and last six thoracic vertebra and inserts onto the spinous processes of T1-6 and C6/7.

The thoracic and cervical muscles receive strands from the transversospinalis muscle and so it is collectively called spinal and semispinal muscle. This muscle group is responsible for stabilization of the spine, elevation of the neck when working bilaterally and when working unilaterally is responsible for flexion of the back and lateral flexion of the neck. It is generally poorly developed and not clinically

Erector Spinae or Paraspinals

relevant. It is also very difficult to needle and is therefore not going to be covered in this text.

Origin: Iliocostalis thoracis: Upper end of the cranial edge of the ribs.

Iliocostalis lumborum: Iliac crest and transverse processes of the lumbar vertebra.

Longissimus thoracis and lumborum: Spinous processes of all thoracic, lumbar and sacral vertebrae and the sacrum.

Insertion: Iliocostalis thoracis: angles of the 1st to the 12th ribs. Transverse processes of the last cervical vertebra C7.

Iliocostalis lumborum: Caudal border of the 11-13th ribs.
Longissimus thoracis and lumborum: Articular, mamillary and transverse processes of the thoracic spine, and the associated ribs.

Action:
Iliocostalis thoracis: Bends the vertebral column sideways.

Iliocostalis lumborum: Fixes the loin and the ribs. Assists with forward propulsion when running.
Both portions of iliocostalis aid in expiration by pulling the ribs caudally and is a major stabilizer of the vertebral column.

Longissimus thoracis and lumborum:
Bilateral: Extension and stabilization of the vertebral column. It reaches the greatest amount of extension when the hindlimb is in its swing phase. It plays an essential part in assisting in transmitting the thrust of the hindlimbs to the back in this phase.

Extension and raising up of the cranial aspect of the body when the hindlimb is fixed (i.e.: jumping up onto hindlegs). Raises the caudal aspect of the body at the same time when the forelimbs are fixed (i.e.: kicking)
Unilateral: Lateral bending to the same side and rotates the head.

Erector Spinae or Paraspinals

Innervation: Iliocostalis: Dorsal branches of the thoracic and lumbar nerves.
Longissimus: Dorsal branches of the cervical, thoracic and lumbar nerves.
Palpation and trigger point location: The erector spinae muscles are the most superficial layer of the paraspinals and the most important postural muscles. They are very difficult to distinguish from each other. Digital palpation is the most effective way of determining the location of myofascial trigger points. These muscles can be very ropey in their feel. There are lots of very distinctive hard nodular trigger points in these muscles that jump out at you. Palpate through the trapezius and the latissimus dorsi.

Iliocostalis thoracis is found just lateral to the transverse processes of the T1-12 vertebrae and refers pain both cranially and caudally. Iliocostalis lumborum is more pronounced from T7-12, and then down towards the iliac crests.

There are three iliocostalis MFTPs.
TP1 is found at the mid thoracic level and refers pain to the shoulder, the pectoral area and the chest wall.
TP2 is found caudal to TP1 lateral to T12/13 and refers pain upward to the shoulder, down towards the lumbar region or around towards the abdomen.
This trigger point is so powerful that it can be mistaken for visceral pain. This trigger point may be classified as iliocostalis lumborum as it is where the two iliocostalis muscles overlap.
Iliocostalis lumborum has a MFTP (sometimes more than one) located in the cranial portion of the muscle and these refer to the mid-buttock, the ipsilateral hip and the lower back.

Longissimus thoracis and lumborum have two trigger points.
TP1 is found lateral to the spine at L1 and refers pain into the lumbar region caudal to the trigger point and to the iliac crest.

Erector Spinae or Paraspinals

TP2 is found in the lower thoracic region (approx. at T12/13), medial to Iliocostalis thoracis TP2. It refers pain to the lower buttock area and if bad enough may cause lameness.

Pain pattern: Pain just lateral to the spine from the upper thoracic region to the gluteal muscles.
Iliocostalis thoracis: from the lower cervical area to the abdomen.
Iliocostalis lumborum: Low in the buttock and along the iliac crest, into the lower back.

Longissimus thoracis and lumborum: buttock pain. Patient has difficulty climbing stairs and walking. Difficulty in standing on hind legs and jumping.

Needling technique: Palpate using the flat portions of the fingers over the length of the area needing treatment. The ropiness of the muscle will allow you to trap the muscle so that the trigger point is isolated between the fingers. Angle the needle toward the relevant area within the muscle preferably toward the vertebra so as to make sure you are not going to pierce any organs.

Causative and perpetuating factors: Iliocostalis thoracis is linked to dysfunction in the latissimus dorsi muscle. If there is dysfunction in either muscle, check the other for associated MFTPs.

Chronic or acute overloading of the erector spinae- a sudden bend and twisting of the back activates MFTPs in the iliocostalis muscle. This is exacerbated if the muscle is fatigued or cold. Leg length inequality, sacroiliac syndrome, any degree of lameness, hip or stifle pathology, immobility, muscle atrophy and any biomechanical change that creates an uneven gait is a causative or perpetuating factor in establishing MFTPs in these muscles.

Associated trigger points: Quadratus lumborum
                                    Iliopsoas
                                    Latissimus dorsi.

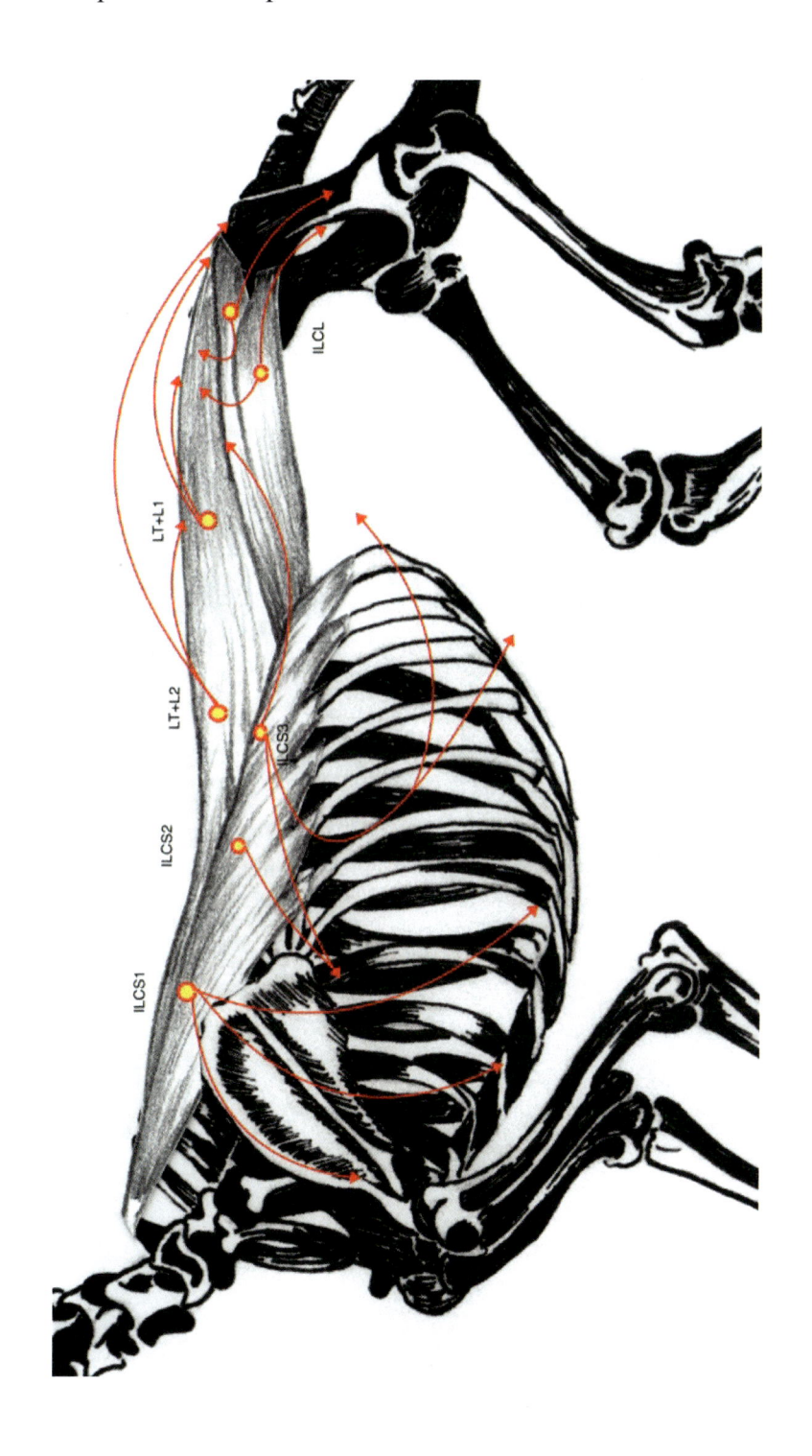

Erector Spinae or Paraspinals

Erector Spinae or Paraspinals

CRANIAL TIBIAL

The cranial tibial muscle is found on the craniolateral surface of the leg and its medial margin is in contact with the tibia. It arises from the cranial border and the articular margin of the tibia. Its tendon inserts on the plantar surface of the base of the 1st and 2nd metatarsals.

The patient may present with weakness in extension of the tarsus, tripping or exhibiting a drag on the affected foot. There is often general tarsal weakness without swelling which should give you cause to look at the cranial tibial muscle for MFTPs.

Origin: Extensor groove and the adjacent articular margin of the tibia, lateral edge of the cranial tibial border.

Distal attachment: Plantar surface of the base of the 1st and 2nd metatarsals.

Action: Flex the tarsus and rotate the paw laterally.

Innervation: Peroneal nerve

Palpation and trigger point location: Patient is lying lateral recumbent. Palpate from the tibial border all the way to the base of the 1st and 2nd metatarsals. Use a flat finger pad to palpate for these trigger points. They are generally superficial and do not require a lot of pressure.

There is one big trigger point in this muscle, and it is found in the upper third of the muscle in the middle of the muscle belly. There are often smaller trigger points that can be found and treated accordingly.

Pain pattern: Pain refers to the cranio-medial aspect of the tarsus and over the dorsal aspect of the foot and 1st and 2nd metatarsals.

Needling technique: Patient must be placed in a lateral recumbent position. Palpate and isolate the trigger points with the index and middle

Cranial Tibial

fingers, trapping the points with gentle pressure. Needle at a 45-degree angle caudal direction. A small needle is required here, and needle shallowly.

Causative and perpetuating factors: The causative factors are due to gross trauma, as opposed to overload. MFTPs here are often associated with a severe tarsal ligament trauma or a fracture. Walking on cambered surfaces may play a role in developing trigger points here, as well as dogs that are prone to tripping or falling while the muscle is contracted and active may develop MFTPs here.

Associated trigger points: All other extensors of the leg.

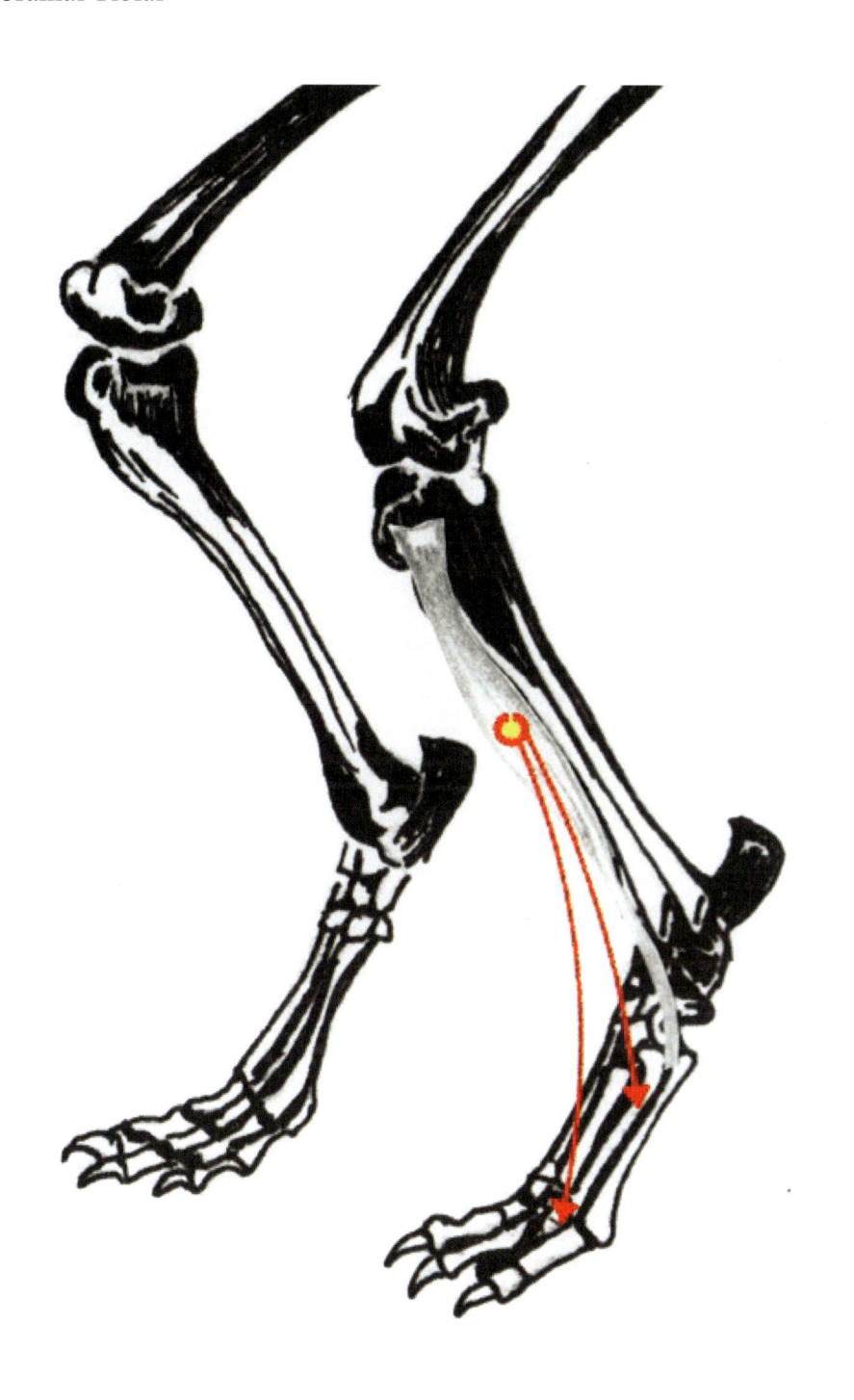

Cranial Tibial

GASTROCNEMIUS

The gastrocnemius muscle consists of two heads that have the superficial digital flexor running between them. It forms the big caudal muscle of the lower leg (calf) and is a major contributor to the common calcaneal tendon.

The two heads arise from the medial and lateral supracondylar tuberosities of the femur. In each tendon there is a fabella that articulates with the caudo-dorsal aspect of the femoral condyle.

The superficial digital flexor muscle that sits between the two heads emerges distally and passes over the medial surface of the gastrocnemius tendon, the tuber calcanei and over the plantar surface of the paw.

Origin: Medial and lateral supracondylar tuberosities of the femur.

Distal attachment: Proximal dorsal surface of tuber calcanei.

Action: Extend the tarsus and flex the stifle

Innervation: Tibial nerve

Palpation: Patient is lying lateral recumbent or standing. Palpate the lateral and medial heads of the gastrocnemius and follow them up to their union at the common calcaneal tendon that inserts onto the tuber calcanei. Use a flat finger pad to palpate the fleshy muscular portion of this muscle and identify the trigger points. They are generally found in the cranial and mid-section of the muscle and do require a moderate amount of pressure.

There are four major trigger points that occur in the gastrocnemius. There are two trigger points (1 & 2) that sit in each muscle belly. They are found in the middle of the muscle. The other two trigger points (3

Gastrocnemius

& 4) are located behind the knee where the medial and lateral heads attach to the femoral condyles.

Trigger point 1 is found on the medial aspect of the gastrocnemius in the middle of the muscle belly refers to the caudo-medial aspect of the leg, the lower portion of the caudal thigh, the ipsilateral foot and the back of the stifle.

Trigger point 2 is slightly more ventral, near the lateral border of the lateral muscle. This trigger point refers pain locally to the lateral leg.

Trigger point 3 refers pain to the caudal aspect of the stifle on the medial side, and trigger point 4 refers pain to the caudal aspect of the stifle on the lateral side.

Pain pattern: Pain extends from the ipsilateral foot, over the caudo-medial aspect of the tarsus, over the gastrocnemius muscle and to the back of the stifle and the caudal aspect of the hindleg just above the stifle. TP1 has the most pronounced referral pattern.

Needling technique: Needling this muscle may lead to post needling soreness. The medial trigger points appear to be more tender, due to the fact that TP1 is a very active and intense trigger point. You may want to needle the medial head on one visit and the lateral head on the next visit to prevent soreness. Needle at a 90-degree angle and be aware of the vasculature in the area.

Causative and perpetuating factors: Climbing uphill, steep slopes, rocky terrain, jogging uphill, tarsus or hock injury- compensation. Casting or immobilization of the limb.

Cambered surface walking will aggravate the medial aspect of the gastrocnemius on the lower side of the slanted surface. This may present as an apparent stifle issue and the patient will lilt towards the low side which results in a shortening of the gastrocnemius on that side.

Gastrocnemius

Long continual climbs and constantly needing to push off the hindleg from a flexed stifle and an extended tarsus will perpetuate these trigger points.

Associated trigger points: Gracilis
Semitendinosus
Biceps femoris
Superficial digital flexor muscle.

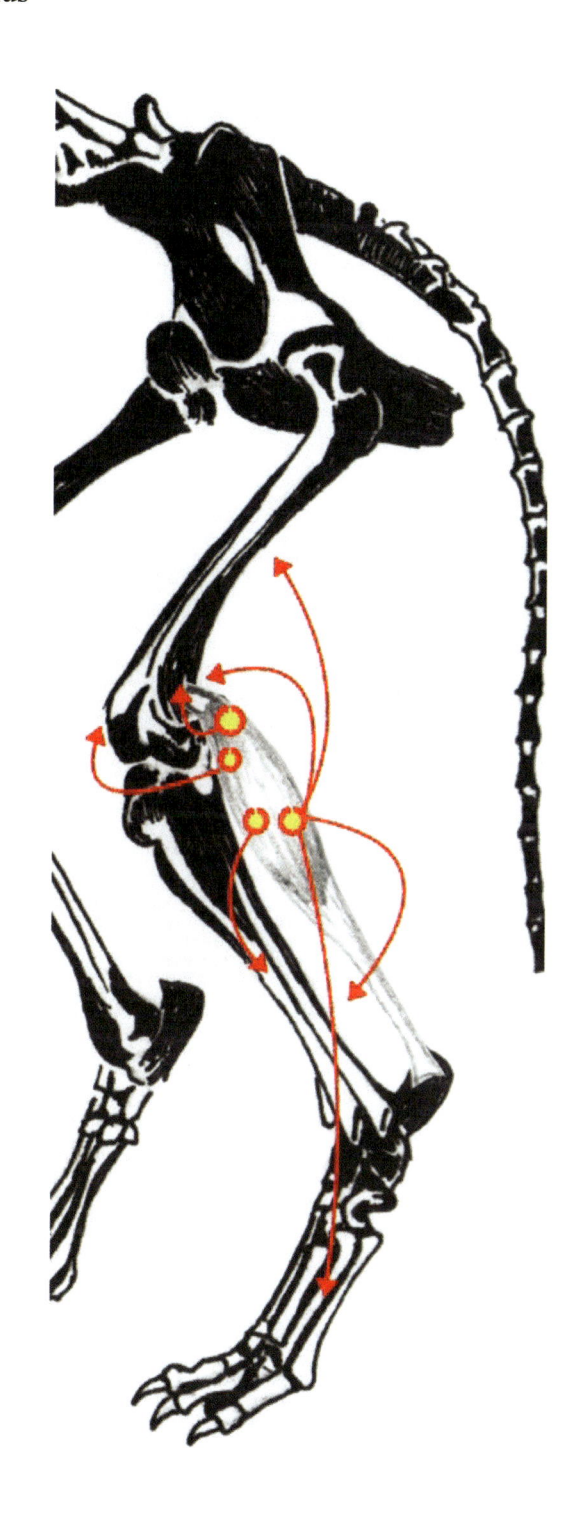

Gastrocnemius

CONCLUSION

Like most manuals or textbooks there is never a real conclusion, more of a "to be continued". As I spoke about at the beginning of this book, myofascial pain syndromes, myofascial trigger points and the treatment thereof is still in its infancy. I hope that this helps guide you on your journey to be a better practitioner, that it opens your mind to look beyond the obvious and keep searching for answers when you are feeling stumped. The changes you can make and the improvement in the quality and quantity of life that you can provide for your patient is testimony to this incredible process that I have been privileged to be involved with for the last 16 years.

I look very forward to meeting many of you over the next few years, at seminars or at my courses and hearing your incredible stories and testimonies about how this simple and wonderful tool has changed the lives of your patients.

For more information on courses and other books go to:
www.drmicheleb.com.

BIBLIOGRAPHY

1. Travell, Janet and David Simons. *Myofascial Pain and Dysfunction: The trigger point manual Vol1*. Baltimore: Williams and Wilkins, 1983.
2. Ballyns JJ, Turo D, Otto P, et al. Office-based elastographic technique for quantifying mechanical properties of skeletal muscle. *J. Ultrasound Med.* Aug 2012;31(8):1209-1219.
3. Ballyns JJ, Shah JP, Hammond J, Gebreab T, Gerber LH, Sikdar S. Objective sonographic measures for characterizing myofascial trigger points associated with cervical pain. *J Ultrasound Med.* Oct 2011;30(10):1331-1340.
4. Chen Q, Bensamoun S, Basford JR, Thompson JM, An KN. Identification and quantification of myofascial taut bands with magnetic resonance elastography. *Arch Phys Med Rehabil.* 2007;88(12):1658-1661.
5. Chen Q, Basford J, An KN. Ability of magnetic resonance elastography to assess taut bands. *Clin Biomech (Bristol, Avon).* 2008;23(5):623-629.
6. Sikdar S, Shah JP, Gebreab T, et al. Novel applications of ultrasound technology to visualize and characterize myofascial trigger points and surrounding soft tissue. *Arch Phys Med Rehabil.* Nov 2009;90(11):1829-1838.
7. Mense S. Morphology of myofascial trigger points: what does a trigger point look like? In: Mense S, Gerwin R, D., eds. *Muscle pain; diagnosis and treatment.* Heidelberg: Springer; 2010:85-102.
8. Brückle W, Sückfull M, Fleckenstein W, Weiss C, Müller W. Gewebe-pO2-Messung in der verspannten Rückenmuskulatur (m. erector spinae). *Z. Rheumatol.* 1990;49:208-216.
9. Shah JP, Gilliams EA. Uncovering the biochemical milieu of myofascial trigger points using in vivo microdialysis: an application of muscle pain concepts to myofascial pain syndrome. *J Bodyw Mov Ther.* Oct 2008;12(4):371-384.
10. Shah J, Phillips T, Danoff JV, Gerber LH. A novel microanalytical technique for assaying soft tissue demonstrates significant quantitative biomechanical differences in 3 clinically distinct groups: normal, latent and active. *Arch Phys Med Rehabil.* 2003;84:A4.
11. Shah JP, Danoff JV, Desai MJ, et al. Biochemicals associated with pain and inflammation are elevated in sites near to and remote from active myofascial trigger points. *Arch Phys Med Rehabil.* Jan 2008;89(1):16-23.
12. Fernández-de-las-Peñas C, Ge HY, Alonso-Blanco C, González-Iglesias J, Arendt-Nielsen L. Referred pain areas of active myofascial trigger points in head, neck, and shoulder muscles, in chronic tension type headache. *J Bodyw Mov Ther.* Oct 2010;14(4):391-396.
13. Fernández-Carnero J, Fernández de las Peñas CF, de la Llave-Rincón AI, Ge HY, Arendt- Nielsen L. Prevalence of and referred pain from myofascial trigger points in the forearm muscles in patients with lateral epicondylalgia. *Clin J Pain.* May 2007;23(4):353-360.
14. Fernández de las Peñas C, Ge HY, Arendt-Nielsen L, Cuadrado ML, Pareja JA. The local and referred pain from myofascial trigger points in the temporalis muscle contributes to pain profile in chronic tension-type headache. *Clin J Pain.* Nov-Dec 2007;23(9):786-792.
15. Lucas KR, Rich PA, Polus BI. Muscle activation patterns in the scapular positioning muscles during loaded scapular plane elevation: the effects of latent myofascial trigger points. *Clin Biomechanics.* 2010;25(8):765-770.
16. Lucas KR, Polus BI, Rich PS. Latent myofascial trigger points: their effects on muscle activation and movement efficiency. *J Bodyw Mov Ther.* 2004;8:160-166.
17. Simons DG, Hong C-Z, Simons LS. Endplate potentials are common to midfiber myofascial trigger points. *Am J Phys Med Rehabil.* 2002;81(3):212-222.
18. Simons DG. Review of enigmatic MTrPs as a common cause of enigmatic musculoskeletal pain and dysfunction. *J Electromyogr Kinesiol.* 2004;14:95-107.
19. Kuan TS, Hsieh YL, Chen SM, Chen JT, Yen WC, Hong CZ. The myofascial trigger point region: correlation between the degree of irritability and the prevalence of endplate noise. *Am J Phys Med Rehabil.* 2007;86(3):183-189.
20. Gerwin RD, Dommerholt J, Shah JP. An expansion of Simons' integrated hypothesis of trigger point formation. *Curr Pain Headache Rep.* Dec 2004;8(6):468-475.
21. McPartland JM, Simons DG. Myofascial trigger points: translating molecular theory into manual therapy. *J Man Manip Ther* 2006;14(4):232-239.
22. Hong CZ, Simons DG. Pathophysiologic and electrophysiologic mechanisms of myofascial trigger points. *Arch Phys Med Rehabil.* 1998;79(7):863-872.
23. Bukharaeva EA, Salakhutdinov RI, Vyskocil F, Nikolsky EE. Spontaneous quantal and non-quantal release of acetylcholine at mouse endplate during onset of hypoxia. *Physiol Res.* 2005;54(2):251-255.
24. Simons DG. New views of myofascial trigger points: etiology and diagnosis. *Arch Phys Med Rehabil.* Jan 2008;89(1):157-159.
25. Dommerholt J. Dry needling — peripheral and central considerations. *J Man Manip Ther.* 2011;19(4):223-237.
26. Mense S. How do muscle lesions such as latent and active trigger points influence central nociceptive neurons? *J Musculokelet Pain.* 2010;18(4):348-353.

Bibliography

27. Fernández de las Peñas C, Cuadrado M, Arendt-Nielsen L, Simons D, Pareja J. Myofascial trigger points and sensitization: an updated pain model for tension-type headache. *Cephalalgia.* 2007;27(5):383-393.
28. Xu YM, Ge HY, Arendt-Nielsen L. Sustained nociceptive mechanical stimulation of latent myofascial trigger point induces central sensitization in healthy subjects. *J Pain.* 2010;11(12):1348-1355.
29. Niddam DM, Chan RC, Lee SH, Yeh TC, Hsieh JC. Central representation of hyperalgesia from myofascial trigger point. *Neuroimage.* Feb 1 2008;39(3):1299-1306.
30. Niddam DM, Chan RC, Lee SH, Yeh TC, Hsieh JC. Central modulation of pain evoked from myofascial trigger point. *Clin J Pain.* Jun 2007;23(5):440-448.
31. Svensson P, Minoshima S, Beydoun A, Morrow TJ, Casey KL. Cerebral processing of acute skin and muscle pain in humans. *J Neurophysiol.* Jul 1997;78(1):450-460.
32. Langevin HM, Bouffard NA, Badger GJ, Churchill DL, Howe AK. Subcutaneous tissue fibroblast cytoskeletal remodeling induced by acupuncture: Evidence for a mechanotrans- duction-based mechanism. *J Cell Physiol.* May 2006;207(3):767-774.
33. Langevin HM, Bouffard NA, Badger GJ, Iatridis JC, Howe AK. Dynamic fibroblast cytoskel- etal response to subcutaneous tissue stretch ex vivo and in vivo. *Am J Physiol Cell Physiol.* Mar 2005;288(3):C747-756.
34. Hong CZ. Lidocaine injection versus dry needling to myofascial trigger point. The impor- tance of the local twitch response. *Am J Phys Med Rehabil.* 1994;73(4):256-263.
35. Travell, Janet and David Simons. *Myofascial Pain and Dysfunction: The trigger point manual Vol2.* . Baltimore: Williams and Wilkins , 1992.
36. Tekin L, Akarsu S, Durmus O, Cakar E, Dincer U, Kiralp MZ. The effect of dry needling in the treatment of myofascial pain syndrome: a randomized double-blinded placebo-controlled trial. *Clin Rheumatol.* Nov 9 2012.
37. Hong C-Z, Yu J. Spontaneous electrical activity of rabbit trigger spot after transection of spinal cord and peripheral nerve. *J Musculoskelet Pain.* 1998;6(4):45-58.
38. Hong CZ, Torigoe Y, Yu J. The localized twitch responses in responsive bands of rabbit skeletal muscle are related to the reflexes at spinal cord level. *J Muscoskelet Pain.* 1995;3:15-33.
39. Hong CZ. Persistence of local twitch response with loss of conduction to and from the spinal cord. *Arch Phys Med Rehabil.* Jan 1994;75(1):12-16.
40. Rha DW, Shin JC, Kim YK, Jung JH, Kim YU, Lee SC. Detecting local twitch responses of myofascial trigger points in the lower-back muscles using ultrasonography. *Arch Phys Med Rehabil.* Oct 2011;92(10):1576-1580 e1571.
41. Hong CZ, Kuan TS, Chen JT, Chen SM. Referred pain elicited by palpation and by needling of myofascial trigger points: a comparison. *Arch Phys Med Rehabil.* 1997;78(9):957-960.
42. Simons DG, Dexter JR. Comparison of local twitch responses elicited by palpation and needling of myofascial trigger points. *J Musculoskelet Pain.* 1995;3:49-61.
43. Ge HY, Fernandez-de-Las-Penas C, Yue SW. Myofascial trigger points: spontaneous electri- cal activity and its consequences for pain induction and propagation. *Chinese Medicine.* 2011;6:13.
44. Hsieh YL, Chou LW, Joe YS, Hong CZ. Spinal cord mechanism involving the remote effects of dry needling on the irritability of myofascial trigger spots in rabbit skeletal muscle. *Arch Phys Med Rehabil.* Jul 2011;92(7):1098-1105.
45. Shah JP, Phillips TM, Danoff JV, Gerber LH. An in-vivo microanalytical technique for measuring the local biochemical milieu of human skeletal muscle. *J Appl Physiol.* 2005;99:1977-1984.
46. Majlesi J, Unalan H. Effect of treatment on trigger points. *Curr Pain Headache Rep.* Oct 2010;14(5):353-360.
47. Affaitati G, Costantini R, Fabrizio A, Lapenna D, Tafuri E, Giamberardino MA. Effects of treat- ment of peripheral pain generators in fibromyalgia patients. *Eur J Pain.* Jan 2011;15(1):61-69.
48. Srbely JZ, Dickey JP, Lee D, Lowerison M. Dry needle stimulation of myofascial trigger points evokes segmental anti-nociceptive effects. *J Rehabil Med.* 2010;42(5):463-468.
49. Chen JT, Chung KC, Hou CR, Kuan TS, Chen SM, Hong CZ. Inhibitory effect of dry needling on the spontaneous electrical activity recorded from myofascial trigger spots of rabbit skeletal muscle. *Am J Phys Med Rehabil.* Oct 2001;80(10):729-735.
50. Tsai C-T, Hsieh L-F, Kuan T-S, Kao M-J, Chou L-W, Hong C-Z. Remote effects of dry needling on the irritability of the myofascial trigger point in the upper trapezius muscle. *Am J Phys Med Rehabil.* 2010;89(2):133-140.
51. Simons DG. Understanding effective treatments of myofascial trigger points. *J Bodyw Mov Ther.* 2002;6(2):81-88.
52. Olausson H, Lamarre Y, Backlund H, et al. Unmyelinated tactile afferents signal touch and project to insular cortex. *Nat Neurosci* Sep 2002;5(9):900-904.
53. Baldry PE. *Acupuncture, Trigger Points and Musculoskeletal Pain.* Edinburgh: Churchill Livingstone; 2005.
54. Ceccherelli F, Rigoni MT, Gagliardi G, Ruzzante L. Comparison between superficial and deep acupuncture in the treatment of lumbar myofascial pain: a double-blind randomized controlled study. *Clin J Pain.* 2002;18:149-153.
55. Edwards J, Knowles N. Superficial dry needling and active stretching in the treatment of myofascial pain--a randomised controlled trial. *Acupunct Med.* 2003/9 2003;21(3 SU):80-86.
56. Simons DG, Mense S. Understanding and measurement of muscle tone as related to clinical muscle pain. *Pain.* 1998;75(1):1-17.

Bibliography

57. Whisler SL, Lang DM, Armstrong M, Vickers J, Qualls C, Feldman JS. Effects of myofascial release and other advanced myofascial therapies on children with cerebral palsy: six case reports. *Explore.* May-Jun 2012;8(3):199-205.
58. Dilorenzo L, Traballesi M, Morelli D, et al. Hemiparetic shoulder pain syndrome treated with deep dry needling during early rehabilitation: a prospective, open-label, randomized investigation. *J Musculoskelet Pain.* 2004;12(2):25-34.
59. Lewit K, Olsanska S. Clinical importance of active scars: abnormal scars as a cause of myofascial pain. *J Manipulative Physiol Ther.* 2004;27(6):399-402.
60. Iqbal SA, Sidgwick GP, Bayat A. Identification of fibrocytes from mesenchymal stem cells in keloid tissue: a potential source of abnormal fibroblasts in keloid scarring. *Arch. Dermatol Res.* Oct 2012;304(8):665-671.
61. Eto H, Suga H, Aoi N, et al. Therapeutic potential of fibroblast growth factor-2 for hypertro- phic scars: upregulation of MMP-1 and HGF expression. *Lab Invest.* Feb 2012;92(2):214-223.
62. Findley TW. Fascia Research from a Clinician/Scientist's Perspective. *Int J Ther Massage Bodywork.* 2011;4(4):1-6.
63. Grinnell F. Fibroblast biology in three-dimensional collagen matrices. *Trends Cell Biol.* May 2003;13(5):264-269.
64. Hicks MR, Cao TV, Campbell DH, Standley PR. Mechanical strain applied to human fibroblasts differentially regulates skeletal myoblast differentiation. *J Appl Physiol.* Aug 2012;113(3):465-472.
65. Langevin HM, Bouffard NA, Fox JR, et al. Fibroblast cytoskeletal remodeling contributes to connective tissue tension. *J Cell Physiol.* May 2011;226(5):1166-1175.
66. Fu ZH, Wang JH, Sun JH, Chen XY, Xu JG. Fu's subcutaneous needling: possible clinical evidence of the subcutaneous connective tissue in acupuncture. *J Altern Complement Med.* Jan-Feb 2007;13(1):47-51.
67. Fu ZH, Chen XY, Lu LJ, Lin J, Xu JG. Immediate effect of Fu's subcutaneous needling for low back pain. *Chin Med J. (Engl).* Jun 5 2006;119(11):953-956.
68. Chiquet M, Renedo AS, Huber F, Fluck M. How do fibroblasts translate mechanical signals into changes in extracellular matrix production? *Matrix Biol.* Mar 2003;22(1):73-80.
69. Langevin HM, Storch KN, Snapp RR, et al. Tissue stretch induces nuclear rem
70. Evans HE, de Lahunta A: *Miller's Anatomy of the Dog*, 4th Edition. Elsevier Saunders, 2013, St. Louis, Missouri
71. Dommerholt J, Shah JP: "Myofascial Pain Syndrome" In: Ballantyne JC, Rathmell JP, Fishman SM, Editors: *Bonica's Pain Management*, 4th Edition, Lippincott, Williams & Wilkins, 2010. Baltimore, Maryland. Chapter 35:450-471
72. Svensson P, Minoshima S, Beydoun A, et al: Cerebral processing of acute skin and muscle pain in humans. *J Neurophysiol* 1997; 78(1):450-460
73. Niddam DM, Chan RC, Lee SH, et al: Central modulation of pain evoked from myofascial trigger point. *Clin J Pain* 2007; 23(5): 440-448
74. Hagglund M, Walden M, Bahr R, et al: Methods of epidemiological study of injuries to professional football players: developing the UEFA model. *Br J Sports Med* 2005; 39:340-346
75. Mueller-Wohlfahrt HW, Haensel L, Mithoefer K, et al: Terminology and classification of muscle injuries in sport: the Munich consensus statement. *Br J Sports Med* 2013; 47(6):342-350
76. Evans J, Levesque D, Shelton GD: Canine inflammatory myopathies: a clinicopathologic review of 200 cases. *J Vet Intern Med* 2004; 18(5):679-691
77. Shelton GD: Routine and specialized laboratory testing for the diagnosis of neuromuscular diseases in dogs and cats. *Vet Clin Path* 2010; 39(3):278-295
78. Dommerholt J, Huijbregts P: *Myofascial Trigger Points – Pathophysiology and Evidence-Informed Diagnosis and Management* 2011; Jones and Bartlett Publishers,Sudbury, Massachusetts
79. Gerwin R: A study of 96 subjects examined for both fibromyalgia and myofascial pain. *J Musculoskel Pain* 1995; 3:121
80. Gerwin R: A review of myofascial pain and fibromyalgia: Factors that promote their persistence. *Acupunct Med* 2005; 23:121-134
81. Lieber RL: *Skeletal Muscle Structure, Function, and Plasticity – The Physiological Basis of Rehabilitation*, 3rd Edition 2010; Lippincott Williams & Wilkins, Baltimore, Maryland and Philadelphia, Pennsylvania
82. Simons DG, Travell JG, Simons LS: *Myofascial Pain and Dysfunction: The Trigger Point Manual. Volume 1. Upper Half of Body* 1999; Lippincott Williams & Wilkins, Baltimore, Maryland
83. Simons DG, Stolov WC: Microscopic Features of Transient Contraction of Palpable Bands in Canine Muscle. *Am J of Physical Med* 1776; 55(2):65-88
84. Gerwin RD, Shannon S, Hong CZ, et al: Interrater reliability in myofascial trigger point examination. *Pain* 1997; 69:65-73.
85. Mense S, Gerwin RD: *Muscle Pain: Diagnosis and Treatment* 2010; Springer-Verlag Berlin Heidelberg.
86. Lucas KR, Rich PA, Polus BI: Muscle Activation patterns in the scapular positioning muscles during loaded scapular plane elevation: The effects of Latent Myofascial Trigger Points. *Clin Biomech* 2010; 8:765-70
87. Simons DG. (2004) Review of enigmatic MTrPs as a common cause of enigmatic musculoskeletal pain and dysfunction. *J Electromyogr Kinesiol* 2004; 14:95-107
88. Bron C, Dommerholt J: Etiology of myofascial trigger points. *Curr Pain Headache Rep* 2012; 16(5):439-444

Bibliography

89. Gerwin R: Myofascial pain syndrome: here we are, where we must go? *J Musculoskeletal Pain* 2010; 18:329-347
90. Simons DG, Travell JG: Myofascial trigger points, a possible explanation. *Pain* 1981; 10:106-109
91. Gerwin RD, Dommerholt J, Shah JP: An Expansion of Simon's Integrated Hypothesis for Trigger Point Formation. *Current Pain and Headache Rep* 2004; 8:468-475
92. Gerwin RD: Myofascial and Visceral Pain Syndromes: Visceral-Somatic Pain Representations. *J Musculoskel Pain* 2002; 10(1/2):165-175
93. Tough EA, White AR, Richards S, et al: Variability of criteria used to diagnose myofascial trigger point pain syndrome – evidence from a review of the literature. *Clinical Journal of Pain* 2007; 23(3):278-286
94. Hakguder A, Birtane M, Gurcan S, et al: Efficacy of low level laser therapy in myofascial pain syndrome: An algometric and thermographic evaluation. *Lasers in Surgery and Medicine* 2003; 33:339-343
95. Gur A, Sarac AJ, Cevik R, et al: Efficacy of 904nm gallium arsenide low-level laser therapy in the management of pain in the neck: A double-blind and randomize-controlled trial. *Lasers in Surgery and Medicine,* 35:229-235
96. Ilbuldu E., Cakmak A, Disci R, et al: Comparison of laser, dry needling, and placebo laser treatments in myofascial pain syndrome. *Photmedicine and Laser Surgery* 2004; 22:306-311.
97. Altan L, Bingol, U, Aykac M, et al: Investigation of the effect of GaAs laser therapy on cervical myofascial pain syndrome. *Rheumatology* International 2005; 25(1):23-7.
98. Dundar U, Eveik D, Samili F, et al: The effect of gallium arsenide aluminum laser therapy in the management of cervical myofascial pain syndrome: A double blind, placebo-controlled study. *Clinical Rheumatology* 2007; 26:930-934
99. Chang WD, Wu JH, and Jiang JA: Therapeutic effects of low-level laser on lateral epicondylitis from differential interventions of Chinese-Western medicine: systematic review. *Photomed Laser Surg*, 28(3):327-36
100. Steiss JE: Muscle Disorders and Rehabilitation in Canine Athletes. *Veterinary Clinics of North America: Small Animal Practic* 2002 32(1):267-285
101. Mlacnik E, Bockstahler B, Muller M, et al: Effect of caloric restriction and moderate or intense physiotherapy program for treatment of lameness in overweight dogs with osteoarthritis. *Journal of the American Veterinary Medical Association* 2006; 229:1756-1760.
102. Canapp DA: Select modalities. *Clinical Techniques in Small Animal Practice* 2007; 22(4):160-165
103. Hou CR, Tsai LC, Cheng KF, et al: Immediate effects of various physical therapeutic modalities on cervical myofascial pain and trigger-point sensitivity. *Archives of Physical Medicine and Rehabilitation* 2002; 83(10):1406-1414
104. Dommerholt J, Huijbregts P: *Myofascial Trigger Points – Pathophysiology and Evidence-Informed Diagnosis and Management* 2011; Jones and Bartlett Publishers,Sudbury, Massachusetts
105. Aguilera FJ, Martin DP, Masanet RA, et al: Immediate effect of ultrasound and ischemic compression techniques for the treatment of trapezius latent myofascial trigger points in healthy subjects: a randomized controlled study. *Journal of Manipulative Physiology and* Therapy 2009; 32(7):515-520
106. Draper DO, Mahaffey C, Kaiser D, et al: Thermal ultrasound decreases tissue stiffness of trigger points in upper trapezius muscles. *Physiotherapy Theory and Practice* 2010; 26(3):167-172
107. Gam AN, Warming S, Larsen LE., et al: Treatment of myofascial trigger-points with ultrasound combined with massage and exercise—a randomized controlled trial. *Pain* 1998 77(1):73-79
108. Lee JC, Lin DT, Hong C: The effectiveness of simultaneous thermotherapy with ultrasound and electrotherapy with combined AC and DC current on the immediate pain relief of myofascial trigger points. *Journal of Musculoskeletal Pain* 1997 5:81-90
109. Mense S, Gerwin RD: *Muscle Pain: Diagnosis and Treatment* 2010; Springer-Verlag Berlin Heidelberg
110. Hains G, Descarreaux M, Hains F: Chronic Shoulder pain of myofascial origin: a randomized clinical trial using ischemic compression therapy. *Journal of Manipulative and Physiological Therapy* 2010; 33(5):362-369
111. Hains G, Descarreaux M, Lamy AM, et al: A randomized controlled (intervention) trial of ischemic compression therapy for chronic carpal tunnel syndrome. *Journal of the Canadian Chiropractic Association* 2010; 54(3):155-163
112. Montanez-Aguilera FJ, Valtuena-Gimeno N, Pecos-Martin D, et al: Changes in a patient with neck pain after application of ischemic compression as a trigger point therapy. *Journal of Back and Musculoskeletal* Rehabilitation 2010; 23(2):101-104
113. Physical Therapists & the Performance of Dry Needling – An Educational Resource Paper. Produced by the APTA Department of Practice and APTA State Government Affairs January 2012
114. Amaro JA:When Acupuncture Becomes "Dry Needling". Dynamic *Chiropractic* 2008; 26(12)
115. Bowsher D: Mechanisms of acupuncture. In: Filshie J, White A, Editors. *Medical Acupuncture – A Western Scientific Approach.* First edition. Edinburgh: ChurchillLivingstone 1998; 69-82
116. Le Bars D, Dickenson AH, Benson JM: Diffuse noxious inhibitory control (DNIC). IEffects on dorsal horn convergent neurons in the rat; II – Lack of effect on nonconvergent neurons, supraspinal involvement and theoretical implications. *Pain* 1979; 6:305-327
117. Schliessbach J, van der Klift E, Siegenthaler A, Arendt-Nielson L, Curatolo M, Streitberger K: Does Acupuncture Needling Induce Analgesic Effects Comparable to Diffuse Noxious Inhibitory Controls? *Evidence-Based Complementary and Alternative*Medicine 2012; 785613
118. Dommerholt, Jan; Fernández de las Peñas, César: *Trigger Point Dry Needling: An Evidence and Clinical-Based Approach* (Kindle) 2013; Churchill Livingstone. KindleEdition

Bibliography

119. Furlan A.D, van Tulder M, Cherkin D, et al: Acupuncture and dry-needling for low back pain: an updated systemic review within the framework of the Cochrane collaboration. *Spine* 2005; 30(8):944-963
120. Tough EA, White A.R, Cummings TM, et al: Acupuncture and dry needling in the management of myofascial trigger point pain: A systematic review and meta-analysis of randomized controlled trials. *European Journal of Pain* 2009; 13:3-10
121. Fernandez-Carnero J, La Touche R, Ortega-Santiago R, et al: Short-term effects of dry needling of active myofascial trigger points in the masseter muscle in patients with temporomandibular disorders. *Journal of Orofacial Pain* 2010; 24(1):106-112
122. Srbely JZ, Dickey JP, Lee D, et al: Dry needle stimulation of myofascial trigger points evokes segmental anti-nociceptive effects. *Journal of Rehabilitation Medicine* 2010; 42(5):463-468
123. Tsai CT, Hsieh LF, Kuan TS, et al: Remote effects of dry needling on the irritability of the myofascial trigger point in the upper trapezius muscle. *American Journal of Physical Medicine and Rehabilitation* 2010; 89(2):133-140
124. Osborne NJ, Gatt IT: Management of shoulder injuries using dry needling in elite volleyball players. *Acupuncture Medicine* 2010; 28(1):42-45
125. Shah JP, Phillips TM, Danoff JV, et; alAn in vivo microanalytical technique for measuring the local biochemical milieu of human skeletal muscle. *Journal of Applied Physiology* 2005 99:1977-1984
126. Shah JP, Danoff JV, Desai MJ, et al: Biochemicals Associated With Pain and Inflammation are Elevated in Sites Near to and Remote From Active Myofascial Trigger Points. *Archives of Physical Medicine and Rehabilitation* 2008; 89:16-23
127. Wheeler AH: Myofascial pain disorders: theory to therapy. *Drugs* 2004;64(1):45-62
128. Janssens LA: Trigger points in 48 dogs with myofascial pain syndromes. *Veterinary Surgery* 1991; 20(4):274-8
129. Janssens LA: Trigger point therapy. *Problems in Veterinary Medicine* 1992; 4(1):117-124
130. Simons DG, Stolov WC: Microscopic Features of Transient Contraction of Palpable Bands in Canine Muscle. *Am J of Physical Med* 1776; 55(2):65-88
131. Macgregor J, Graf von Schjweinitz D: Needle electromyographic activity of myofascial trigger points and control sites in equine cleidobrachialis muscle-an observational study. *Acupunct Med* 2006; 24(2):61-70
132. Wright B: Management of Chronic Soft Tissue Pain. *Topics in Companion Animal Medicine* 2010 25(1):26-31.
133. Lucas KR, Rich PA, Polus Bl: Muscle activation patterns in the scapular positioning muscles during loaded scapular plane elevation: the effects of Latent Myofascial Trigger Points. *Clin Biomech* 2010; 25(8):765-70
134. Hidalgo-Lozano A, Fernandez-de-las-Penas C, Calderon-Soto C, et al: Elite swimmers with and without unilateral shoulder pain: mechanical hyperalgesia and active/latent muscle trigger points in neck-shoulder muscles. *Scand J Med Sci Sports* 2013; 23(1):66-73
135. Osborne NJ, Gatt IT: Management of shoulder injuries using dry needling in elite volleyball players. *Acupunct Med* 2010; 28(1):42-45
136. Redskins' Dry Needles Speed Recovery Time. http://www.redskins.com/news-and-events/article-1/Redskins%E2%80%99-Dry-Needles-Speed-Recovery-Time/744d3f1e-b8c2-4f5d-8735-c4f8c8a2c468
137. Woolf CJ. Central sensitization: implications for the diagnosis and treatment of pain.Pain. 2011 Mar; 152(3 Suppl):S2-15. doi: 10.1016/j.pain.2010.09.030.
138. Galer BS, Argoff CE. Defeat Chronic Pain Now. Fair Winds Press; 1 edition (December 1, 2010).
139. Xies Veterinary Acupuncture, Huisheng Xie, 2007, Blackwell Publishing USA. Pg. 14-16.
140. Extracorporeal Shock Wave therapy- Application for trigger points. Part three of a three part series examining the role of extracorporeal shock wave therapy in pain management. Marovino Tiziano
141. The Role of Extracorporeal Shockwave Treatment in Musculoskeletal Disorders Moya, Daniel MD[1,a]; Ramón, Silvia MD, PhD[2]; Schaden, Wolfgang MD[3]; Wang, Ching-Jen MD[4]; Guiloff, Leonardo MD[5]; Cheng, Jai-Hong MD[4]JBJS: February 7, 2018 - Volume 100 - Issue 3 - p 251-263 doi: 10.2106/JBJS.17.00661
142. Muller-Ehrenberg H. Diagnosis and therapy of myofascial pain with focused shock waves. Medizibisch-Orthopadische Technik 2005;5:1-6.
143. Cheng JH, Wang CJ. Biological mechanism of shockwave in bone. Int J Surg. 2015 Dec;24(Pt B):143-6. Epub 2015 Jun 25.
144. 3. D Agostino MC, Frairia R, Romeo P, Amelio E, Berta L, Bosco V, Gigliotti S, Guerra C, Messina S, Messuri L, Moretti B, Notarnicola A, Maccagnano G, Russo S, Saggini R, Vulpiani MC, Buselli P. Extracorporeal shockwaves as regenerative therapy in orthopedic traumatology: a narrative review from basic research to clinical practice. J Biol Regul Homeost Agents. 2016 Apr-Jun;30(2):323-32.Ioppolo F, Rompe JD, Furia JP, Cacchio A. Clinical application of shock wave therapy (SWT) in musculoskeletal disorders. Eur J Phys Rehabil Med. 2014 Apr;50(2):217-30. Epub 2014 Mar 26.
145. Wang CJ. An overview of shock wave therapy in musculoskeletal disorders. Chang Gung Med J. 2003 Apr;26(4):220-32.
146. Cleveland RO, McAteer JA. Physics of shock-wave lithotripsy. In: Smith AD, Badlani G, Preminger GM, Kavoussi LR, editors. Smith's textbook of endourology. 3rd ed. Cichester: Wiley-Blackwell; 2012. p 529-58.
147. Loske AM. Medical and biomedical applications of shock waves. Cham, Switzerland: Springer International; 2017.

Bibliography

148. Cleveland RO, Chitnis PV, McClure SR. Acoustic field of a ballistic shock wave therapy device. Ultrasound Med Biol. 2007 Aug;33(8):1327-35. Epub 2007 Apr 27.
149. Császár NB, Angstman NB, Milz S, Sprecher CM, Kobel P, Farhat M, Furia JP, Schmitz C. Radial shock wave devices generate cavitation. PLoS One. 2015 Oct 28;10(10):e0140541.
150. Haupt G. Use of extracorporeal shock waves in the treatment of pseudarthrosis, tendinopathy and other orthopedic diseases. J Urol. 1997 Jul;158(1):4-11.
151. Ogden JA, Tóth-Kischkat A, Schultheiss R. Principles of shock wave therapy. Clin Orthop Relat Res. 2001 Jun;387:8-17.
152. Holfeld J, Tepeköylü C, Reissig M, Lobenwein D, Scheller B, Kirchmair E, Kozaryn R, Albrecht-Schgoer K, Krapf C, Zins K, Urbschat A, Zacharowski K, Grimm M, Kirchmair R, Paulus P. Toll-like receptor 3 signalling mediates angiogenic response upon shock wave treatment of ischaemic muscle. Cardiovasc Res. 2016 Feb 1;109(2):331-43. Epub 2015 Dec 16.
153. Holfeld J, Tepeköylü C, Kozaryn R, Urbschat A, Zacharowski K, Grimm M, Paulus P. Shockwave therapy differentially stimulates endothelial cells: implications on the control of inflammation via toll-like receptor 3. Inflammation. 2014 Feb;37(1):65-70.
154. Xu JK, Chen HJ, Li XD, Huang ZL, Xu H, Yang HL, Hu J. Optimal intensity shock wave promotes the adhesion and migration of rat osteoblasts via integrin β1-mediated expression of phosphorylated focal adhesion kinase. J Biol Chem. 2012 Jul 27;287(31):26200-12. Epub 2012 May 31.
155. Yu T, Junger WG, Yuan C, Jin A, Zhao Y, Zheng X, Zeng Y, Liu J. Shockwaves increase T-cell proliferation and IL-2 expression through ATP release, P2X7 receptors, and FAK activation. Am J Physiol Cell Physiol. 2010 Mar;298(3):C457-64. Epub 2009 Nov 4.
156. Weihs AM, Fuchs C, Teuschl AH, Hartinger J, Slezak P, Mittermayr R, Redl H, Junger WG, Sitte HH, Rünzler D. Shock wave treatment enhances cell proliferation and improves wound healing by ATP release-coupled extracellular signal-regulated kinase (ERK) activation. J Biol Chem. 2014 Sep 26;289(39):27090-104. Epub 2014 Aug 12.
157. Jan CR, Huang JK, Tseng CJ. High-energy shock waves alter cytosolic calcium mobilization in single MDCK cells. Nephron. 1998;78(2):187-94.
158. Frairia R, Berta L. Biological effects of extracorporeal shock waves on fibroblasts. A review. Muscles Ligaments Tendons J. 2012 Apr 1;1(4):138-47.
159. Wang CJ, Wang FS, Yang KD, Weng LH, Hsu CC, Huang CS, Yang LC. Shock wave therapy induces neovascularization at the tendon-bone junction. A study in rabbits. J Orthop Res. 2003 Nov;21(6):984-9.
160. Wang CJ, Wang FS, Yang KD. Biological effects of extracorporeal shockwave in bone healing: a study in rabbits. Arch Orthop Trauma Surg. 2008 Aug;128(8):879-84. Epub 2008 Jun 17.
161. Kuo YR, Wang CT, Wang FS, Chiang YC, Wang CJ. Extracorporeal shock-wave therapy enhanced wound healing via increasing topical blood perfusion and tissue regeneration in a rat model of STZ-induced diabetes. Wound Repair Regen. 2009 Jul-Aug;17(4):522-30.
162. Wang CJ, Yang YJ, Huang CC. The effects of shockwave on systemic concentrations of nitric oxide level, angiogenesis and osteogenesis factors
163. Wang CJ, Hsu SL, Weng LH, Sun YC, Wang FS. Extracorporeal shockwave therapy shows a number of treatment related chondroprotective effect in osteoarthritis of the knee in rats. BMC Musculoskelet Disord. 2013 Jan 28;14:44.
164. Mariotto S, de Prati AC, Cavalieri E, Amelio E, Marlinghaus E, Suzuki H. Extracorporeal shock wave therapy in inflammatory diseases: molecular mechanism that triggers anti-inflammatory action. Curr Med Chem. 2009;16(19):2366-72.
165. Fu M, Sun CK, Lin YC, Wang CJ, Wu CJ, Ko SF, Chua S, Sheu JJ, Chiang CH, Shao PL, Leu S, Yip HK. Extracorporeal shock wave therapy reverses ischemia-related left ventricular dysfunction and remodeling: molecular-cellular and functional assessment. PLoS One. 2011;6(9):e24342. Epub 2011 Sep 6.
166. Wang CJ. Extracorporeal shockwave therapy in musculoskeletal disorders. J Orthop Surg Res. 2012 Mar 20;7:11.
167. Abe Y, Ito K, Hao K, Shindo T, Ogata T, Kagaya Y, Kurosawa R, Nishimiya K, Satoh K, Miyata S, Kawakami K, Shimokawa H. Extracorporeal low-energy shock-wave therapy exerts anti-inflammatory effects in a rat model of acute myocardial infarction. Circ J. 2014;78(12):2915-25. Epub 2014 Oct 2.
168. Yu TC, Liu Y, Tan Y, Jiang Y, Zheng X, Xu X. Shock waves increase T-cell proliferation or IL-2 expression by activating p38 MAP kinase. Acta Biochim Biophys Sin (Shanghai). 2004 Nov;36(11):741-8.
169. Chen YJ, Wurtz T, Wang CJ, Kuo YR, Yang KD, Huang HC, Wang FS. Recruitment of mesenchymal stem cells and expression of TGF-beta 1 and VEGF in the early stage of shock wave-promoted bone regeneration of segmental defect in rats. J Orthop Res. 2004 May;22(3):526-34.
170. Wang FS, Yang KD, Chen RF, Wang CJ, Sheen-Chen SM. Extracorporeal shock wave promotes growth and differentiation of bone-marrow stromal cells towards osteoprogenitors associated with induction of TGF-beta1. J Bone Joint Surg Br. 2002 Apr;84(3):457-61.
171. Wang FS, Yang KD, Kuo YR, Wang CJ, Sheen-Chen SM, Huang HC, Chen YJ. Temporal and spatial expression of bone morphogenetic proteins in extracorporeal shock wave-promoted healing of segmental defect. Bone. 2003 Apr;32(4):387-96.
172. Wang CJ, Wang FS, Ko JY, Huang HY, Chen CJ, Sun YC, Yang YJ. Extracorporeal shockwave therapy shows regeneration in hip necrosis. Rheumatology (Oxford). 2008 Apr;47(4):542-6.
173. Wang CJ, Sun YC, Wu CT, Weng LH, Wang FS. Molecular changes after shockwave therapy in osteoarthritic knee in rats. Shock Waves. 2016;26(1):45-51.

216

Bibliography

174. Wang CJ, Sun YC, Siu KK, Wu CT. Extracorporeal shockwave therapy shows site-specific effects in osteoarthritis of the knee in rats. J Surg Res. 2013 Aug;183(2):612-9. Epub 2013 Feb 26.35. Takahashi K, Yamazaki M, Saisu T, Nakajima A, Shimizu S, Mitsuhashi S, Moriya H. Gene expression for extracellular matrix proteins in shockwave-induced osteogenesis in rats. Calcif Tissue Int. 2004 Feb;74(2):187-93. Epub 2003 Nov 6.
175. Sun D, Junger WG, Yuan C, Zhang W, Bao Y, Qin D, Wang C, Tan L, Qi B, Zhu D, Zhang X, Yu T. Shockwaves induce osteogenic differentiation of human mesenchymal stem cells through ATP release and activation of P2X7 receptors. Stem Cells. 2013 Jun;31(6):1170-80.
176. Maier M, Averbeck B, Milz S, Refior HJ, Schmitz C. Substance P and prostaglandin E2 release after shock wave application to the rabbit femur. Clin Orthop Relat Res. 2003 Jan;406:237-45.
177. Yuen CM, Chung SY, Tsai TH, Sung PH, Huang TH, Chen YL, Chen YL, Chai HT, Zhen YY, Chang MW, Wang CJ, Chang HW, Sun CK, Yip HK. Extracorporeal shock wave effectively attenuates brain infarct volume and improves neurological function in rat after acute ischemic stroke. Am J Transl Res. 2015 Jun 15;7(6):976-94.
178. Ochiai N, Ohtori S, Sasho T, Nakagawa K, Takahashi K, Takahashi N, Murata R, Takahashi K, Moriya H, Wada Y, Saisu T. Extracorporeal shock wave therapy improves motor dysfunction and pain originating from knee osteoarthritis in rats. Osteoarthritis Cartilage. 2007 Sep;15(9):1093-6. Epub 2007 Apr 26.
179. Hu J, Liao H, Ma Z, Chen H, Huang Z, Zhang Y, Yu M, Chen Y, Xu J. Focal adhesion kinase signaling mediated the enhancement of osteogenesis of human mesenchymal stem cells induced by extracorporeal shockwave. Sci Rep. 2016 Feb 11;6:20875.
180. Wang CJ, Huang KE, Sun YC, Yang YJ, Ko JY, Weng LH, Wang FS. VEGF modulates angiogenesis and osteogenesis in shockwave-promoted fracture healing in rabbits. J Surg Res. 2011 Nov;171(1):114-9. Epub 2010 Feb 21.
181. Sun CK, Shao PL, Wang CJ, Yip HK. Study of vascular injuries using endothelial denudation model and the therapeutic application of shock wave: a review. Am J Transl Res. 2011 May 15;3(3):259-68. Epub 2011 Apr 8.
182. Yamaya S, Ozawa H, Kanno H, Kishimoto KN, Sekiguchi A, Tateda S, Yahata K, Ito K, Shimokawa H, Itoi E. Low-energy extracorporeal shock wave therapy promotes vascular endothelial growth factor expression and improves locomotor recovery after spinal cord injury. J Neurosurg. 2014 Dec;121(6):1514-25. Epub 2014 Oct 3.
183. Holfeld J, Tepeköylü C, Kozaryn R, Mathes W, Grimm M, Paulus P. Shock wave application to cell cultures. J Vis Exp. 2014 Apr 8;(86).
184. Holfeld J, Tepeköylü C, Blunder S, Lobenwein D, Kirchmair E, Dietl M, Kozaryn R, Lener D, Theurl M, Paulus P, Kirchmair R, Grimm M. Low energy shock wave therapy induces angiogenesis in acute hind-limb ischemia via VEGF receptor 2 phosphorylation. PLoS One. 2014 Aug 5;9(8):e103982.
185. Ciampa AR, de Prati AC, Amelio E, Cavalieri E, Persichini T, Colasanti M, Musci G, Marlinghaus E, Suzuki H, Mariotto S. Nitric oxide mediates anti-inflammatory action of extracorporeal shock waves. FEBS Lett. 2005 Dec 19;579(30):6839-45. Epub 2005 Nov 28.
186. Chen YL, Chen KH, Yin TC, Huang TH, Yuen CM, Chung SY, Sung PH, Tong MS, Chen CH, Chang HW, Lin KC, Ko SF, Yip HK. Extracorporeal shock wave therapy effectively prevented diabetic neuropathy. Am J Transl Res. 2015 Dec 15;7(12):2543-60.
187. Waugh CM, Morrissey D, Jones E, Riley GP, Langberg H, Screen HR. In vivo biological response to extracorporeal shockwave therapy in human tendinopathy. Eur Cell Mater. 2015 May 15;29:268-80, discussion :280.
188. Han SH, Lee JW, Guyton GP, Parks BG, Courneya JP, Schon LCJJ. J.Leonard Goldner Award 2008. Effect of extracorporeal shock wave therapy on cultured tenocytes. Foot Ankle Int. 2009 Feb;30(2):93-8.
189. Dias dos Santos PR, De Medeiros VP, Freire Martins de Moura JP, da Silveira Franciozi CE, Nader HB, Faloppa F. Effects of shock wave therapy on glycosaminoglycan expression during bone healing. Int J Surg. 2015 Dec;24(Pt B):120-3. Epub 2015 Sep 30.
190. Schuh CM, Hercher D, Stainer M, Hopf R, Teuschl AH, Schmidhammer R, Redl H. Extracorporeal shockwave treatment: a novel tool to improve Schwann cell isolation and culture. Cytotherapy. 2016 Jun;18(6):760-70. Epub 2016 Apr 5
191. Murata R, Ohtori S, Ochiai N, Takahashi N, Saisu T, Moriya H, Takahashi K, Wada Y. Extracorporeal shockwaves induce the expression of ATF3 and GAP-43 in rat dorsal root ganglion neurons. Auton Neurosci. 2006 Jul 30;128(1-2):96-100. Epub 2006 May 23.
192. International Society for Medical Shockwave Treatment. Consensus statement on ESWT indications and contraindications. https://www.shockwavetherapy.org/fileadmin/user_upload/dokumente/PDFs/Formul are/ISMST_consensus_statement_on_indications_and_contraindications_20161012_final.pdf. Accessed 2017 Nov 6.
193. Gärtner J, Simons B. Analysis of calcific deposits in calcifying tendinitis. Clin Orthop Relat Res. 1990 May;254:111-20.
194. Moya D, Ramón S, Guiloff L, Gerdesmeyer L. Current knowledge on evidence-based shockwave treatments for shoulder pathology. Int J Surg. 2015 Dec;24(Pt B):171-8. Epub 2015 Sep 9.
195. Albert JD, Meadeb J, Guggenbuhl P, Marin F, Benkalfate T, Thomazeau H, Chalès G. High-energy extracorporeal shock-wave therapy for calcifying tendinitis of the rotator cuff: a randomised trial. J Bone Joint Surg Br. 2007 Mar;89(3):335-41.
196. Cacchio A, Paoloni M, Barile A, Don R, de Paulis F, Calvisi V, Ranavolo A, Frascarelli M, Santilli V, Spacca G. Effectiveness of radial shock-wave therapy for calcific tendinitis of the shoulder: single-blind, randomized clinical study. Phys Ther. 2006 May;86(5):672-82.

Bibliography

197. Gerdesmeyer L, Wagenpfeil S, Haake M, Maier M, Loew M, Wörtler K, Lampe R, Seil R, Handle G, Gassel S, Rompe JD. Extracorporeal shock wave therapy for the treatment of chronic calcifying tendonitis of the rotator cuff: a randomized controlled trial. JAMA. 2003 Nov 19;290(19):2573-80.
198. Cosentino R, De Stefano R, Selvi E, Frati E, Manca S, Frediani B, Marcolongo R. Extracorporeal shock wave therapy for chronic calcific tendinitis of the shoulder: single blind study. Ann Rheum Dis. 2003 Mar;62(3):248-50.
199. Hsu CJ, Wang DY, Tseng KF, Fong YC, Hsu HC, Jim YF. Extracorporeal shock wave therapy for calcifying tendinitis of the shoulder. J Shoulder Elbow Surg. 2008 Jan-Feb;17(1):55-9.
200. Ioppolo F, Tattoli M, Di Sante L, Venditto T, Tognolo L, Delicata M, Rizzo RS, Di Tanna G, Santilli V. Clinical improvement and resorption of calcifications in calcific tendinitis of the shoulder after shock wave therapy at 6 months' follow-up: a systematic review and meta-analysis. Arch Phys Med Rehabil. 2013 Sep;94(9):1699-706. Epub 2013 Mar 13.
201. Bannuru RR, Flavin NE, Vaysbrot E, Harvey W, McAlindon T. High-energy extracorporeal shock-wave therapy for treating chronic calcific tendinitis of the shoulder: a systematic review. Ann Intern Med. 2014 Apr 15;160(8):542-9.
202. Huisstede BM, Gebremariam L, van der Sande R, Hay EM, Koes BW. Evidence for effectiveness of extracorporeal shock-wave therapy (ESWT) to treat calcific and non-calcific rotator cuff tendinosis—a systematic review. Man Ther. 2011 Oct;16(5):419-33. Epub 2011 Mar 10.
203. Louwerens JK, Sierevelt IN, van Noort A, van den Bekerom MP. Evidence for minimally invasive therapies in the management of chronic calcific tendinopathy of the rotator cuff: a systematic review and meta-analysis. J Shoulder Elbow Surg. 2014 Aug;23(8):1240-9. Epub 2014 Apr 26.
204. Speed C. A systematic review of shockwave therapies in soft tissue conditions: focusing on the evidence. Br J Sports Med. 2014 Nov;48(21):1538-42. Epub 2013 Aug 5.
205. Verstraelen FU, In den Kleef NJ, Jansen L, Morrenhof JW. High-energy versus low-energy extracorporeal shock wave therapy for calcifying tendinitis of the shoulder: which is superior? A meta-analysis. Clin Orthop Relat Res. 2014 Sep;472(9):2816-25. Epub 2014 May 29.
206. Kim YS, Lee HJ, Kim YV, Kong CG. Which method is more effective in treatment of calcific tendinitis in the shoulder? Prospective randomized comparison between ultrasound-guided needling and extracorporeal shock wave therapy. J Shoulder Elbow Surg. 2014 Nov;23(11):1640-6. Epub 2014 Sep 12.
207. Moya D, Ramón S, d'Agostino MC, Leal C, Aranzabal JR, Eid J, Schaden W. Incorrect methodology may favor ultrasound-guided needling over shock wave treatment in calcific tendinopathy of the shoulder. J Shoulder Elbow Surg. 2016 Aug;25(8):e241-3.
208. Rompe JD, Zoellner J, Nafe B. Shock wave therapy versus conventional surgery in the treatment of calcifying tendinitis of the shoulder. Clin Orthop Relat Res. 2001 Jun;387:72-82.
209. Rebuzzi E, Coletti N, Schiavetti S, Giusto F. Arthroscopy surgery versus shock wave therapy for chronic calcifying tendinitis of the shoulder. J Orthop Traumatol. 2008 Dec;9(4):179-85. Epub 2008 Aug 8.
210. Speed CA, Richards C, Nichols D, Burnet S, Wies JT, Humphreys H, Hazleman BL. Extracorporeal shock-wave therapy for tendonitis of the rotator cuff. A double-blind, randomised, controlled trial. J Bone Joint Surg Br. 2002 May;84(4):509-12.
211. Engebretsen K, Grotle M, Bautz-Holter E, Ekeberg OM, Juel NG, Brox JI. Supervised exercises compared with radial extracorporeal shock-wave therapy for subacromial shoulder pain: 1-year results of a single-blind randomized controlled trial. Phys Ther. 2011 Jan;91(1):37-47. Epub 2010 Nov 18.
212. Zhang JY, Fabricant PD, Ishmael CR, Wang JC, Petrigliano FA, Jones KJ. Utilization of platelet-rich plasma for musculoskeletal injuries: an analysis of current treatment trends in the United States. Orthop J Sports Med. 2016 Dec 21;4(12):2325967116676241.
213. Buchbinder R, Johnston RV, Barnsley L, Assendelft WJJ, Bell SN, Smidt N. Surgery for lateral elbow pain. Cochrane Database Syst Rev. 2011 Mar 16;3:CD003525.
214. Green S, Buchbinder R, Barnsley L, Hall S, White M, Smidt N, Assendelft W. Acupuncture for lateral elbow pain. Cochrane Database Syst Rev. 2002;1:CD003527.
215. Krogh TP, Bartels EM, Ellingsen T, Stengaard-Pedersen K, Buchbinder R, Fredberg U, Bliddal H, Christensen R. Comparative effectiveness of injection therapies in lateral epicondylitis: a systematic review and network meta-analysis of randomized controlled trials. Am J Sports Med. 2013 Jun;41(6):1435-46. Epub 2012 Sep 12.
216. Loew LM, Brosseau L, Tugwell P, Wells GA, Welch V, Shea B, Poitras S, De Angelis G, Rahman P. Deep transverse friction massage for treating lateral elbow or lateral knee tendinitis. Cochrane Database Syst Rev. 2014 Nov 8;11:CD003528.
217. Silagy M, O'Bryan E, Johnston RV, Buchbinder R. Autologous blood and platelet rich plasma injection therapy for lateral elbow pain. Cochrane Database Syst Rev. 2014;2:CD010951.
218. Speed CA, Nichols D, Richards C, Humphreys H, Wies JT, Burnet S, Hazleman BL. Extracorporeal shock wave therapy for lateral epicondylitis—a double blind randomised controlled trial. J Orthop Res. 2002 Sep;20(5):895-8.
219. Thiele S, Thiele R, Gerdesmeyer L. Lateral epicondylitis: this is still a main indication for extracorporeal shockwave therapy. Int J Surg. 2015 Dec;24(Pt B):165-70. Epub 2015 Oct 9.
220. Sims SE, Miller K, Elfar JC, Hammert WC. Non-surgical treatment of lateral epicondylitis: a systematic review of randomized controlled trials. Hand (N Y). 2014 Dec;9(4):419-46.
221. Buchbinder R, Green SE, Youd JM, Assendelft WJ, Barnsley L, Smidt N. Shock wave therapy for lateral elbow pain. Cochrane Database Syst Rev. 2005 Oct 19;4:CD003524.

Bibliography

222. Dingemanse R, Randsdorp M, Koes BW, Huisstede BM. Evidence for the effectiveness of electrophysical modalities for treatment of medial and lateral epicondylitis: a systematic review. Br J Sports Med. 2014 Jun;48(12):957-65. Epub 2013 Jan 18.
223. Rompe JD, Maffulli N. Repetitive shock wave therapy for lateral elbow tendinopathy (tennis elbow): a systematic and qualitative analysis. Br Med Bull. 2007;83:355-78. Epub 2007 Jul 11.
224. Pettrone FA, McCall BR. Extracorporeal shock wave therapy without local anesthesia for chronic lateral epicondylitis. J Bone Joint Surg Am. 2005 Jun;87(6):1297-304.
225. Lee SS, Kang S, Park NK, Lee CW, Song HS, Sohn MK, Cho KH, Kim JH. Effectiveness of initial extracorporeal shock wave therapy on the newly diagnosed lateral or medial epicondylitis. Ann Rehabil Med. 2012 Oct;36(5):681-7. Epub 2012 Oct 31.
226. Radwan YA, ElSobhi G, Badawy WS, Reda A, Khalid S. Resistant tennis elbow: shock-wave therapy versus percutaneous tenotomy. Int Orthop. 2008 Oct;32(5):671-7. Epub 2007 Jun 6.
227. Rompe JD, Segal NA, Cacchio A, Furia JP, Morral A, Maffulli N. Home training, local corticosteroid injection, or radial shock wave therapy for greater trochanter pain syndrome. Am J Sports Med. 2009 Oct;37(10):1981-90. Epub 2009 May 13.
228. Furia JP, Rompe JD, Maffulli N. Low-energy extracorporeal shock wave therapy as a treatment for greater trochanteric pain syndrome. Am J Sports Med. 2009 Sep;37(9):1806-13. Epub 2009 May 13.
229. Mani-Babu S, Morrissey D, Waugh C, Screen H, Barton C. The effectiveness of extracorporeal shock wave therapy in lower limb tendinopathy: a systematic review. Am J Sports Med. 2015 Mar;43(3):752-61. Epub 2014 May 9.
230. Leal C, Ramon S, Furia J, Fernandez A, Romero L, Hernandez-Sierra L. Current concepts of shockwave therapy in chronic patellar tendinopathy. Int J Surg. 2015 Dec;24(Pt B):160-4. Epub 2015 Oct 9.
231. Figueroa D, Figueroa F, Calvo R. Patellar tendinopathy: diagnosis and treatment. J Am Acad Orthop Surg. 2016 Dec;24(12):e184-92.
232. Gaida JE, Cook J. Treatment options for patellar tendinopathy: critical review. Curr Sports Med Rep. 2011 Sep-Oct;10(5):255-70.
233. Larsson ME, Käll I, Nilsson-Helander K. Treatment of patellar tendinopathy—a systematic review of randomized controlled trials. Knee Surg Sports Traumatol Arthrosc. 2012 Aug;20(8):1632-46. Epub 2011 Dec 21.
234. Visnes H, Bahr R. The evolution of eccentric training as treatment for patellar tendinopathy (jumper's knee): a critical review of exercise programmes. Br J Sports Med. 2007 Apr;41(4):217-23. Epub 2007 Jan 29.
235. Wang CJ, Ko JY, Chan YS, Weng LH, Hsu SL. Extracorporeal shockwave for chronic patellar tendinopathy. Am J Sports Med. 2007 Jun;35(6):972-8. Epub 2007 Feb 16.
236. Furia JP, Rompe JD, Cacchio A, Del Buono A, Maffulli N. A single application of low-energy radial extracorporeal shock wave therapy is effective for the management of chronic patellar tendinopathy. Knee Surg Sports Traumatol Arthrosc. 2013 Feb;21(2):346-50. Epub 2012 May 25.
237. Everhart JS, Cole D, Sojka JH, Higgins JD, Magnussen RA, Schmitt LC, Flanigan DC. Treatment options for patellar tendinopathy: a systematic review. Arthroscopy. 2017 Apr;33(4):861-72. Epub 2017 Jan 16.
238. Peers KH, Lysens RJJ, Brys P, Bellemans J. Cross-sectional outcome analysis of athletes with chronic patellar tendinopathy treated surgically and by extracorporeal shock wave therapy. Clin J Sport Med. 2003 Mar;13(2):79-83.
239. Vulpiani MC, Vetrano M, Savoia V, Di Pangrazio E, Trischitta D, Ferretti A. Jumper's knee treatment with extracorporeal shock wave therapy: a long-term follow-up observational study. J Sports Med Phys Fitness. 2007 Sep;47(3):323-8.
240. Zwerver J, Hartgens F, Verhagen E, van der Worp H, van den Akker-Scheek I, Diercks RL. No effect of extracorporeal shockwave therapy on patellar tendinopathy in jumping athletes during the competitive season: a randomized clinical trial. Am J Sports Med. 2011 Jun;39(6):1191-9. Epub 2011 Feb 1.
241. Thijs KM, Zwerver J, Backx FJ, Steeneken V, Rayer S, Groenenboom P, Moen MH. Effectiveness of shockwave treatment combined with eccentric training for patellar tendinopathy: a double-blinded randomized st
242. Järvinen TA, Kannus P, Maffulli N, Khan KM. Achilles tendon disorders: etiology and epidemiology. Foot Ankle Clin. 2005 Jun;10(2):255-66.
243. Alfredson H, Cook J. A treatment algorithm for managing Achilles tendinopathy: new treatment options. Br J Sports Med. 2007 Apr;41(4):211-6. Epub 2007 Feb 20.
244. Scott A, Huisman E, Khan K. Conservative treatment of chronic Achilles tendinopathy. CMAJ. 2011 Jul 12;183(10):1159-65. Epub 2011 Jun 13.
245. Rowe V, Hemmings S, Barton C, Malliaras P, Maffulli N, Morrissey D. Conservative management of midportion Achilles tendinopathy: a mixed methods study, integrating systematic review and clinical reasoning. Sports Med. 2012 Nov 1;42(11):941-67.
246. Kearney RS, Parsons N, Costa ML. Achilles tendinopathy management: A pilot randomised controlled trial comparing platelet-richplasma injection with an eccentric loading programme. Bone Joint Res. 2013 Oct 17;2(10):227-32.108. Gerdesmeyer L, Mittermayr R, Fuerst M, Al Muderis M, Thiele R, Saxena A, Gollwitzer H. Current evidence of extracorporeal shock wave therapy in chronic Achilles tendinopathy. Int J Surg. 2015 Dec;24(Pt B):154-9. Epub 2015 Aug 29.
247. Costa ML, Shepstone L, Donell ST, Thomas TL. Shock wave therapy for chronic Achilles tendon pain: a randomized placebo-controlled trial. Clin Orthop Relat Res. 2005 Nov;440:199-204.
248. Rasmussen S, Christensen M, Mathiesen I, Simonson O. Shockwave therapy for chronic Achilles tendinopathy: a double-blind, randomized clinical trial of efficacy. Acta Orthop. 2008 Apr;79(2):249-56.

Bibliography

249. Furia JP. High-energy extracorporeal shock wave therapy as a treatment for insertional Achilles tendinopathy. Am J Sports Med. 2006 May;34(5):733-40.
250. Furia JP. High-energy extracorporeal shock wave therapy as a treatment for chronic noninsertional Achilles tendinopathy. Am J Sports Med. 2008 Mar;36(3):502-8. Epub 2007 Nov 15.
251. Rompe JD, Furia J, Maffulli N. Eccentric loading compared with shock wave treatment for chronic insertional Achilles tendinopathy. A randomized, controlled trial. J Bone Joint Surg Am. 2008 Jan;90(1):52-61.
252. Rompe JD, Furia J, Maffulli N. Eccentric loading versus eccentric loading plus shock-wave treatment for midportion Achilles tendinopathy: a randomized controlled trial. Am J Sports Med. 2009 Mar;37(3):463-70. Epub 2008 Dec 15.
253. Al-Abbad H, Simon JV. The effectiveness of extracorporeal shock wave therapy on chronic Achilles tendinopathy: a systematic review. Foot Ankle Int. 2013 Jan;34(1):33-41.
254. Kearney R, Costa ML. Insertional Achilles tendinopathy management: a systematic review. Foot Ankle Int. 2010 Aug;31(8):689-94.
255. Roche AJ, Calder JD. Achilles tendinopathy: a review of the current concepts of treatment. Bone Joint J. 2013 Oct;95-B(10):1299-307.
256. Lemont H, Ammirati KM, Usen N. Plantar fasciitis: a degenerative process (fasciosis) without inflammation. J Am Podiatr Med Assoc. 2003 May-Jun;93(3):234-7.
257. Buchbinder R, Ptasznik R, Gordon J, Buchanan J, Prabaharan V, Forbes A. Ultrasound-guided extracorporeal shock wave therapy for plantar fasciitis: a randomized controlled trial. JAMA. 2002 Sep 18;288(11):1364-72.
258. Haake M, Buch M, Schoellner C, Goebel F, Vogel M, Mueller I, Hausdorf J, Zamzow K, Schade-Brittinger C, Mueller HH. Extracorporeal shock wave therapy for plantar fasciitis: randomised controlled multicentre trial. BMJ. 2003 Jul 12;327(7406):75.
259. Chuckpaiwong B, Berkson EM, Theodore GH. Extracorporeal shock wave for chronic proximal plantar fasciitis: 225 patients with results and outcome predictors. J Foot Ankle Surg. 2009 Mar-Apr;48(2):148-55. Epub 2009 Jan 9.
260. Wang CJ, Wang FS, Yang KD, Weng LH, Ko JY. Long-term results of extracorporeal shockwave treatment for plantar fasciitis. Am J Sports Med. 2006 Apr;34(4):592-6.
261. . Gerdesmeyer L, Frey C, Vester J, Maier M, Weil L Jr, Weil L Sr, Russlies M, Stienstra J, Scurran B, Fedder K, Diehl P, Lohrer H, Henne M, Gollwitzer H. Radial extracorporeal shock wave therapy is safe and effective in the treatment of chronic recalcitrant plantar fasciitis: results of a confirmatory randomized placebo-controlled multicenter study. Am J Sports Med. 2008 Nov;36(11):2100-9. Epub 2008 Oct 1.
262. Ibrahim MI, Donatelli RA, Schmitz C, Hellman MA, Buxbaum F. Chronic plantar fasciitis treated with two sessions of radial extracorporeal shock wave therapy. Foot Ankle Int. 2010 May;31(5):391-7.
263. Gollwitzer H, Saxena A, DiDomenico LA, Galli L, Bouché RT, Caminear DS, Fullem B, Vester JC, Horn C, Banke IJ, Burgkart R, Gerdesmeyer L. Clinically relevant effectiveness of focused extracorporeal shock wave therapy in the treatment of chronic plantar fasciitis: a randomized, controlled multicenter study. J Bone Joint Surg Am. 2015 May 6;97(9):701-8.
264. Ogden JA, Alvarez RG, Levitt RL, Johnson JE, Marlow ME. Electrohydraulic high-energy shock-wave treatment for chronic plantar fasciitis. J Bone Joint Surg Am. 2004 Oct;86(10):2216-28.
265. Rompe JD, Furia J, Cacchio A, Schmitz C, Maffulli N. Radial shock wave treatment alone is less efficient than radial shock wave treatment combined with tissue-specific plantar fascia-stretching in patients with chronic plantar heel pain. Int J Surg. 2015 Dec;24(Pt B):135-42. Epub 2015 May 1.
266. Aqil A, Siddiqui MRS, Solan M, Redfern DJ, Gulati V, Cobb JP. Extracorporeal shock wave therapy is effective in treating chronic plantar fasciitis: a meta-analysis of RCTs. Clin Orthop Relat Res. 2013 Nov;471(11):3645-52. Epub 2013 Jun 28.
267. Chang KV, Chen SY, Chen WS, Tu YK, Chien KL. Comparative effectiveness of focused shock wave therapy of different intensity levels and radial shock wave therapy for treating plantar fasciitis: a systematic review and network meta-analysis. Arch Phys Med Rehabil. 2012 Jul;93(7):1259-68. Epub 2012 Mar 12.
268. Dizon JN, Gonzalez-Suarez C, Zamora MT, Gambito ED. Effectiveness of extracorporeal shock wave therapy in chronic plantar fasciitis: a meta-analysis. Am J Phys Med Rehabil. 2013 Jul;92(7):606-20.
269. Othman AM, Ragab EM. Endoscopic plantar fasciotomy versus extracorporeal shock wave therapy for treatment of chronic plantar fasciitis. Arch Orthop Trauma Surg. 2010 Nov;130(11):1343-7. Epub 2009 Dec 24.
270. Radwan YA, Mansour AM, Badawy WS. Resistant plantar fasciopathy: shock wave versus endoscopic plantar fascial release. Int Orthop. 2012 Oct;36(10):2147-56. Epub 2012 Jul 11.
271. Saxena A, Fournier M, Gerdesmeyer L, Gollwitzer H. Comparison between extracorporeal shockwave therapy, placebo ESWT and endoscopic plantar fasciotomy for the treatment of chronic plantar heel pain in the athlete. Muscles Ligaments Tendons J. 2013 Jan 21;2(4):312-6.134. Weil LS Jr, Roukis TS, Weil LS, Borrelli AH. Extracorporeal shock wave therapy for the treatment of chronic plantar fasciitis: indications, protocol, intermediate results, and a comparison of results to fasciotomy. J Foot Ankle Surg. 2002 May-Jun;41(3):166-72.
272. Thomas JL, Christensen JC, Kravitz SR, Mendicino RW, Schuberth JM, Vanore JV, Weil LS Sr, Zlotoff HJ, Bouché R, Baker J; American College of Foot and Ankle Surgeons Heel Pain Committee. The diagnosis and treatment of heel pain: a clinical practice guideline-revision 2010. J Foot Ankle Surg. 2010 May-Jun;49(3)(Suppl):S1-19.

Bibliography

273. Wang FS, Wang CJ, Chen YJ, Chang PR, Huang YT, Sun YC, Huang HC, Yang YJ, Yang KD. Ras induction of superoxide activates ERK-dependent angiogenic transcription factor HIF-1alpha and VEGF-A expression in shock wave-stimulated osteoblasts. J Biol Chem. 2004 Mar 12;279(11):10331-7. Epub 2003 Dec 16.
274. Chen YJ, Kuo YR, Yang KD, Wang CJ, Sheen Chen SM, Huang HC, Yang YJ, Yi-Chih S, Wang FS. Activation of extracellular signal-regulated kinase (ERK) and p38 kinase in shock wave-promoted bone formation of segmental defect in rats. Bone. 2004 Mar;34(3):466-77.
275. Ha CH, Kim S, Chung J, An SH, Kwon K. Extracorporeal shock wave stimulates expression of the angiogenic genes via mechanosensory complex in endothelial cells: mimetic effect of fluid shear stress in endothelial cells. Int J Cardiol. 2013 Oct 9;168(4):4168-77. Epub 2013 Aug 1.
276. Wang CJ, Yang KD, Ko JY, Huang CC, Huang HY, Wang FS. The effects of shockwave on bone healing and systemic concentrations of nitric oxide (NO), TGF-beta1, VEGF and BMP-2 in long bone non-unions. Nitric Oxide. 2009 Jun;20(4):298-303. Epub 2009 Mar 10.
277. Gerdesmeyer L, Schaden W, Besch L, Stukenberg M, Doerner L, Muehlhofer H, Toepfer A. Osteogenetic effect of extracorporeal shock waves in human. Int J Surg. 2015 Dec;24(Pt B):115-9. Epub 2015 Oct 9.
278. Ingber DE. Cellular mechanotransduction: putting all the pieces together again. FASEB J. 2006 May;20(7):811-27.
279. Valchanou VD, Michailov P. High energy shock waves in the treatment of delayed and nonunion of fractures. Int Orthop. 1991;15(3):181-4.143. Beutler S, Regel G, Pape HC, Machtens S, Weinberg AM, Kremeike I, Jonas U, Tscherne H. [Extracorporeal shock wave therapy for delayed union of long bone fractures - preliminary results of a prospective cohort study]. Unfallchirurg. 1999 Nov;102(11):839-47. German.
280. Rompe JD, Rosendahl T, Schöllner C, Theis C. High-energy extracorporeal shock wave treatment of nonunions. Clin Orthop Relat Res. 2001 Jun;387:102-11.
281. Wang CJ, Chen HS, Chen CE, Yang KD. Treatment of nonunions of long bone fractures with shock waves. Clin Orthop Relat Res. 2001 Jun;387:95-101.
282. Schaden W, Fischer A, Sailler A. Extracorporeal shock wave therapy of nonunion or delayed osseous union. Clin Orthop Relat Res. 2001 Jun;387:90-4.
283. Wang CJ, Liu HC, Fu TH. The effects of extracorporeal shockwave on acute high-energy long bone fractures of the lower extremity. Arch Orthop Trauma Surg. 2007 Feb;127(2):137-42. Epub 2006 Oct 13.
284. Bara T, Synder M. Nine-years experience with the use of shock waves for treatment of bone union disturbances. Ortop Traumatol Rehabil. 2007 May-Jun;9(3):254-8.149. Xu ZH, Jiang Q, Chen DY, Xiong J, Shi DQ, Yuan T, Zhu XL. Extracorporeal shock wave treatment in nonunions of long bone fractures. Int Orthop. 2009 Jun;33(3):789-93. Epub 2008 Apr 25.
285. Elster EA, Stojadinovic A, Forsberg J, Shawen S, Andersen RC, Schaden W. Extracorporeal shock wave therapy for nonunion of the tibia. J Orthop Trauma. 2010 Mar;24(3):133-41.
286. Zelle BA, Gollwitzer H, Zlowodzki M, Bühren V. Extracorporeal shock wave therapy: current evidence. J Orthop Trauma. 2010 Mar;24(Suppl 1):S66-70.
287. Cacchio A, Giordano L, Colafarina O, Rompe JD, Tavernese E, Ioppolo F, Flamini S, Spacca G, Santilli V. Extracorporeal shock-wave therapy compared with surgery for hypertrophic long-bone nonunions. J Bone Joint Surg Am. 2009 Nov;91(11):2589-97.
288. Furia JP, Rompe JD, Cacchio A, Maffulli N. Shock wave therapy as a treatment of nonunions, avascular necrosis, and delayed healing of stress fractures. Foot Ankle Clin. 2010 Dec;15(4):651-62
289. . Furia JP, Juliano PJ, Wade AM, Schaden W, Mittermayr R. Shock wave therapy compared with intramedullary screw fixation for nonunion of proximal fifth metatarsal metaphyseal-diaphyseal fractures. J Bone Joint Surg Am. 2010 Apr;92(4):846-54.
290. Notarnicola A, Moretti L, Tafuri S, Gigliotti S, Russo S, Musci L, Moretti B. Extracorporeal shockwaves versus surgery in the treatment of pseudoarthrosis of the carpal scaphoid. Ultrasound Med Biol. 2010 Aug;36(8):1306-13.
291. Kuo SJ, Su IC, Wang CJ, Ko JY. Extracorporeal shockwave therapy (ESWT) in the treatment of atrophic non-unions of femoral shaft fractures. Int J Surg. 2015 Dec;24(Pt B):131-4. Epub 2015 Jul 9.
292. Schaden W, Mittermayr R, Haffner N, Smolen D, Gerdesmeyer L, Wang CJ. Extracorporeal shockwave therapy (ESWT)—first choice treatment of fracture non-unions? Int J Surg. 2015 Dec;24(Pt B):179-83. Epub 2015 Oct 9.
293. Lyon R, Liu XC, Kubin M, Schwab J. Does extracorporeal shock wave therapy enhance healing of osteochondritis dissecans of the rabbit knee. a pilot study. Clin Orthop Relat Res. 2013 Apr;471(4):1159-65.
294. Moretti B, Notarnicola A, Moretti L, Giordano P, Patella V. A volleyball player with bilateral knee osteochondritis dissecans treated with extracorporeal shock wave therapy. Chir Organi Mov. 2009 May;93(1):37-41. Epub 2009 Apr 28.
295. Thiele S, Thiele R, Gerdesmeyer L. Adult osteochondritis dissecans and focussed ESWT: a successful treatment option. Int J Surg. 2015 Dec;24(Pt B):191-4. Epub 2015 Oct 9.
296. Dubs B. Efficacy and economical aspects: comparison ESWT versus alternate therapies in the treatment of calcifying tendinitis. Read at the 6th International Congress of the International Society for Musculoskeletal Shockwave Therapy;; 2003; Orlando, Florida.
297. Haake M, Rautmann M, Wirth T. Assessment of the treatment costs of extracorporeal shock wave therapy versus surgical treatment for shoulder diseases. Int J Technol Assess Health Care. 2001 Fall;17(4):612-7.

Bibliography

298. Ramón S, Moya D, Alvarez P, Cugat R, Corbella X. Efficiency in treatment of calcifying tendinopathy of the shoulder: extracorporeal shockwave therapy vs. surgery. Read at the 13th International Congress of Shoulder and Elbow Surgery; 2016 May 18-20; Jeju, Korea.
299. Wright JG. Revised grades of recommendation for summaries or reviews of orthopaedic surgical studies. J Bone Joint Surg Am. 2006 May;88(5):1161-2.
300. Lingshu, Jing. *Classic of the Miraculous Pivot*. Shi Song of the Southern Song Dynasty. 1155.
301. Wu, Jing Nuan. *Lingshu or the Spiritual Pivot*. University of Hawaii Press.. 2002.
302. Xinnong, Cheng. *Chinese Acupuncture and Moxibustion*. Foreign Language Press Beijing.1999.
303. Amaro, John A. *When the student is ready the teacher shall appear*. Dynamic Chiropractic 1992.
304. Maashing, Ni. *The Yellow Emperors Inner Classic*. Shambhala. 1995.
305. Van Nghi, Nguyen. *Medecine Traditionnelle Clinoise. Acupuncture-moxibusion and massages*. Marseille, edition NVN. 1984.
306. Maciocia, Giovanni *The foundations of Chinese Medicine*. Edinburgh/London: Churchill Livingston 1989.
307. Matsumoto, Kiiko; Euler David. *Kiiko Matsumotos Clinical Strategies. In the Spirit of Master Nagano. Volume 1*. Kiiko Matsumoto International 2002.
308. Matsumoto, Kiiko. *Kiiko Matsumotos Clinical Strategies. In the Spirit of Master Nagano. Volume 2*. Kiiko Matsumoto International 2008.
309. Nielson, Arya *Gua Sha: A traditional Technique for modern practice*. New York: Churchill Livingstone 1995.
310. Amaro, John A. *Meridian therapy Pain Management*. Dynamic Chiropractic January 15th,1993.
311. Peter E. Baldry; Acupuncture Trigger Points and Musculoskeletal Pain (Edinburgh/London: Churchill Livingstone 1989).
312. Clemente, Carmine. *Anatomy*. Urban and Schwarzenberg (3rd edition). 1987.Magee, David J. *Orthopedic Physical Assessment*. Philadelphia: Saunders, 1992.
313. Mennell, John McMillan *The musculoskeletal system*. Gaithersburg,Md: Aspen, 1992.
314. Moore, Keith L. *Clinically Orientated Anatomy *2nd edition)*. Baltimore: Williams and Wilkins, 1985.
315. Netter, Frank H. *Atlas of Human Anatomy*. Ciba Geigy Corp. 1989.
316. Platzer, Werner MD. *Color Atlas: Textbook of Human Anatomy vol 1 (4th edition)*. New York: Thieme Medical 1992.
317. Reid, David. *Sports Injury Assessment and Rehabilitation*. Churchill Livingston. 1992.
318. Reider, Bruce. *The Orthopedic Physical Examination*. WB Saunders.1999.Shafer, RC; Faye LJ. *Motion Palpation and Chiropractic Technic*. The Motion Palpation Institute. 1989.
319. Sieg, Kay and Sandra Adams. *Illustrated Essentials of Musculoskeletal Anatomy*. Gainsville FL: Megabooks,1985.
320. Janet Travell and David Simons. Myofascial Pain and Dysfunction. Williams and Wilkins, 1982-1992.
321. Enwemeka CS, Parker JC, Dowdy DS, et al. The efficacy of low-power lasers in tissue repair and pain control: a meta-analysis study. *Photomed Laser Surg* 2004;22:323-329.
322. Karu TI. Multiple roles of cytochrome c oxidase in mammalian cells under action of red and IR-A radiation. *IUBMB Life* 2010;62:607-610.
323. Baxter GD, McDonough SM. Principles of electrotherapy in veterinary physiotherapy. In: *Animal physiotherapy: assessment, treatment and rehabilitation of animals*. Hoboken, New Jersey: Blackwell Publishing, 2007.
324. Abergel RP, Meeker CA, Lam TS, et al. Control of connective tissue metabolism by lasers: recent developments and future prospects. *J Am Acad Dermatol* 1984;11:1142-1150.
325. Pourreau-Schneider N, Ahmed A, Soudry M, et al. Helium-neon laser treatment transforms fibroblasts into microfibroblasts. *Am J Pathol* 1990;137:171-178.
326. Corazza AV, Jorge J, Kurachi C, et al. Photobiomodulation on the angiogenesis of skin wounds in rats using different light sources. *Photomed Laser Surg* 2007;25:102-106.
327. Vasilenko T, Slezák M, Kovác I, et al. The effect of equal daily dose achieved by different power densities of low-level therapy at 635 and 670 nm on wound tensile strength in rats: a short report. *Photomed Laser Surg* 2010;28:281-283.
328. Hopkins JT, McLoda TA, Seegmiller JG, et al. Low-level laser therapy facilitates superficial wound healing in humans: a triple-blind, sham-controlled study. *J Athl Train* 2004;39:223-229.
329. Honmura A, Ishii A, Yanase M, et al. Analgesic effect of Ga-Al-As diode laser irradiation on hyperalgesia in carrageenan-induced inflammation. *Lasers Surg Med*1993;13:463-469.
330. Sakurai Y, Yamaguchi M, Abiko Y. Inhibitory effect of low-level laser irradiation on LPS-stimulated prostaglandin E2 production and cyclooxygenase-2 in human gingival fibroblasts. *Eur J Oral Sci* 2000;108:29-34. 25.
331. Hakguder A, Birtane M, Gurcan S, et al: Efficacy of low level laser therapy in myofascial pain syndrome: An algometric and thermographic evaluation. *Lasers in Surgery and Medicine* 2003; 33:339-343
332. Gur A, Sarac AJ, Cevik R, et al: Efficacy of 904nm gallium arsenide low-level laser therapy in the management of pain in the neck: A double-blind and randomize-controlled trial. *Lasers in Surgery and Medicine*, 35:229-235. 2
333. Ilbuldu E., Cakmak A, Disci R, et al: Comparison of laser, dry needling, and placebo laser treatments in myofascial pain syndrome. *Photmedicine and Laser Surgery* 2004; 22:306-311.
334. Altan L, Bingol, U, Aykac M, et al: Investigation of the effect of GaAs laser therapy on cervical myofascial pain syndrome. *Rheumatology* International 2005; 25(1):23-7.

Bibliography

335. Dundar U, Eveik D, Samili F, et al: The effect of gallium arsenide aluminum laser therapy in the management of cervical myofascial pain syndrome: A double blind, placebo-controlled study. *Clinical Rheumatology* 2007; 26:930-934.
336. Chang WD, Wu JH, Jiang JA: Therapeutic effects of low level laser on lateral epicondylitis from differential interventions of Chinese western medicine: systematic review. Photomed laser surg 28(3):327-36.
337. Ilbuldu E, Cakmak A, Disci R, Aydin R (2004) Comparison of laser, dry needling, and placebo laser treatments in myofascial pain syndrome. Photomed Laser Surg 22, 306-311.
338. Venancio RA, Camparis CM, Lizarelli RFZ (2002) Laser in the treatment of temporomandibular disorders. J Brasileiro de Oclusão 2, 229-234.
339. Simunovic Z (1996) Low level laser therapy with trigger points technique: a clinical study on 243 patients. J Clin Laser Med Surg 14, 163-16
340. Simunovic Z (2000) Lasers in medicine and dentistry: basic science and up-to-date clinical application of low energy-level laser therapy LLLT. Vitagraf, Rijeka.
341. Fricton JR, Kroening R, Haley D, Siegert R (1985) Myofascial pain syndrome of the head and neck: a review of clinical characteristics of 164 patients. Oral Surg Oral Med Oral Pathol 60, 615-623.
342. Steiss JE: Muscle Disorders and Rehabilitation in Canine Athletes. *Veterinary Clinics of North America: Small Animal Practic* 2002 32(1):267-285
343. Mlacnik E, Bockstahler B, Muller M, et al: Effect of caloric restriction and moderate or intense physiotherapy program for treatment of lameness in overweight dogs with osteoarthritis. *Journal of the American Veterinary Medical Association* 2006; 229:1756-1760.
344. Canapp DA: Select modalities. *Clinical Techniques in Small Animal Practice* 2007; 22(4):160-165
345. Hou CR, Tsai LC, Cheng KF, et al: Immediate effects of various physical therapeutic modalities on cervical myofascial pain and trigger-point sensitivity. *Archives of Physical Medicine and Rehabilitation* 2002; 83(10):1406-1414
346. Dommerholt J, Huijbregts P: *Myofascial Trigger Points – Pathophysiology and Evidence-Informed Diagnosis and Management* 2011; Jones and Bartlett Publishers,Sudbury, Massachusetts
347. Aguilera FJ, Martin DP, Masanet RA, et al: Immediate effect of ultrasound and ischemic compression techniques for the treatment of trapezius latent myofascial trigger points in healthy subjects: a randomized controlled study. *Journal of Manipulative Physiology and* Therapy 2009; 32(7):515-520
348. Draper DO, Mahaffey C, Kaiser D, et al: Thermal ultrasound decreases tissue stiffness of trigger points in upper trapezius muscles. *Physiotherapy Theory and Practice* 2010; 26(3):167-172
349. Gam AN, Warming S, Larsen LE., et al: Treatment of myofascial trigger-points with ultrasound combined with massage and exercise—a randomized controlled trial. *Pain* 1998 77(1):73-79
350. Lee JC, Lin DT, Hong C: The effectiveness of simultaneous thermotherapy with ultrasound and electrotherapy with combined AC and DC current on the immediate pain relief of myofascial trigger points. *Journal of Musculoskeletal Pain* 1997 5:81-90
351. Mense S, Gerwin RD: *Muscle Pain: Diagnosis and Treatment* 2010; Springer-Verlag Berlin Heidelberg
352. Hains G, Descarreaux M, Hains F: Chronic Shoulder pain of myofascial origin: a randomized clinical trial using ischemic compression therapy. *Journal of Manipulative and Physiological Therapy* 2010; 33(5):362-369
353. Hains G, Descarreaux M, Lamy AM, et al: A randomized controlled (intervention) trial of ischemic compression therapy for chronic carpal tunnel syndrome. *Journal of the Canadian Chiropractic Association* 2010; 54(3):155-163
354. Montanez-Aguilera FJ, Valtuena-Gimeno N, Pecos-Martin D, et al: Changes in a patient with neck pain after application of ischemic compression as a trigger point therapy. *Journal of Back and Musculoskeletal* Rehabilitation 2010; 23(2):101-104
355. Physical Therapists & the Performance of Dry Needling – An Educational Resource Paper. Produced by the APTA Department of Practice and APTA State Government Affairs January 2012
356. Amaro JA:When Acupuncture Becomes "Dry Needling". Dynamic *Chiropractic* 2008; 26(12)
357. Bowsher D: Mechanisms of acupuncture. In: Filshie J, White A, Editors. *Medical Acupuncture – A Western Scientific Approach.* First edition. Edinburgh: ChurchillLivingstone 1998; 69-82
358. . White A. A cumulative review of the range and incidence of significant adverse events associated with acupuncture. Acupunct Med. 2004;22(3) (September):122-133.
359. Park J-E, Lee M, Choi J-Y, Kim B-Y, Choi S-M. Adverse events Associated with Acupuncture: A Prospective Survey. J Altern Complement Med. 2010;16(9) (Sept 14):959-63.
360. Witt CM, Pach D, Brinkhaus B et al. Safety of acupuncture: results of a prospective observational study with 229,230 patients and introduction of a medical information and consent form. Forsch Komplementmed. 2009;16(2) (April):91-97.
361. Ernst E, White AR. Prospective studies of the safety of acupuncture: a systematic review. Am J Med. 2001;110(6) (April 15):481-485.
362. Lao L, Hamilton GR, Fu J, Berman BM. Is acupuncture safe? A systematic review of case reports. Altern Ther Health Med. 2003;9(1) (February):72-83.

Bibliography

363. Xu S, Wang L, Cooper E et al. Adverse events of acupuncture: a systematic review of case reports. Evid Based Complement Alternat Med. 2013;2013:581203.
364. White A, Hayhoe S, Hart A, Ernst E. Survey of adverse events following acupuncture (SAFA): A prospective study of 32,000 consultations. Acupunct Med. 2001;19:84-92.
365. MacPherson H, Thomas K, Walters S, Fitter M. A prospective survey of adverse events and treatment reactions following 34,000 consultations with professional acupuncturists. Acupunct Med. 2001;19(2):93-102.
366. . Yamashita H, Tsukayama H, Tanno Y, Nishijo K. Adverse events in Acupuncture and Moxibustion Treatment: a Six-Year Survey at a National Clinic in Japan. J Altern Complement Med. 1999;5(3):229-236.
367. Yamashita H, Tsukayama H. Safety of acupuncture practice in Japan: patient reactions, therapist negligence and error reduction strategies. Evid Based Complement Alternat Med. 2007;5(4) (Dec):391-8.
368. Butterfield T, Best T, Merrick M. The Dual Roles of Neutrophils and Macrophages in Inflammation: A Critical Balance Between Tissue Damage and Repair. J Athl Train. 2006;41(4) (Oct-Dec):457-465.
369. Pape H, Marcucio R, Humphery C, Colnot C, Knobe M, Harvery E. Trauma-induced inflammation and fracture healing. J Orthop Trauma. 2010;24(9):522-5.
370. David S., López-Vales R, Wee Yong V. Harmful and beneficial effects of inflammation after spinal cord injury: potential therapeutic implications. Handb Clin Neurol. 2012;109:485- 502.
371. Kimura A, Kanazawa N, Li H, Yonei N, Yamamoto Y, Furukawa F.Influence of chemical peeling on the skin stress response system. Exp Dematol. 2012;Suppl 1 (Jul):8-10.
372. Xu S, Wang L, Cooper E et al. Adverse events of acupuncture: a systematic review of case reports. Evid Based Complement Alternat Med. 2013;2013:581203.
373. . McCutcheon L, Yelland M. Iatrogenic pneumothorax: safety concerns when using acupuncture or dry needling in the thoracic region. Physical therapy reviews. 2001;16(2):126-32.
374. Cummings M, Ross-Marrs R, Gerwin R. Pneumothorax complication of deep dry needling demonstration: Supplementary Data Online Video. Acupunct Med. 2014; http://aim.bmj.com/content/32/6/517/suppl/DC1; Accessed Jan 18, 2014 (Oct 3).
375. Evans H, de La Hunta A. Miller's guide to the dissection of the dog. WB Saunders co. 1996.
376. Done S, Goody P, Evans S, Stickland N. Color atlas of Veterinary anatomy the dog and cat. Mosby 2006.
377. Konig H, Liebich H. Veterinary anatomy of Domestic Animals. Third edition. Schattauer. 2007
378. Millis D, Levine D. Canine rehabilitation and Physical therapy second edition. Elsevier. 2014

Printed by Amazon Italia Logistica S.r.l.
Torrazza Piemonte (TO), Italy